UNDERSTANDING AND ADDRESSING

GIRLS' AGGRESSIVE BEHAVIOUR PROBLEMS

UNDERSTANDING AND ADDRESSING GIRLS' AGGRESSIVE BEHAVIOUR PROBLEMS
A FOCUS ON RELATIONSHIPS

EDITED BY DEBRA PEPLER AND H. BRUCE FERGUSON

WILFRID LAURIER UNIVERSITY PRESS

SickKids®

Wilfrid Laurier University Press acknowledges the financial support of the Government of Canada through the Canada Book Fund for our publishing activities.

Library and Archives Canada Cataloguing in Publication

   Understanding and addressing girls' aggressive behaviour problems : a focus on relationships / Debra J. Pepler and H. Bruce Ferguson, editors.

(SickKids community and mental health series)
Co-published by: Hospital for Sick Children
Includes bibliographical references and index.
Also issued in electronic format.
ISBN 978-1-55458-838-1

   1. Aggressiveness in girls. 2. Aggressiveness in girls—Treatment. 3. Interpersonal relations in children.
I. Pepler, Debra June II. Ferguson, H. Bruce III. Series: SickKids community and mental health series
BF723.A35U54 2013   155.4'124708342   C2012-904268-4

———

Electronic monograph issued in multiple formats.
Also issued in print format.
ISBN 978-1-55458-872-5 (PDF).—ISBN 978-1-55458-873-2 (EPUB)

   1. Aggressiveness in girls. 2. Aggressiveness in girls—Treatment. 3. Interpersonal relations in children.
I. Pepler, Debra June II. Ferguson, H. Bruce III. Series: SickKids community and mental health series
(Online)

BF723.A35U54 2013   155.4'124708342   C2012-904269-2

DISCLAIMER: This book is a general guide only and should never be a substitute for the skill, knowledge, and experience of a qualified medical professional dealing with the facts, circumstances, and symptoms of a particular case.

Cover design by Chris Rowat Design. Front-cover image: *Blue Harmony* by Roberto Louis Foz. Text design by Daiva Villa, Chris Rowat Design.

This book is printed on FSC recycled paper and is certified Ecologo. It is made from 100% post-consumer fibre, processed chlorine free, and manufactured using biogas energy.

Printed in Canada

Every reasonable effort has been made to acquire permission for copyright material used in this text, and to acknowledge all such indebtedness accurately. Any errors and omissions called to the publisher's attention will be corrected in future printings.

Published by Wilfrid Laurier University Press
Waterloo, Ontario, Canada
www.wlupress.wlu.ca

RECYCLED
Paper made from
recycled material
FSC   FSC® C103567
www.fsc.org

CONTENTS

A FOCUS ON RELATIONSHIPS: UNDERSTANDING AND ADDRESSING GIRLS' AGGRESSIVE BEHAVIOUR PROBLEMS

DEBRA PEPLER AND BRUCE FERGUSON

For this book, we challenged the contributors to focus on the relationships of aggressive girls, often in comparison with boys, to provide a lens for understanding the development and treatment of aggressive behaviour problems. From an ecological (Bronfenbrenner, 1979) or developmental-contextual perspective (Lerner, 1995), we have long recognized that children develop in a variety of influential contexts including the family, peer group, school, community, and broader society. In this volume, we explore the notion that it is not so much the contexts themselves but the relationships that children have with others in those contexts that shape development. In its first working paper, the National Scientific Council on the Developing Child focused on young children's development and argued that relationships are the "'active ingredients' of the environment's influence on healthy development" (2004, p. 1). The authors continued by noting that it is children's continuous give-and-take with significant others that provides experiences that are tailored to individual children's personality styles, interests, abilities, and initiative. Through these interactions, children develop knowledge, self-awareness, social understanding, and empathy. In this book, the contributors provide us with fresh insights into research and interventions that enable us to explore how healthy development depends on healthy relationships, or conversely, how unhealthy relationships may contribute to the development of aggressive behaviour and associated problems. The authors cover a broad developmental span from the early years through adulthood; they cover a broad range of relationships within the family, peer group, school, and community; and they point to potential relationship solutions to the relationship problems that aggressive girls and boys experience.

In the first chapter, Dale Hay, Lisa Mundy, and Kathryn Hudson ask why some girls deviate from the typical girls' pathway to controlled aggression; and why they carry on using physical as well as verbal aggression into adolescence. By examining the research on the interplay of biological and social factors, Hay and colleagues build the argument that relatively small, biologically based sex differences in temperament and rate of maturation are amplified in the context of relationships with parents and peers. These authors suggest that girls who do not follow the gender-normative developmental pathway are at particular risk for aggression and its associated deleterious outcomes. Hay and colleagues also note the salient role of peer relationships: if aggressive girls are rejected by their same-sex peers because they are out of step in a variety of ways, they may be at increased risk for affiliation with boys. In relationships with boys, girls may increase in aggressive behaviour and accelerate earlier into the developmental transitions into sexual relationships, for which they may be ill prepared because their social development has lagged behind that of their same-sex peers. Hay and colleagues provide preliminary evidence suggesting that the predicted pathway from very early biological risk to problems in peer relationships, such as peer rejection, is one followed by many aggressive girls.

In the second chapter, Candice Odgers continues with the theme of examining both biological and social aspects of aggressive girls' development. Using longitudinal data, Odgers describes the developmental pathways of anti-social behaviour among girls along with the associated risks for relationship violence and poor physical health in adulthood. She highlights two main themes to support concerns for girls who exhibit anti-social behaviour. First, numerous studies have shown a strong association between children's early patterns of anti-social behaviour and poor adult physical health, even after controlling for a wide range of individual, family, and other potentially confounding factors. Second, although the link between early anti-social behaviour and poor adult health holds for both girls and boys, there are reasons to be highly concerned about girls. The physical health consequences for anti-social girls growing up in risky families may be more severe due to higher rates of victimization and the greater tendency for girls to internalize stressful life events. Against the empirical backdrop of anti-social girls in troubled relationships, Odgers calls for more research to identify why there are connections between early behavioural problems and poor health, and to examine how these pathways differ for boys and girls. To inform programming and policy, Odgers argues for an assessment of the costs of early-onset and persistent anti-social behaviour in terms of a wide range of medical and health-care expenses.

In Chapter 3, a commentary on the first two chapters, Magda Stouthamer-Loeber emphasizes the importance of studying anti-social girls, given the harm that anti-social behaviour inflicts on society. She points to the need for future research to explore the processes that influence different developmental pathways for girls and boys to provide direction for prevention and intervention strategies. Stouthamer-Loeber notes that this type of research has been done extensively for boys, but is only slowly starting for girls. The largest longitudinal study of the development of anti-social behaviour in girls is currently being conducted in Pittsburgh by Stouthamer-Loeber and her colleagues.

The Pittsburgh Girls Study is highlighted in the following chapter by Rolf Loeber, Magda Stouthamer-Loeber, Alison Hipwell, Jeffrey Burke, and Deena Battista. In particular they explore the developmental ordering of conduct problems and depression. For boys, conduct problems have been shown to precede depression; in their study, Loeber and colleagues examine the developmental sequence among girls. After analyzing oppositional behaviours, relational aggression, and conduct problems, they made two developmental constructs: one for irritability (losing temper, annoying others, and blaming others) and the other for anger (spiteful behaviour, vindictive behaviour, anger, and resentful behaviour). Their data show an increase in irritability and anger with age. The pattern of conduct problems preceding depression in preadolescent girls is most distinct when girls' oppositional behaviour is taken into account. This chapter concludes with a set of intriguing questions for future research regarding critical links between the developmental timing of girls' emotional states and their experiences in social relationships.

In her chapter on Aboriginal adolescent girls telling their stories, Susan Dion takes a positive youth development or strengths perspective to explore girls' aggression. Using qualitative data from interviews with girls, Dion shares with us a view that aggression may not be a trait of the individual girl, but a strategy that Aboriginal girls might use for a range of purposes. She illustrates this view through the stories that the girls tell to help the reader understand how and why Aboriginal girls sometimes use aggression. With the lens of strength and an open ear, Dion reflects on the girls' stories not as experiences of violence and poverty, but as girls doing the work of adolescence, cultivating a sense of themselves in relationship with their families, friends, community, and culture. The girls' stories reflect their emerging sense of self in relationship with the community and in their culture, rather than in isolation. Using the girls' own words, Dion shares her understanding of the legacy of colonialism as it is reflected in the girls' stories of anger, frustration, hopes, and dreams. Grandmothers are particularly important in the lives of these girls, helping them learn about interdependence, survival, and resistance. The girls themselves identify time with friends and other trusted people as critical to their well-being. Dion suggests that promoting this form of "relationship solution" might provide an alternative to the anger and aggression that the girls are expressing.

In Chapter 6, Wendy Craig's commentary identifies three findings related to the development of girls' aggression and anger that are common to both the chapter by Loeber and colleagues and the chapter by Dion. They are: (a) individual mechanisms that underlie girls' aggression transcend cultural contexts; (b) different relationships can act as protective or risk factors; and (c) anger and depression may have an important role in the development of aggressive behaviour. Craig notes that the research provides guidance for early identification and prevention of conduct problems and depression. Those girls who are persistently irritable are at risk for developing emotional difficulties as well as oppositional behaviour. Craig argues that early intervention to disrupt these troubled and troubling developmental pathways will provide youth with positive relationship experiences that promote their capacities to regulate and understand their emotions and behaviours. Positive experiences will also contribute to the development of the resilience to cope more positively with highly stressful relationship contexts in their lives, both currently and into the future.

Bonnie Leadbeater's chapter leads the second section of this volume with a focus on prevention and intervention approaches to support the healthy development of girls and boys with aggressive behaviour problems. Against the backdrop of many changes during early adolescence and research linking these changes to concerns about interpersonal aggression, Leadbeater identifies potential elements for prevention programs to reduce interpersonal aggression and victimization among middle school students. Specifically, Leadbeater provides evidence of the protective or risk processes associated with various developmental changes in early adolescents' concerns about popularity, group membership, and social status, as well as changes in the intimacy of their friendships, and increases in perspective-taking abilities and consequence-based reasoning. Leadbeater has led the development of the *WITS* and *WITS-LEADS* bullying prevention programs for elementary school children and draws from this experience to lay out a framework for developmentally appropriate, ecologically valid strategies for early adolescents. She highlights the need to promote socially responsible and interpersonally respectful behaviours across the many relationship contexts in which youth live. The focus of support is not just on the youth: Leadbeater argues that interventions are needed to assist the important adults in youths' lives. The adults responsible for socializing children and youth must be supported to develop awareness so that they are not modelling aggression and indicating that they perceive aggression to be normative in peer relationships. The important adults in youths' lives need support to understand how to respond proactively to aggressive behaviours in early adolescence and how to respond to youths who are victimized and require help.

Donna Cross, Therese Shaw, Helen Monks, Stacey Waters, and Leanne Lester frame their chapter on bullying prevention programming for girls by providing an understanding of the similarities and differences in girls' and boys' bullying. They review research with a particular focus on gender differences in individual and social processes related to bullying, as well as on the differential effectiveness of bullying prevention programs. Based on this empirical foundation, they consider how school-based interventions may need to be tailored to adequately protect both girls and boys from bullying. Drawing from their own research on the Australian *Friendly Schools, Friendly Families Program* for elementary school students and the related *Supportive Schools Project* for secondary school students, Cross and her colleagues examine the effectiveness of the interventions on the bullying experiences of girls and boys. The authors provide suggestions for "promising" school-based intervention strategies for girls. They also provide a focus on girls' relationships: programs with enhanced parent involvement appear to be more effective in reducing girls' bullying. Cross and colleagues conclude with recommendations for school-based policy and practice, to help address the factors associated with girls' bullying experiences and to enable girls to take positive action to reduce potential harm from bullying behaviour.

In their commentary on the preceding two chapters on school-based interventions, Leena Augimeri and Margaret Walsh highlight several common themes: (a) the need to promote prosocial leadership and social responsibility; (b) the importance of taking an ecological perspective encompassing the individual child's characteristics, family relationships, and school relationships (including teacher and peer interactions, and climate); and (c) the need to consider how developmental and relationship processes are influenced by broader social contexts including the community, media, politics, and culture. Augimeri and Walsh highlight research indicating the cost of not intervening to ameliorate aggressive behaviour problems in children and note that school is the ideal place to focus interventions because all children pass through this system. Based on the positive outcomes of the *SNAP®* gender-sensitive treatment models, developed at the Child Development Institute, they have adapted *SNAP®* for school-based settings. Emerging evidence indicates promising results: children participating in the program have significantly fewer behavioural and discipline problems and show overall behavioural improvement in the classroom and on the playground.

In Chapter 10, Tina Daniels and Danielle Quigley review research on girls' social aggression to describe the nature of elementary school girls' peer relationships. They point out a challenge for those of us interested in curbing girls' aggression: the use of socially aggressive strategies often leads to highly desirable ends for many girls including popularity, status, power, and control. Daniels and Quigley contend that prevention and intervention strategies must focus on replacing this source of power and control with a more socially desirable alternative and a way to meet salient social needs in a more prosocial way. They review the elements and effectiveness of five programs designed to address girls' social aggression and promote girls' use of prosocial strategies. Based on their review, the authors provide guidelines for programming to address girls' social aggression: (a) include only girls and design programs to include all girls rather than only those at risk; (b) start early because social aggression begins to develop in the fourth and fifth grades; (c) continue the program over an extended period of time to ensure change; and (d) promote awareness and develop skills that are incompatible with social aggression. Daniels and Quigley suggest that using older girls as peer mentors may be more effective than using adult leaders to deliver programming to promote girls' healthy relationships and prevent aggression.

Marlene Moretti and Ingrid Obsuth have extensive experience in focusing on relationships as a means of diverting youth from an anti-social pathway. In this next chapter, the authors discuss the facets of parenting and parent–child relationships that may pose risks for the development of aggression and violence into the teen years. They focus on how parents' behaviours shape their children's attachment representations, which in turn regulate children's cognitive, affective, and behavioural functioning, particularly in the context of relationships. Moretti and Obsuth draw upon evidence from their innovative intervention program *Connect*, which is a brief manualized program that supports parents and caregivers of high-risk teens. They illustrate how effective it can be to focus on enhancing parent–youth relationships as a means of reducing youth violence and promoting healthy youth development. The *Connect* program is based on the finding that attachment mediates the association between parenting and risk for aggression and violence. This is an excellent example of how a developmental mechanism, such as attachment, can be tested within the context of an intervention. In the *Connect* program, parents learn how to foster the core components of secure attachment: parental sensitivity, parental reflective function and mindfulness, and dyadic affect regulation. The authors provide promising evidence of the effectiveness of the program in improving parent–child relationships, thereby reducing youths' anti-social behaviour.

In her commentary on the previous two chapters concerning interventions, Isabela Granic notes that the authors lead us from research considering the mechanisms that underlie the development of girls' aggression to the application of this understanding. The latter is geared toward the task of tailoring and implementing prevention and intervention strategies that will effectively target troubled girls' problem behaviours. Drawing out the common themes of the chapters, Granic highlights the clear argument for thinking about the development and treatment of aggressive behaviour as a "relationship" problem. She relies on a developmental perspective by identifying the importance of focusing on the relationship between the times of transition and the emergence of problems. She also emphasizes the importance of understanding the developmental contexts of the family and peer group within which girls' aggression is developing. Granic pushes the reader's thinking further by identifying the differences between the approaches represented in these two chapters. Whereas Moretti and Obsuth provide evidence of the effectiveness of an attachment-based program for both girls and boys, Daniels and Quigley point to the need to tailor interventions to meet girls' specific needs. In support of the latter position, Granic points out some of the gender-specific needs of aggressive girls including: experiences with sexual objectification, sexual abuse, and a view of relationships as constituting alliances of power. She notes that girls often find themselves vulnerable in dating relationships and subsequently advises that prevention and intervention programs may need to focus on problems in the context of romantic relationships. Granic calls for more research on comprehensive interventions that take into account all the relationships that are central to girls' lives, as well as the multi-faceted risk profiles which they present.

Together the chapters in this volume weave a tapestry of what we now know about the development and treatment of girls' aggression. There are biological bases that place some girls at risk for following developmental pathways in which aggressive behaviour patterns are established. Girls' experiences within relationships shape not only their behavioural style, but also their emotional character and physical health, which in turn may place girls at increased risk for a wide range of individual and relationship problems. After exploring the concerns highlighted for aggressive girls, the reader can consider how these may be addressed by the prevention and intervention programs described by the contributors—all of which focus on girls' relationships to promote healthy development and reduce aggression. The contributions in this book provide an understanding and direction for programs and policies to reduce the significant individual, family, social, health, and other costs associated with girls' aggression.

REFERENCES

Bronfenbrenner, U. (1979). *The ecology of human development*. Boston: Harvard University Press.

Lerner, R.M. (1995). Developing individuals within changing contexts: Implications of developmental contextualism for human development research, policy, and programs. In T.A. Kindermann & J. Valsiner (Eds.), *Development of person-context relations* (pp. 13–37). Hillsdale, NJ: Lawrence Erlbaum Associates.

National Scientific Council on the Developing Child. (2004). *Young children develop in an environment of relationships* (Working Paper No. 1). Retrieved from http://www.developingchild.net

CHAPTER ONE

DIFFERENT PATHS TO AGGRESSION FOR GIRLS AND BOYS

DALE F. HAY, LISA MUNDY, AND KATHRYN HUDSON

CARDIFF UNIVERSITY

INTRODUCTION

Most people believe that aggression is a natural part of boyhood and that girls are naturally less aggressive than their male peers. However, girls and boys both use force during infancy and early childhood (e.g., Caplan, Vespo, Pedersen, & Hay, 1991; Hay, Castle, & Davies, 2000; Hay & Ross, 1982); sex differences in the rate of physical aggression only begin to appear in early childhood, after the second year of life (for reviews see Hay, 2007; Keenan & Shaw, 1997). Even once the sex differences emerge, some girls persist in showing physical aggression; trajectory analyses show that in subgroups of persistently aggressive children, a substantial minority are girls (Côté, Vaillancourt, LeBlanc, Nagin, & Tremblay, 2006; Tremblay et al., 2004). However, during the childhood years, for most girls, aggression comes under control—girls' aggression tends to be restricted to close relationships (Moffitt, Caspi, Rutter, & Silva, 2001), it is often covert (Pepler & Craig, 1991), and it is more often expressed through words than deeds (e.g., Crick, Casas, & Mosher, 1997). This suggests that girls begin to use aggression tactically, and that emotional, angry aggression may be more often seen with family members or romantic partners than in the public sphere.

However, some women remain physically aggressive, and an increasing number of women commit violent crimes. The aim of this chapter is to examine why some girls deviate from the typical girls' pathway to controlled aggression and carry on using physical as well as verbal aggression into adolescence.

BIOLOGICAL AND SOCIAL INFLUENCES ON GIRLS' AND BOYS' AGGRESSION

Why do girls and boys become so different? The emergence of the sex difference in rates of aggression and violent crime is no doubt due to the interplay of biological and social factors. We propose that relatively small, biologically based sex differences in temperament and rate of maturation are amplified in the context of socialization by parents and peers (see Figure 1.1 on p. 17 below for a depiction of the developmental model we propose).

Biological Hypotheses: Do Sex Differences Derive from Individual Differences?

Some theorists contend that aggression is a sex-linked adaptive trait, maintained in the population through processes of sexual selection (Archer & Côté, 2005). It is certainly the case that sex-linked biological traits are not necessarily evident in infancy or early childhood; for example, secondary sex characteristics emerge in adolescence, and male baldness typically emerges in later adulthood. The fact that sex differences are not present in early life does not necessarily refute the evolutionary argument.

However, if aggression were a late-emerging, sex-linked trait, it would seem unlikely that both sexes would display physical aggression in the early years of life. Furthermore, there is striking evidence for individual differences in trajectories toward problem aggression (Broidy et al., 2003; Côté et al., 2006; Tremblay et al., 2004), and there is also evidence for a genetic contribution to individual differences in early aggression (Dionne, Tremblay, Boivin, Laplante, & Pérusse, 2003). This latter finding suggests that biological influences may contribute to individual variation within each sex. The trajectory analyses show clearly that many boys are never very aggressive. The emerging sex difference may therefore derive from a relatively small number of boys who are at high levels of biological and social risk. Thus, boys may become more aggressive than girls because boys are more vulnerable to biological insults and risky environments.

Aggressive Interactions: The Role of Temperament.

Aggression is best seen as a social phenomenon in social species, not as an individual trait, as demonstrated by analyses of fighting in a number of mammalian species (Cairns, 1979). However, the characteristics of individuals heighten the probability of aggression and conflict in social situations. Heightened activity levels and emotional reactivity to frustration promote aggression in mice and men (Cairns, 1979; Dodge & Coie, 1987; Raine, 2002; van Goozen, Fairchild, Snoek, & Harold, 2007). Conversely, the young child's growing capacity for self-regulation promotes desistance from conflict and aggression (Calkins & Fox, 2002; Kochanska, Coy, & Murray, 2001; Kopp, 1982). Harmonious social interaction depends on individual self-control.

Self-regulation of attention, activity, and emotion is underpinned by individual temperament in both sexes (Goldsmith et al., 1987). Evidence for sex differences is mixed, with few temperamental differences between girls and boys typically not identified before one year of age (Pauli-Pott, Mertesacker, Bade, Haverlock, & Beckermann, 2003; Hane, Fox, Polak-Toste, Ghera, & Guner, 2006), although many studies of infant temperament are underpowered. In large epidemiological samples, based on maternal ratings, there is evidence that girls hold the advantage over boys in the ability to persist at tasks, regulate their activity, and maintain emotional equanimity (e.g., Rothbart & Hwang, 2002; Oberklaid, Prior, Sanson, Sewell, & Kyrios, 1990).

Because the most substantial differences are found in maternal reports, not observed behaviour, it is unclear whether the sex differences reflect mothers' attributions about gender-typical behaviour, or true behavioural differences. However, informants' reports of temperament show substantial heritability (Goldsmith, Buss, & Lemery, 1996), and the biological basis of temperament is also supported by molecular genetic analyses (e.g., Auerbach, Faroy, Ebstein, Kahana, & Levine, 2001). Thus it is possible that, in large samples, with the power to detect small effect sizes, biological differences between infant girls and boys can be detected in the temperamental dimensions that are likely to foster the occurrence of aggressive interactions. However, a meta-analysis of studies of temperament in infancy and childhood found differences favouring girls in self-regulatory abilities, but no differences in negative emotionality (Else-Quest, Hyde, Goldsmith, & Van Hulle, 2006). This suggests that girls' growing ability to control their aggression is related to sex differences in self-regulatory capacities, and not in the negative emotion that might underpin aggression. However, more detailed analyses of different forms of negative emotionality are needed.

Are Males More Vulnerable to Early Insults?
It is well known that, during fetal development and infancy, mortality and morbidity rates are higher for males than for females; the decreasing sex ratio from conception to childhood reflects this fact. Aggressive tendencies

are associated with neurobiological deficits that may derive from early developmental insults (Raine, Moffitt, Caspi, Loeber, Stouhamer-Loeber, & Lynam, 2005; van Goozen et al., 2007). It is possible that males are especially vulnerable to perinatal risk factors that disrupt normal development, increase the rate of developmental disorders, and interfere with the ability to achieve self-regulation.

In recent years, many investigations have provided evidence for links between prenatal experiences and disruptive behaviour (for reviews see Raine, 2002; van Goozen et al., 2007). In particular, disruptive behaviour disorders are predicted by exposure to nicotine in pregnancy (e.g., Brennan, Grekin, & Mednick, 1999; Maughan, Taylor, Caspi, & Moffitt, 2004; Mick, Biederman, Faraone, Sayer, & Kleinman, 2002; Orlebeke, Knol & Verhulst, 1999; Thapar et al., 2003; Wakschlag, Pickett, Kasza, & Loeber, 2006). Disruptive behaviour in childhood and adolescence is also associated with maternal stress and psychopathology in pregnancy (e.g., Hay, Pawlby, Waters, Perra, & Sharp, 2010; O'Connor, Heron, Golding, Beveridge, & Glover, 2002). It is not clear, however, whether males are especially vulnerable to adverse prenatal experiences. For example, some investigations of the effects of smoking and pregnancy only study boys (e.g., Brennan et al., 1999; Wakschlag et al., 2006). Although animal studies suggest that prenatal exposure to nicotine has a stronger effect on males than females (Schlumpf, Gähwiler, Ribary, & Lichtensteigner, 1988; Slotkin et al., 2007), there is little evidence for interactions between exposure to smoking and sex in humans. For example, in a nationally representative sample of twins at environmental risk for disruptive behaviour (Maughan et al., 2004), daughters and sons of women who smoked during pregnancy were both at risk for conduct problems, and there was no interaction between exposure and the child's sex.

There is some evidence that boys who were exposed to prenatal smoking were at heightened risk for ADHD, and that this was not the case with girls (Rodriquez & Bohlin, 2005); however, other work suggests that prenatal smoking interacts with the child's genotype to influence ADHD symptoms (Kahn, Khoury, Nichols, & Lanphear, 2003), and the 2:1 sex ratio in prevalence of ADHD (Arcia & Connors, 1998) suggests that girls and boys may be at different levels of genetic risk. This finding in turn suggests that boys may be at increased risk for aggression and other forms of disruptive behaviour because of the interplay between genetic risk and prenatal insults.

Female Precocity and Male Developmental Delay
Maturation rate is another biologically based phenomenon that may contribute to eventual sex differences in aggression. In general, girls mature at

a faster rate than their male counterparts, as seen in their earlier acquisition of language and other developmental milestones. Female precocity in the early years of life may promote self-regulation and help girls desist from physical aggression. This does not mean that girls will necessarily refrain from aggressive encounters with family members and peers; however, girls may be better able than boys to learn how to control their aggressive impulses and pursue their self-interest in different ways. It should be noted, however, that female precocity also implies that girls enter into puberty earlier than their male counterparts; individuals who experience menarche sooner than other girls are at elevated risk for conduct problems, especially if they had experienced behavioural or emotional problems prior to puberty. Thus female precocity may serve as a protective factor in infancy and early childhood but a risk factor in later childhood and adolescence.

The differential maturational rate implies that young girls and boys are not equally prepared for socialization. Consider, for example, the implications of the well-established advantage held by girls with respect to language acquisition (e.g., Dale et al., 1998). Highly verbal children of either sex are less likely to display physical aggression; at 19 months, vocabulary level is negatively associated with informants' reports of physical aggression, even though there is no significant sex difference in the rate of aggression (Dionne et al., 2003). Children with better levels of receptive and productive language will be better able to understand other people's speech, and therefore can understand and respond appropriately to other people's requests and demands (Kochanska, 1993; Rheingold, Cook, & Kolowitz, 1987) and profit from parents' inductive reasoning during disciplinary encounters (Kuczynski, Kochanska, Radke-Yarrow, & Girnius-Brown, 1987); a lower ability to respond to verbal information may be one reason why boys are more likely than girls to receive harsh punishment from their parents (e.g., Pinderhughes, Dodge, Bates, Pettit, & Zelli, 2000).

In early childhood, verbal children may also be more likely to engage in the type of private speech that promotes self-regulation (Meichenbaum & Goodman, 1969). Verbal children are also better able to listen to and understand the needs of other children. For example, young girls develop the art of conversation with peers sooner than boys do (Hay, 2006); this provides a means to settle disputes and pursue their own ends without recourse to the use of force. To the extent that two-year-old girls as a group have stronger language skills and are less likely to experience specific language impairment (Dale et al., 1998), they are better placed to profit from their socialization experiences. Girls as a group may therefore be better able to pick up on the verbal nuances that explain the rules of social life, and come to understand that physical aggression needs to be brought under control. Girls' verbal skills may make the transition to classroom life and larger peer groups easier to handle; it is perhaps not a coincidence that the sex difference in aggression emerges around the time that children in the industrialized world move into group-based education.

Within each sex, some individuals will mature faster than others. Thus some boys attain language early, and some girls show delayed development. Individual differences in the rate of development will no doubt be influenced by genetic factors. Furthermore, during fetal development and in the first postnatal months, genetic males undergo hormonal reorganization, as revealed in the prenatal and postnatal testosterone surges. It has been argued, on the basis of animal studies, that early hormonal reorganization affects brain maturation (e.g., Denenberg, Fitch, Schrott, Cowell, & Waters, 1991). Specific prenatal experiences may also disrupt maturational processes in both sexes. In particular, two well-known prenatal risk factors for aggression and related problems, maternal smoking and psychopathology in pregnancy, also delay the course of development. It is clear that smoking in pregnancy is associated with preterm delivery and low birth weight (Windham, Hopkins, Fenster, & Swan, 2000), which in turn are associated with developmental delay (Vohr et al., 2000). Furthermore, in a large community sample of British children (the ALSPAC study), mothers' reports of depressive symptoms in pregnancy were associated with delayed development, even after controlling for the effects of prenatal smoking (Deave, Heron, Evans, & Emond, 2008). To the extent that girls as well as boys are affected by prenatal risk factors (e.g., Hay et al., 2010; Maughan et al., 2004), girls who have experienced prenatal risk may not experience the maturational advantage held by other girls, and are thus at elevated risk for aggression.

Gender Segregation: How Young Children Socialize Their Peers
To the extent that young girls and boys differ in temperament, maturational rate, and verbal ability; prefer to play in different ways, with different types of toys (Ruble, Martin, & Berebaum, 2006); and experience explicit gender-role socialization (e.g., Fagot, Leinbach, & O'Boyle, 1992; Rheingold & Cook, 1975), it is perhaps not surprising that the two sexes become increasingly incompatible and that gender segregation in childhood peer groups becomes the norm (Maccoby, 1998). The origins of gender segregation lie in infancy; even before the first birthday, same-sex, familiar peers are less likely to engage in conflict than opposite-sex peers (Hay et al., 2007). Toddler girls are more likely to share with other girls (Hay, Castle, Davies, Demetriou, & Stimson, 1999). Gradually, the two sexes draw apart to the extent that they can be characterized as dwelling in two separate worlds of childhood (Maccoby, 1998).

Within gender-segregated peer groups, children socialize their peers to conform to the gender-role expectations of their societies. Young children develop strong views about the essential nature of sex differences (e.g., Gelman, Taylor, & Nguyen, 2004), and they enforce those rules of behaviour. In preschool classrooms, violation of gender stereotypes provokes conflicts with peers. This implies that male and female peer groups develop different social norms.

Social psychological theorists have long drawn attention to processes of majority influence (e.g., Asch, 1956) and minority influence (Moscovici & Personnaz, 1980) in small groups. Both processes of influence are likely to be at work in the gender-segregated peer groups that form in early childhood. To the extent that most members of each sex respond to gender-role socialization and adhere to gender stereotypes, the behaviour of the majority will foster conformity in their same-sex peers. In this way, peers' behaviour is likely to bolster gender-role socialization that is undertaken by parents.

In addition, minority influence may also play an important role in creating quantitative and qualitative differences in girls' and boys' aggression. Based on the trajectory analyses of aggressive tendencies from infancy to childhood (Broidy et al., 2003), we can assume that, in boys' groups, there is likely to be a minority of highly aggressive boys (e.g., Côté et al., 2006; Tremblay et al., 2004). These highly aggressive boys will have been affected by biological and environmental risk factors that foster aggression; they now are likely to increase the rate of conflict and aggression in boys' groups. The trajectory studies show that, in the early years, most boys are not very aggressive; however, those less aggressive boys may have to learn to engage in some aggression, just in self-defence, in response to the minority of highly aggressive boys. Ultimately highly aggressive boys may suffer from peer rejection (Dodge & Coie, 1987); however, their aggressive actions are likely to raise the overall mean level of aggression in boys' groups. This in turn would create different norms for aggressiveness in boys' as opposed to girls' peer relations. Furthermore, to the extent that aggressive boys foster each other's aggressive tendencies (Dishion, Bullock, & Granic, 2002), their own behaviour may become more violent.

Meanwhile, what might be happening in the girls' groups? Again, the studies of the early development of aggression indicate that a majority of the children who are never or rarely physically aggressive are girls (Broidy et al., 2003). Although most girls show some aggression in the early years, this minority of girls may exert important levels of social influence. They may be the enforcers of gender-segregation, rejecting disruptive male peers. To the extent that physical aggression is inversely correlated with vocabulary level (Dionne et al., 2003), girls who do not use physical aggression may have higher levels of verbal skill. If so, they may find alternate ways of solving problems; they may also find effective ways of deploying verbal or relational aggression (Crick et al., 1997). In their gender-segregated groups, girls may learn new ways of causing psychological harm to others.

It seems likely that the minority of physically aggressive girls will be rejected by their same-sex peers, and thus will have fewer opportunities to be socialized into "proper girl behaviour." Such girls may experience loneliness and associated emotional problems (e.g., Cassidy & Asher, 1992); they may also choose to affiliate with boys, and perhaps especially with aggressive boys. Because of their maturational advantage vis-à-vis same-aged peers, they may be particularly likely to affiliate with older boys—which opens up many opportunities for the development of additional conduct symptoms, as well as increased likelihood of early sexual relationships and pregnancy, which in turn may be one mechanism of transmission of risk from one generation to the next (Zoccolillo, Meyers, & Assister, 1997).

SUMMARY OF THE DEVELOPMENTAL MODEL

On the basis of the foregoing evidence and speculation, we propose a theoretical model whereby biological differences between the sexes are amplified through socialization processes into more extreme differences in the quantity and quality of male and female aggression (see Figure 1.1). Differences in temperament, vulnerability to early adversity, and maturation rate mean that girls are more amenable to socialization pressures at earlier ages. Differences in attention, temperament, and verbal ability promote different interests, which makes opposite-sex peers increasingly incompatible. Due to this growing incompatibility, both girls and boys may begin to feel more comfortable in same-sex groups. As Maccoby (1998) has long pointed out, peers may be more effective than parents in creating very different norms and patterns of behaviour for girls and boys. We propose that the socialization pressures exerted by parents and peers contribute to the widely diverging pathways taken by girls and boys and their emerging differences in levels of aggression.

We see aggression not as a simple individual trait, but rather as a social behaviour that emerges from the interplay of biological tendencies, environmental risk, and social learning processes (Cairns, 1979). For boys, there may be many factors that promote aggression; for girls, there may be many factors preventing its occurrence. However, due to genetic risk and social circumstance, it is possible for individual girls and boys to "fall off" their gender-normative developmental pathway. In the remainder of

FIGURE 1.1 A THEORY: PATHWAYS TO SEX DIFFERENCES

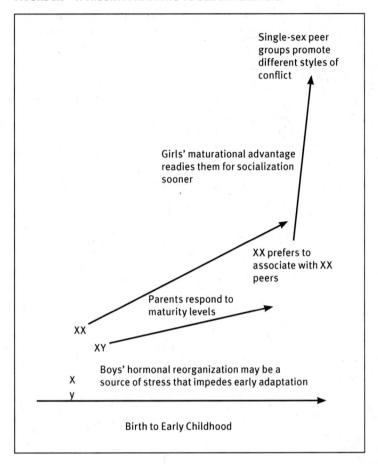

the chapter, we examine some illustrative data to explore whether highly aggressive girls have indeed fallen off the female pathway, due to *prenatal insults, maturational delay,* and *poor peer relationships.*

Preliminary Evidence for the Developmental Model

To illustrate the proposed developmental model, and to identify some directions for subsequent research on girls' development, we have examined illustrative longitudinal data from the South London Child Development Study (SLCDS; e.g., Pawlby, Hay, Waters, & Sharp, 2008). These analyses were undertaken after the development of the model presented in Figure 1.1, which was based on speculations derived from reading the literature on the development of aggression and our observational studies of girls and boys in the first years of life (Hay, 2007). Thus these preliminary analyses on the SLCDS data set represent our first attempt to find empirical evidence that is consonant with the model.

We have identified girls and boys who show higher than average levels of aggressiveness in early adolescence, and examine the extent to which the girls in particular have not experienced the protective influences of the "female pathway." More specifically, we have enquired whether highly aggressive girls have experienced early adversity in the perinatal period, whether they have shown any disruption of maturational processes, and whether they have experienced any problems in peer relations that may have interfered with gender-normative socialization processes in childhood peer groups.

The Sample

The SLCDS is a prospective, longitudinal study of a representative community sample of British women who were recruited during pregnancy while receiving routine prenatal care in general practices in two areas of South London. In the UK, only 5% of births take place in private hospitals, and 90% to 95% of all adults are registered with the National Health Service, at a GP practice. This means that this sampling frame—the list of consecutive prenatal patients at those two practices—identifies the vast majority of children born in those catchment areas during 1986. From a list of 252 consecutive patients, a random sample of 70% (177) was selected for intensive study at two points in pregnancy. Of this sample, 171 women gave birth to live infants, and were followed up at 3 months and at 1, 4, 11, and 16 years postpartum. No attempt had been made to follow up women who had moved out of the area at 3 and 12 months postpartum, but at the subsequent assessments all families who had participated at 12 months were traced. At 16 years, 90% of the original random sample was still participating in the study.

Aggression in Early Adolescence

Physically aggressive girls and boys were identified at 11 years of age on the basis of parents' and children's joint reports of aggressive conduct symptoms (bullying, fighting, cruelty to people, stealing with confrontation and use of weapons) on the Child and Adolescent Psychiatric Assessment (CAPA; Angold & Costello, 2000) and/or teachers' reports of fighting or bullying on the Strengths and Difficulties Questionnaire (SDQ; Goodman, 1997). In line with the literature, 11-year-old boys were significantly more likely than 11-year-old girls to show such signs of physical aggression: 21 boys and 13 girls met these criteria at age 11, $\chi^2_{(1)} = 8.26$, $p < .005$. Of 13 girls who met criteria for physical aggression, one girl did so solely on the basis of one incident of self-reported fighting with one particular sibling, in a dispute over spillage of flour in the family kitchen. Because the other girls who met criteria showed more pervasive and severe aggressive symptoms, that (scrupulously honest) child was excluded from the sample, and the following comparisons focus on N = 12 aggressive girls, in comparison with girls who show no physical aggression.

Prenatal experiences that disrupt maturational and self-regulatory processes.
In the SLCDS sample, girls who were physically aggressive at age 11 had suffered from less optimal environments before birth (Figure 1.2). In comparison with other girls, and in line with our model, most aggressive girls had been exposed to smoking in pregnancy ($\chi^2_{(1)}$ = 9.40, $p < .005$) and to the mother's depression during pregnancy ($\chi^2_{(1)}$ = 6.83, $p < .01$). Moreover, the majority of the aggressive girls (58.3% vs. 28.1% of other girls) had weighed less than 3000 grams at birth, $\chi^2_{(1)}$ = 4.09, $p < .05$. Because lower birth weight is associated with delayed development (Vohr et al., 2000), these perinatal risk factors may have set these girls on a different trajectory from that followed by other, non-aggressive girls.

FIGURE 1.2   PERINATAL RISK FACTORS AND BIRTH WEIGHT

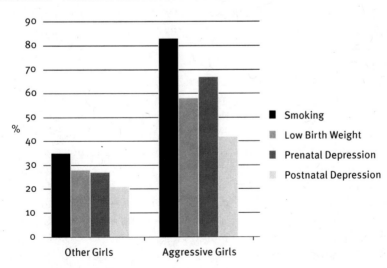

Aggressive girls defined by aggressive conduct symptoms on CAPA or teachers reports of fighting at age 11 (N=12)

FIGURE 1.3   LENGTH OF BREASTFEEDING

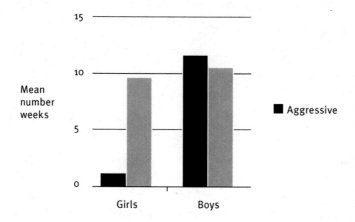

The postnatal environment
The aggressive girls had also suffered from a sub-optimal postnatal environment. They were somewhat more likely to be cared for by a mother suffering from postnatal depression (Figure 1.2). Indeed, all the aggressive girls had mothers who had experienced depression before or immediately after birth. Furthermore, one dimension of the mother-infant relationship was qualitatively different for aggressive girls: in comparison with other girls, and with aggressive and non-aggressive boys, the aggressive girls had been much less likely to experience breastfeeding after birth (Figure 1.3).

Peer rejection
We have argued that most girls have a maturational advantage compared with boys, and greater self-regulatory abilities, which promote gender segregation in the preschool years and gender-specific socialization experiences within same-sex peer groups. We have therefore suggested that girls who do not have the maturational advantage and powers of self-regulation may not succeed in integrating into the gender-segregated peer relations of middle childhood. Some evidence for this claim can be found in teachers' reports on girls' versus boys' peer relationships. According to teachers, aggressive girls were significantly less likely to be liked by their peers than were non-aggressive girls, $\chi^2_{(1)} = 5.87$, $p < .02$ (Figure 1.4). In contrast, according to teachers, peers did not necessarily dislike aggressive boys. This suggests that aggressive girls are indeed likely to be excluded from same-sex peer groups, whereas aggressive boys are indeed likely to influence normative behaviour in male peer groups.

FIGURE 1.4   TEACHERS' REPORTS OF PEER RELATIONS AT AGE 11

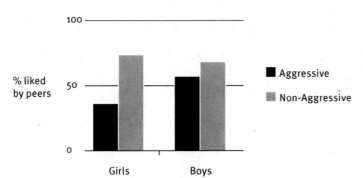

That pattern of peer relations in turn supports our claim that a minority of highly aggressive boys may raise the overall level of "normative aggression" in the male sex as a whole.

SUMMARY AND CONCLUSIONS

The purpose of this book is to focus attention on girls in their own right, and not just as a comparison group in studies of boys. Although, beginning in the early childhood years, boys are more aggressive than girls, there remains a minority of highly aggressive girls. We have proposed a developmental model to explain the increasing divergence between the sexes, and have suggested that girls who do not follow the gender-normative developmental pathway are at particular risk for aggression and its associated deleterious outcomes. To the extent that such girls are rejected by their same-sex peers, they may be at special risk for affiliation with boys, which may increase their levels of aggression and also put them at risk for earlier transitions into sexual relationships. Preliminary evidence from a small sample of aggressive girls and boys, drawn from a representative community sample, suggest that the predicted pathway from perinatal risk to peer rejection is one followed by many aggressive girls.

If the developmental model proposed here is confirmed by evidence in other samples, policy-makers might begin to consider gender-specific screening and prevention strategies. At present, the needs of aggressive girls may be less likely to be identified in the early childhood years. Our preliminary evidence suggests that it might be best to try to identify girls at risk for aggression with respect to the following markers: mothers' depression, smoking, and other substance use during pregnancy; low birth weight and delayed developmental milestones; slower acquisition of language and conversational fluency; and lack of same-sex friends. Even these physically aggressive girls may be more likely than boys to engage in covert aggression (Pepler & Craig, 1991), and so their problems in getting along with same-sex peers may be less visible to teachers and parents. This means that their problems may escalate over the middle childhood years, until they become highly visible, along with other conduct symptoms and comorbid emotional problems, when the girls enter puberty.

KEY MESSAGES
1. Sex differences in aggression emerge in the early childhood years.
2. Girls who have been exposed to prenatal and postnatal insults, and whose development may therefore be delayed, may be especially at risk for aggression.
3. Girls with communication difficulties may be less well accepted by other girls; these problems with same-sex peers increase their risk for aggression.
4. Gender-specific prevention programs might focus on aggressive girls' acquisition of self-regulatory and communicative skills that promote harmonious relations with other girls.

ACKNOWLEDGEMENTS

The preparation of this chapter, as well as the collection of the preliminary data reported within it, has been supported by the Medical Research Council, UK, through MRC Project Grant Nos. G89292999N and G9539876N; MRC Programme Grant No. G0400086; and an MRC postgraduate scholarship for Kathryn Hudson. We are grateful to the children and families who have participated in the South London Child Development Study, which has been led by Professor Deborah Sharp, Dr. Susan Pawlby, and the late Professor R. Kumar.

REFERENCES

Angold, A., & Costello, E.J. (2000). The Child and Adolescent Psychiatric Assessment (CAPA). *Journal of the American Academy of Child Adolescent Psychiatry, 39*, 39–48.

Archer, J., & Côté, S. (2005). Sex differences in aggressive behavior: A developmental and evolutionary perspective. In R. Tremblay, W.W. Hartup, & J. Archer (Eds.), *Developmental Origins of Aggression* (pp. 425–443). New York: Guilford.

Arcia, E., & Conner, C.K. (1998). Gender differences in ADHD? *Journal of Developmental Behavioural Pediatrics, 19,* 77–83.

Asch, S.E. (1956). Studies of independence and conformity: A minority of one against a unanimous majority. *Psychological Monographs: General and Applied, 70,* 1–70 (Whole No. 416).

Auerbach, J.G., Faroy, M., Ebstein, R., Kahana, M., & Levine, J. (2001). The association of the dopamine D4 receptor gene (DRD4) and the serotonin transporter promoter gene (5-HTTLPR) with temperament in 12-month-old infants. *Journal of Child Psychology and Psychiatry, 42,* 777–783.

Brennan, P.A., Grekin, E.R., & Mednick, S.A. (1999). Maternal smoking during pregnancy and adult male criminal outcomes. *Archives of General Psychiatry, 56,* 215–219.

Broidy, L., Nagin, D.S., Tremblay, R.E., Bates, J., Brame, B., Dodge, K.A., Pettit, G.S. (2003). Developmental trajectories of childhood disruptive behaviors and adolescent delinquency: A six-site, cross-national study. *Developmental Psychology, 39,* 222–245.

Cairns, R. (1979). Social development: The origins of plasticity of interchanges. San Francisco: Freeman.

Calkins, S.D., & Fox, N.A. (2002). Self-regulatory processes in early personality development: A multilevel approach to the study of childhood social withdrawal and aggression. *Development and Psychopathology, 14,* 477–498.

Caplan, M., Vespo, J.E., Pedersen, J., & Hay, D.F. (1991). Conflict and its resolution in small groups of one- and two-year-olds. *Child Development, 62,* 1513–1524.

Cassidy, J., & Asher, S. (1992). Loneliness and peer relations in young children. *Child Development, 63,* 350–365.

Côté, S., Vaillancourt, T., LeBlanc, J.C., Nagin, D.S., & Tremblay, R.E. (2006). The development of physical aggression from toddlerhood to pre-adolescence: A nation wide longitudinal study of Canadian children. *Journal of Abnormal Child Psychology, 34,* 71–85.

Crick, N.R., Casas, J.F., & Mosher, M. (1997). Relational and overt aggression in preschool. *Child Development, 33,* 579–588.

Dale, P.S., Simonoff, E., Bishop, D.V.M., Eley, T.C., Oliver, B., Price, T.S., Purcell, S., Stevenson, J., & Plomin, R. (1998). Genetic influence on language delay in two-year-old children. *Nature Neuroscience, 1,* 324–328.

Deave, T., Heron, J., Evans, J., & Emond, A. (2008). The impact of maternal depression in pregnancy on early child development. *British Journal of Obstetrics and Gynecology, 115,* 1043–1051.

Denenberg, V.H., Fitch, R.H., Schrott, L.M., Cowell, P.E., & Waters, N.S. (1991). Corpus callosum: Interactive effects of infantile handling and testosterone in the rat. *Behavioral Neuroscience, 105,* 562–566.

Dionne, G., Tremblay, R.E., Boivin, M., Laplante, D., & Pérusse, D. (2003). Physical aggression and expressive vocabulary in 19-month-old twins. *Developmental Psychology, 39,* 261–273.

Dishion, T.J., Bullock, B.M., & Granic, I. (2002). Pragmatism in modeling peer influence: Dynamics, outcomes, and change processes. *Development and Psychopathology, 14*, 969–981.

Dodge, K.A., & Coie, J.D. (1987). Social information processing factors in reactive and proactive aggression in children's peer groups. *Journal of Personality and Social Psychology, 53*, 1146–1158.

Else-Quest, N.M., Hyde, J.S., Goldsmith, H.H., & Van Hulle, C.A. (2006). Gender differences in temperament: A meta-analysis. *Psychological Bulletin, 132*, 33–72.

Fagot, B.I., Leinbach, M.D., & O'Boyle, C. (1992). Gender labelling, gender stereotyping, and parenting behaviors. *Developmental Psychology, 28*, 225–230.

Gelman, S.A., Taylor, M.G., & Nguyen, S.P. (2004). Mother-child conversations about gender. *Monographs of the Society for Research in Child Development, 69*(1), vii–127.

Goldsmith, H.H., Buss, K.A., & Lemery, K.S. (1996). Toddler and childhood temperament: Expanded content, stronger genetic evidence, new evidence for the importance of environment. *Developmental Psychology, 33*, 891–905.

Goldsmith, H.H., Buss, A.H., Plomifhbart, M.K., Thomas, A., Chess, S.,...McCall, R.B. (1987). Roundtable: What is temperament? Four approaches. *Child Development, 58*, 505–529.

Goodman, R. (1997). The Strengths and Difficulties Questionnaire: A research note. *Journal of Child Psychology and Psychiatry, 38*, 581–586.

Hane, A.A., Fox, N.A., Polak-Toste, C., Ghera, M.M., & Guner, B.M. (2006). Contextual basis of maternal perceptions of infant temperament. *Developmental Psychology, 42*, 1077–1088.

Hay, D.F. (2006). "Yours and mine": Toddlers' talk about possession with familiar peers. *British Journal of Developmental Psychology, 24*, 39–52.

Hay, D.F. (2007). The gradual emergence of sex differences in aggression: Alternative hypotheses. *Psychological Medicine, 37*(11), 1527–1537.

Hay, D.F., Caplan, M.Z., Pedersen, J., Ishikawa, F., Nash, A., & Vespo, J.E. (2007). Young girls and boys in conflict. Manuscript submitted for publication.

Hay, D.F., Castle, J., & Davies, L. (2000). Toddlers' use of force against familiar peers: A precursor of serious aggression? *Child Development, 71*, 457–467.

Hay, D.F., Castle, J., Davies, L., Demetriou, H., & Stimson, C.A. (1999). Prosocial action in very early childhood. *Journal of Child Psychology and Psychiatry, 40*, 905–916.

Hay, D.F., Pawlby, S., Waters, C.S., Perra, O., & Sharp, D. (2010). Mothers' antenatal depression and their children's antisocial outcomes. *Child Development, 81*, 149–165.

Hay, D.F., & Ross, H.S. (1982). The social nature of early conflict. *Child Development, 53*, 105–113.

Kahn, R.S., Khoury, J., Nichols, W.C., & Lanphear, B.P. (2003). Role of dopamine transporter genotype and maternal prenatal smoking in childhood hyperactive-impulsive, inattentive, and oppositional behaviors. *Journal of Pediatrics, 143*, 104–110.

Keenan, K., & Shaw, D. (1997). Developmental and social influences on young girls' early problem behavior. *Psychological Bulletin, 121,* 95–113.

Kochanska, G., Coy, K.C., & Murray, K.T. (2001). The development of self-regulation in the first four years of life. *Child Development, 72,* 1091–1111.

Kopp, C.B (1982). Antecedents of self-regulation: A developmental perspective. *Developmental Psychology, 18,* 199–214.

Kuczynski, L., Kochanska, G., Radke-Yarrow, M., & Girnius-Brown, O. (1987). A developmental interpretation of young children's noncompliance. *Developmental Psychology, 23,* 799–806.

Maccoby, E.E. (1998). *The two sexes: Growing up apart, coming together.* Cambridge, MA: Harvard University Press.

Maughan, B., Taylor, A., Caspi, A., & Moffitt, T.E. (2004). Prenatal smoking and early childhood conduct problems. *Archives of General Psychiatry, 61,* 836–843.

Meichenbaum, D., & Goodman, J. (1969). Reflection-impulsivity and verbal control of motor behavior. *Child Development, 40,* 785–797.

Mick, E., Biederman, J., Faraone, S.V., Sayer, J., & Kleinman, S. (2002). Case-control study of Attention-Deficit Hyperactivity Disorder and maternal smoking, alcohol use, and drug use during pregnancy. *Journal of American Academy of Child and Adolescent Psychiatry, 41,* 378–385.

Moffitt, T.E., Caspi, A., Rutter, M., & Silva, P.A. (2001). *Sex differences in antisocial behaviour: Conduct disorder, delinquency and violence in the Dunedin Longitudinal Study.* Cambridge: Cambridge University Press.

Moscovici, S., & Personnaz, B. (1980). Studies in social influence: Minority influence and conversion behaviour in a perceptual task. *Journal of Experimental Social Psychology, 16,* 279–282.

Oberklaid, F., Prior, M., Sanson, A., Sewell, J., & Kyrios, M. (1990). Assessment of temperament in the toddler age group. *Pediatrics, 85,* 559–566.

O'Connor, T.G., Heron, J., Golding, J., Beveridge, M., & Glover, V. (2002). Maternal antenatal anxiety and children's behavioural/emotional problems at 4 years. Report from the Avon Longitudinal Study of Parents and Children. *British Journal of Psychiatry, 180,* 502–508.

Orlebeke, J.F., Knol, D.L., & Verhulst, F.C. (1999). Child behavior problems increased by maternal smoking during pregnancy. *Archives of Environmental Health, 54,* 15.

Pauli-Pott, U., Mertesacker, B., Bade, U., Haverlock, A., & Beckermann, D. (2003). Parental perceptions and infant temperament development. *Infant Behavior and Development, 26,* 27–48.

Pawlby, S., Hay, D.F., Waters, C.S., & Sharp, D. (2008). Antenatal depression predicts depression in adolescent offspring: Prospective longitudinal community-based study. *Journal of Affective Disorders, 113,* 236–243.

Pepler, D.J., & Craig, W. (1991). A peek behind the fence: Naturalistic observations of aggressive children with remote audiovisual recording. *Developmental Psychology, 31,* 548–553.

Pinderhughes, E.E., Dodge, K.A., Bates, J.E., Pettit, G.S., & Zelli, A. (2000). Discipline responses: Influence of parents' socioeconomic status, ethnicity, beliefs about parenting, stress, and cognitive-emotional processes. *Journal of Family Psychology*, *14*, 380–400.

Raine, A. (2002). Annotation: The role of prefrontal deficits, low autonomic arousal, and early health factors in the development of antisocial and aggressive behavior in children. *Journal of Child Psychology and Psychiatry*, *43*, 417–434.

Raine, A., Moffitt, T.E., Caspi, A., Loeber, R., Stouhamer-Loeber, M., & Lynam, D. (2005). Neurocognitive impairments in boys on the life-course persistent antisocial path. *Journal of Abnormal Psychology*, *114*, 38–49.

Rheingold, H.L., & Cook, K.V. (1975). The contents of boys' and girls' rooms as an index of parents' behaviour. *Child Development*, *46*, 459–463.

Rheingold, H.L., Cook, K.V., & Kolowitz, V. (1987). Commands activate the behavior and pleasure of 2-year-old children. *Developmental Psychology*, *23*, 146–151.

Rodriquez, A., & Bohlin, G. (2005). Are maternal smoking and stress during pregnancy related to ADHD symptoms in children? *Journal of Child Psychology and Psychiatry*, *46*, 246–254.

Rothbart, M.K., & Hwang, J. (2002). Measuring infant temperament. *Infant Behavior and Development*, *25*, 113–116.

Ruble, D.N., Martin, C., & Berebaum, S.A. (2006). Gender development. In W. Damon, R. Lerner, & N. Eisenberg (Eds.), *Handbook of child psychology*, Vol. 3 (pp. 858–932). Chichester: Wiley.

Schlumpf, M., Gähwiler, M., Ribary, U., & Lichtensteigner, W. (1988). A new device for monitoring early motor development: Prenatal nicotine-induced changes. *Pharmacology, Biochemistry and Behavior*, *30*, 199–203.

Slotkin, T.A., MacKillop, E.A., Rudder, C.L., Ryde, I.T., Tate, C.A., & Seidler, F.J. (2007). Permanent, sex-selective effects of prenatal or adolescent nicotine exposure, separately or sequentially, in rat brain regions: Indices of cholinergic and serotonergic synaptic function, cell signaling, and neural cell number and size at 6 months of age. *Neuropsychopharmacology*, *32*(5), 1082–1097.

Thapar, A., Fowler, T., Rice, F., Scourfield, J., van den Bree, M., Thomas, H., & Hay, D.F. (2003). Maternal smoking during pregnancy and attention deficit hyperactivity disorder symptoms in offspring. *American Journal of Psychiatry*, *160*, 1985–1989.

Tremblay, R., Nagin, D.S., Séguin, J.R., Zoccolillo, M., Zelazo, P.D., Boivin, M.,...Japel, C. (2004). Physical aggression during early childhood: Trajectories and predictors. *Pediatrics*, *114*, e43–e50.

van Goozen, S.H.M., Fairchild, G., Snoek, H., & Harold, G.T. (2007). The evidence for a neurobiological model of childhood antisocial behavior. *Psychological Bulletin*, *133*, 149–182.

Vohr, B.R., Wright, L.L., Dusick, A.M., Mele, L., Verter, J., Steicher, J.J., ... Kaplan, M.D. (2000). Neurodevelopmental and functional outcomes in very low-birth-weight infants in the National Institute of Child Health and Human Development National Research Network, 1993–1994. *Pediatrics, 105*, 1216–1226.

Wakschlag, L.S., Pickett, K.E., Kasza, K.E., & Loeber, R. (2006). Is prenatal smoking associated with a developmental pattern of conduct problems in young boys? *Journal of the American Academy of Child and Adolescent Psychiatry, 45*, 461–467.

Windham, G., Hopkins, B., Fenster, L., & Swan, S. (2000). Prenatal active or passive tobacco smoke exposure and the risk of preterm delivery or low birth weight. *Epidemiology, 11*, 427–433.

Zoccolillo, M., Meyers, J., & Assiter, S. (1997). Conduct disorder, substance dependence, and adolescent motherhood. *American Journal of Orthopsychiatry, 67*, 152–157.

CHAPTER TWO

ADULT HEALTH OUTCOMES OF GIRLS WITH ANTI-SOCIAL BEHAVIOUR PROBLEMS

CANDICE L. ODGERS

DUKE UNIVERSITY

Girls who engage in aggressive and anti-social behaviour are at increased risk for a number of social and emotional problems. While there is already good reason to direct resources towards these young women, new research linking adult relationship violence and poor physical health to early behaviour problems is providing new cause for concern. This chapter describes the developmental pathways of anti-social behaviour among girls along with the associated risks for relationship violence and poor physical health in adulthood. Potential mechanisms underlying the association between anti-social behaviour in childhood and poor health in adulthood are reviewed, with an emphasis on gender-specific mechanisms and priorities for future research.

THE DEVELOPMENTAL COURSE OF ANTI-SOCIAL BEHAVIOUR AMONG GIRLS

Many researchers have asked whether girls follow the same developmental pathways of anti-social and aggressive behaviour as their male counterparts. Much of this debate has centred on the question of whether the developmental taxonomy of anti-social behaviour (Moffitt, 1993) that has guided research with primarily male samples, can also be extended to understand the developmental pathways and adult outcomes for females.

In a nutshell, the original developmental taxonomy of anti-social behaviour proposed that at least two prototypical subtypes characterize the development of anti-social behaviour over time (Moffitt, 1993): a *life-course-persistent* (LCP) pathway that is characterized by social, familial, and neuro-developmental deficits, onsets in early childhood, and distinguishes a relatively small, yet persistent and pathological subgroup of individuals; and an *adolescence-limited* (AL) pathway that is hypothesized to be more common, relatively transient, and near normative. Adolescence-limited involvement in anti-social behaviour is believed to emerge alongside puberty as a relatively normative response to the role-less years between biological maturation and access to mature privileges and responsibilities, a period of time labelled the "maturity gap." Although those on the LCP pathway are expected to experience multiple problems in adulthood (including violence), adolescence-limited individuals, given the normative nature of their preteen development, are hypothesized to be more successful in their transition to adulthood, provided that they do not encounter snares, such as substance dependency or a criminal record.

The original statement of the taxonomy was intended to apply to females as well as males (Moffitt, 1994; Moffitt, Caspi, Rutter, & Silva, 2001). Within the developmental taxonomy, much of the gender difference in levels of anti-social behaviour is attributed to sex differences in the individual risk factors for persistent anti-social behaviour; research has consistently shown that girls have lower rates than boys of symptoms of nervous system dysfunction, difficult temperament, hyperactivity, reading failure, and learning disabilities (Gorman-Smith & Loeber, 2005; Lahey et al., 2006; Messer, Goodman, Rowe, Meltzer, & Maughan, 2006). Thus, the consequent processes of cumulative continuity ensue for fewer girls than boys, resulting in a smaller number of girls following the LCP pathway, but the childhood correlates of the LCP subtype are assumed to be similar across gender (Moffitt et al., 2001).

While the majority of past research has focused on the developmental course of anti-social behaviour in males, the male-only focus in aggression research is rapidly changing (Moffitt et al., 2001; Moretti, Odgers, & Jackson, 2004; Pepler, Jiang, Craig, & Connolly, 2008; Pepler, Madsen, Webster, & Levene, 2005; Putallaz & Bierman, 2004). As a result, an evidence base regarding the course and consequences of girls' anti-social behaviour and aggression is emerging (Hay, 2007; Hipwell et al., 2002; Keenan, Loeber, & Green, 1999; Keenan, Stouthamer-Loeber, & Loeber, 2005; Pepler & Craig, 2005). For example, prospective cohort studies have identified a childhood-onset and persistent subtype of females who, although fewer in number, look very similar to LCP males on childhood risk factors and who also experience poor prognosis in adolescence and adulthood (Bongers,

Koot, van der Ende, & Verhulst, 2004; Broidy et al., 2003; Coté, Zoccolillo, Tremblay, Nagin, & Vitaro, 2001; Fergusson & Horwood, 2002; Kratzer & Hodgins, 1999; Lahey et al., 2006; Odgers, Moffitt, et al., 2008; Schaeffer et al., 2006; White & Piquero, 2004).

ARE GIRLS ON THE LIFE-COURSE-PERSISTENT AND ADOLESCENCE-LIMITED PATHWAYS AT RISK FOR AGGRESSIVE AND ANTI-SOCIAL BEHAVIOUR AS ADULTS?

Epidemiological studies testing for gender-specific pathways of anti-social behaviour have identified a "childhood-onset" or "early starter" pathway among females (Bongers et al., 2004; Broidy et al., 2003; Coté, Tremblay, Nagin, Zoccolillo, & Vitaro, 2002; Fergusson & Horwood, 2002; Lahey et al., 2006; Schaeffer et al., 2006). For example, in a representative study of 820 Canadian girls, Coté and colleagues (2001) found that approximately 11% of girls followed a medium-high to high trajectory of persistent disruptive behaviours between the ages of 6 to 12 and were at an increased risk for juvenile conduct disorder. Continued follow-up of this sample to age 21 indicated that females with early and persistent behaviour problems (particularly those who were chronically high on both hyperactivity and aggression) were at an increased risk for physical and psychological aggression towards their romantic partners, although they were not more likely to engage in *non-violent* criminal behaviours (Fontaine et al., 2008). Continuity from early aggression to family violence and child abuse has also been documented in a 30-year follow-up of over 1,700 male and female children in the Concordia Longitudinal Risk Project with support for both direct and indirect pathways from childhood aggression to later physical violence towards partners and children (Temcheff et al., 2008).

Similar findings have been found in the United States and elsewhere: in a nationally representative US sample, Lahey and colleagues (2006) reported that 3.5% to 6.9% of females followed an LCP pathway between the ages of 4 and 17. Schaeffer and colleagues (2006) also identified an early starter and persistent subgroup of females (9% of a cohort) among 665 girls from a representative US inner-city sample. This early starter group went on to have the highest levels of anti-social behaviour in adulthood, including increased risk of arrests for violent offences.

A recent report from the Dunedin Multidisciplinary Health and Development Study, a 32-year longitudinal study of a birth cohort of 1,000 New Zealanders, revealed a small group of females (7.5% of the cohort) who exhibited conduct problem symptoms in childhood and persisted in their involvement in anti-social behaviour into young adulthood. At age 32, women on this early-onset and persistent pathway were at an increased risk for violence towards their partners and their children; over 75% of women on this early-onset persistent pathway had engaged in at least one form of physical violence over the past 6 months (e.g., physical violence towards partners, children, or others) (Odgers, Moffitt, et al., 2008). For example, approximately half of the women on the LCP pathway had engaged in physical violence towards partners (44.8%) or their children (41.7%) within the past 6 months. Interestingly, girls on the adolescence-limited pathway in the Dunedin Study were not at an increased risk for aggression against romantic partners or other adults once they reached adulthood; however, they were significantly more likely than the average Dunedin female (14.3% versus 24.4%) to report "hitting their child out of anger."

In sum, emerging research supports the existence of a small, yet significant, subgroup of girls following an early-onset and persistent pathway of anti-social behaviour; young women on this pathway are at an increased risk for anti-social behaviour and aggression in adulthood, including violence towards partners and children. Although girls on the adolescence-limited pathway in the Dunedin Study seemed to be making a successful transition away from violence within intimate partner relationships and against other adults, they were still more likely to engage in physical violence towards their children. Thus, aggressive and anti-social behaviour in *both* childhood and adolescence seems to be an important signal of future risk for violence within family contexts.

These findings suggest that early interventions are required to promote the development of healthy romantic and parenting relationships—particularly for girls on an at-risk developmental trajectory. Newly emerging intervention research suggests that school-based relationship violence prevention programs during the transition to high school may be effective in reducing males' perpetration of partner violence; however, evidence supporting the effectiveness of these programs in reducing girls' violence has been mixed (Wolfe, 2006). Additional research is required to understand both the positive and negative aspects regarding the close relationships of these young women and also to identify leverage points for the promotion of healthy relationships across development.

WHAT ARE THE PHYSICAL HEALTH CONSEQUENCES FOR ANTI-SOCIAL GIRLS GROWN UP?

Researchers and practitioners alike recognize the need to look beyond traditional measures of anti-social behaviour and aggression when evaluating the adult outcomes of high-risk children and adolescents. A number of longitudinal studies have adopted this approach and there is now evidence that early-onset and persistent anti-social behaviour predicts a wide range of poor adult outcomes, including depression, substance use disorders, relationship difficulties, self-harm behaviours, poor educational outcomes, and dependence on social welfare systems (Fergusson, Horwood, & Ridder, 2005; Kim-Cohen et al., 2003; Kratzer & Hodgins, 1997; Moffitt, Caspi, Harrington, & Milne, 2002; Wiesner, Kim, & Capaldi, 2005).

More recently, there has been a renewed interest in understanding the relationship between the development of anti-social behaviour and poor physical health, with the suggestion that anti-social behaviour and aggression may be a particularly important risk factor for poor health among girls (De Genna, Stack, Serbin, Ledingham, & Schwartzman, 2006; Pajer, 1998; Pajer & Gardner, 2004; Pajer, Leininger, & Lourie, 2011). In one study, 93 adolescent girls (41 controls versus 52 girls with conduct disorder) were recruited from the community and followed for three years. At the three-year follow-up, adolescent girls with conduct disorder versus controls self-reported poorer overall health, more discomfort, more health risk behaviours as young adults, and earlier onset of adult reproductive behaviours, even when controlling for demographic factors and pre-existing health history (Pajer, Kazmi, Gardner, & Wang, 2007). Similar results were reported in a representative sample of 1,218 mothers of boys randomly selected from urban public schools in the United States. In this study, women with versus without a history of anti-social behaviour reported higher rates of long-term physical health problems even after controlling for socio-demographic factors (Pajer, Stouthamer-Loeber, Gardner, & Loeber, 2006). Finally, a 10-year follow-up study of more than 700 boys and girls in a population-based sample, found that conduct disorder symptoms in adolescence predicted body mass index (BMI) and obesity in early adulthood, again, after controlling for a range of confounding factors (Pine, Cohen, Brook, & Coplan, 1997).

The hypothesis that anti-social behaviour and physical health are related is not new (Robins & Rutter, 1990). Indeed, there is a significant body of research linking anti-social behaviour and *self-reported* health problems (Bardone et al., 1998; De Genna et al., 2006; Farrington, 1995; Pajer et al., 2006; Piquero, Gibson, Daigle, Leeper-Piquero, & Tibbetts, 2007; Serbin et al., 2004; Shepherd & Farrington, 2003). However, longitudinal cohort studies that include *objective* markers of disease and physical health in adulthood are now becoming available, which corrects for possible bias in prior work where individuals have provided self-reports of both their behaviour and their health. For example, the Dunedin Study assessed physical-health status in adulthood via medical examinations, the collection of blood samples, tests of vital lung capacity via a computerized spirometer and body plethysmograph, and dental examinations.

Findings from the Dunedin Study support a prospective link between anti-social subtypes and adult physical health across the first 32 years of life. Here, women on the LCP pathway were experiencing the worst physical-health outcomes at age 32, and they were more likely than the average Dunedin female cohort member to have contracted type 2 herpes, to smoke, to be dependent on nicotine, and to exhibit signs of chronic bronchitis, gum disease, and decayed tooth surfaces (Odgers, Moffitt, et al., 2008). Similar findings were documented for males on the LCP pathway who, when compared to the average Dunedin male cohort member, had significantly higher rates of sexually transmitted diseases, dental disease, cardiovascular risk factors, inflammatory measures of immune dysfunction, injuries requiring medical treatment, and respiratory lung dysfunctions (Odgers et al., 2007).

It is also important to note that individuals who began engaging in anti-social behaviour in *adolescence* may also be at an elevated risk for poor health. For example, both males and females in the Dunedin Study who began their anti-social behaviour in adolescence were at an increased risk for poor health in adulthood. Although individuals on this pathway were not experiencing the same levels of problems as their life-course-persistent counterparts, it was clear that involvement in anti-social behaviour—even if it was restricted to adolescence—carried residual health risks (Odgers, Moffitt, et al., 2008).

In sum, longitudinal research supports a prospective link between anti-social behaviour in childhood and adolescence and later physical health problems. The association between early behaviour problems and adult physical health problems: (a) has been consistently documented across a number of studies, using both self-report and objective measures of health, (b) holds for both males and females, and (c) is robust after controlling for a range of childhood risk and confounding factors—with evidence that there may be both indirect and direct pathways from childhood behaviour problems to poor adult health (e.g., see De Genna et al., 2006).

From a public health perspective, there is a need to develop a better understanding of the link between anti-social behaviour and poor physical health, not only because it may offer the opportunity to reduce health costs, but also because of the potential for developing joint interventions that may promote positive development related to both behaviour *and* health. However, in order to understand how the robust relationship between childhood behaviour problems and adult health can be disrupted, a more complete understanding of the mechanisms through which antisocial behaviour and poor health may be linked is required.

WHAT ARE THE MECHANISMS UNDERLYING THE ASSOCIATION BETWEEN ANTI-SOCIAL BEHAVIOUR AND POOR PHYSICAL HEALTH?

Unfortunately, we know very little about how anti-social behaviour may "get under the skin" and compromise a child or adolescent's physical health. Four possible explanations for the association between anti-social behaviour and poor physical health are reviewed below. Each theory suggests different intervention and prevention opportunities as well as possibilities for gender-specific theory and programming.

1. Risky Family and Relationship Contexts Predict Both Childhood Anti-Social Behaviour and Poor Adult Health

Exposure to early stressors, including maltreatment and family conflict, is known to influence children's health and development (Gunnar & Quevedo, 2007). This is important because research has consistently demonstrated that the childhood experiences for male and female children on the LCP pathway are characterized by high levels of family adversity, parental conflict, and an increased risk of childhood maltreatment (Moffitt, 2006). Within these contexts, a vulnerable child is often exposed to a cascade of risk that may contribute to both early behaviour problems and poor health outcomes. Repetti, Taylor, and Seeman (2002) describe how these types of "risky families" may get under the skin and compromise present and future health. Risky families are characterized by conflict and aggression and by relationships that are cold, unsupportive, and neglectful. This type of exposure is hypothesized to create vulnerabilities in children or to interact with genetically based predispositions to disrupt psychosocial functioning. In doing so, risky families are believed to produce disruptions in the stress-response system, impede psychosocial development, and encourage poor health behaviours.

Support for the risky families model has been found in large epidemiological studies. For example, results from a large retrospective study of the childhood experiences of approximately 9,500 individuals demonstrated that childhood exposure to abuse or household dysfunction independently predicted a number of adult diseases, including cancer, chronic lung disease, heart disease, skeletal fractures, and liver disease (Felitti et al., 1998). Similarly, a 30-year follow-up of Dunedin Study children into young adulthood also found that experiences of childhood maltreatment independently predicted objective markers of immune function and allostatic load (Danese, Pariante, Caspi, Taylor, & Poulton, 2007).

The risky families model, and its primacy in understanding the origins and course of physical and mental health problems across the lifespan

(Repetti et al., 2002), seems especially important to consider when examining the associated risk factors of anti-social behaviour among girls. That is, research has consistently documented higher rates of maltreatment, including severe physical and sexual victimization (for a review see Odgers & Moretti, 2002) and post-traumatic stress disorder (Cauffman, Feldman, Waterman, & Steiner, 1998), among high-risk girls versus boys. Girls diagnosed with conduct disorder are also more likely to be placed outside the home in foster care and are at a greater risk of being removed from their homes earlier than boys (Moretti, Holland, & McKay, 2001). Increased risk for family-related problems among girls with a developmental history of anti-social behaviour is especially concerning given that females tend to internalize external stressors and symptoms (Quinn, 2005).

Relationship stress and interpersonal conflict across the lifespan have also been linked to compromised physical health (De Vogli, Chandola, & Marmot, 2007; Wickrama et al., 2001). These findings are important because individuals with a history of anti-social behaviour often experience high levels of repeated conflict with parents, teachers, peers, and in extreme cases with the criminal justice system. Moreover, anti-social individuals may lack the types of social support networks that have been shown to buffer many of the ill-health consequences associated with exposure to stressful life events (Cohen, 2004), likely due to the fact that they have alienated friends and family members by engaging in behaviours that persistently violate the rights of others.

In sum, individuals following early-onset and persistent-pathway anti-social behaviour are: (a) more likely to experience early stress and adversity, (b) often exposed to repeated conflict in their interpersonal relationships across childhood and into adulthood, and (c) less likely to have intact social support networks and positive relationships to buffer the effects stressful life events. These types of repeated exposures to stress and interpersonal conflict may be one way that external life events get under the skin and influence individuals with a pervasive history of anti-social behaviour, particularly among young women who may be more likely to internalize relationship problems and stressful life experiences.

2. Anti-Social Children and Adolescents May Engage in More Health-Risk Behaviours

One of the most straightforward explanations for the relationship between anti-social behaviour and poor health is that individuals who engage in anti-social behaviour are also more likely to engage in health-risk behaviours (e.g., substance abuse, reckless driving) and less likely to engage in health-promoting behaviours (e.g., failure to attend regular checkups, poor diet) (Elliot, 1993). Unfortunately, the majority of research on this topic has excluded girls, due in part to low numbers in high-risk childhood clinical groups (e.g., children with ADHD). Nonetheless, available research suggests that children who engage in anti-social and disruptive behaviour are at a higher risk for accidents and unintentional injuries (Brehaut, Miller, Raina, & McGrail, 2003; Schwebel, Speltz, Jones, & Bardina, 2002), including traumatic dental injury (Sabuncuoglu, 2007) and major and minor head injuries (Lalloo & Sheiham, 2003).

The link between anti-social behaviour and poor health seems particularly strong when early behavioural problems include aggression and/ or ADHD symptoms. For example, children with ADHD are significantly more likely to be injured while riding a bicycle, to receive head injuries, to be hospitalized for accidental poisoning, and to utilize medical services across multiple delivery settings (DiScala, Lescohier, Barthel, & Li, 1998; Leibson, Katusic, Barbaresi, Ransom, & O'Brien, 2001). With respect to early physical aggression, Tremblay (2002) has reported that boys who engaged in physical aggression from early childhood to late adolescence were at the highest risk of causing injuries to others and to themselves. Similar findings were reported in the Cambridge Study of Delinquent Development, where injuries at ages 16–18 and 27–32 were concentrated among males with a history of anti-social behaviour and violence (Shepherd, Farrington, & Potts, 2002, 2004).

The increased risk for injury and medical service use among children and adolescents with early behaviour problems is not inconsequential, as unintentional injury is the leading cause of death in children and young adults. Such findings suggest that intervention efforts with at-risk children may have the potential to both reduce violence and alleviate related medical problems. In an effort to test this idea, Borowsky, Mozayeny, Stuenkel, and Ireland (2004) conducted a randomized, controlled trial to evaluate the effects of a physician-administered intervention on children's violent behaviours and violence-related injuries (N = 224). At the nine-month follow-up, children in the intervention versus control group exhibited lower rates of aggression and attention problems, as well as fewer fight-related injuries requiring medical care (Borowsky et al., 2004). Although findings were generally consistent across males and females, separate analyses of intervention effects by sex showed that intervention had a significant effect on parent-reported *aggressive* behaviour for boys but not for girls (although this finding may have been due to low base rates of aggression among girls in the sample). These results provide proof of principle that efforts to reduce childhood aggression and violence may also reduce violence-related injuries and health costs among children, although more research with young girls is sorely needed.

The contribution of social and behavioural factors to chronic disease and premature death—especially during adolescence when many lifestyle habits are forming—has been widely recognized (Millstein, Petersen, & Nightingale, 1993). During adolescence young teens begin to operate in social contexts where their still-developing moral reasoning and perspective-taking skills may put them at risk (Cauffman & Steinberg, 2000). These deficits in psychosocial maturity may have unique consequences for young teens with a history of anti-social behaviour who are already more likely to engage in a range of risk-taking and health-compromising behaviours, including early exposure to substances, dangerous driving, and risky sexual behaviours (Odgers, Caspi, et al., 2008; Raikkonen, Matthews, Sutton-Tyrrell, & Kuller, 2004; Ramrakha et al., 2007). For example, a nine-year follow-up of 625 Canadian boys found that boys high on disruptive behaviour at age 6 were significantly more likely to engage in risky health behaviours in adolescence, including alcohol abuse, tobacco use, problems with drugs, and unsafe sex (Dobkin, Tremblay, & McDuff, 1997). Thus, for teens with a developmental history of anti-social behaviour the "normative" increase in risk-taking that accompanies adolescence may be amplified. In adulthood, these well-developed patterns of health-risk behaviour—including substance use, poor self-care, and general lifestyle choices that damage health—may become heavily entrenched and resistant to change, resulting in cumulative and prolonged exposure to many causes of injury, compromised health, and disease. Moreover, as reviewed in the previous section, these individuals are more likely to enter into abusive and highly conflictual relationships, further increasing the risk for injury and premature death, particularly for females.

3. Anti-Social Males and Females Are Often High on Hostility, Negative Affect, and Depression, Which May Confer Physiological Vulnerability
Anti-social behaviour does not occur in isolation. Rather, children who experience difficulties with anti-social behaviour early in life are also more likely to experience co-occurring mental health and personality difficulties. For example, anti-social children are characterized by under-controlled temperament, irritability, temper tantrums, and impulsivity (Moffitt, 2006). In adolescence and young adulthood, anti-social individuals are more likely to exhibit hostility and anger and are at an elevated risk for both negative affect and depressive symptoms; with evidence of greater co-morbidity between anti-social behaviour and depression among girls (Keenan et al., 1999). This is important because depression and depressive symptoms have been linked to cardiovascular disease, obesity, and related problems (Simon et al., 2006; Whooley, 2006). Likewise, hostility, a closely

associated trait of anti-social behaviour, has been independently related to a number of adverse health outcomes, including cardiovascular disease (CVD), elevated glucose levels, and diabetes (Knox, Weidner, Adelman, Stoney, & Ellison, 2004; Miller, Smith, Turner, Guijarro, & Hallet, 1996; Raikkonen et al., 2004). In fact, Pajer (2007) argues that the relationship between negative emotions and heart disease may onset in adolescence via facilitating the progression of early atherosclerotic lesions (proximal cause of the most common types of CVD). More broadly, Pajer argues that negative emotions in adolescents may be risk factors for the development of CVD via dysregulation of the stress response system (Pajer, 2007); consistent with this hypothesis, anger and aggression in childhood and adolescence have been associated with increases in triglycerides, BMI, and blood pressure reactivity (Gump, Matthews, & Raikkonen, 1999; Ravaja, Keltikangas-Jarvinen, & Keskivaara, 1996). Perhaps most convincingly, one study reported that hostility among adolescents predicted the development of metabolic syndrome characteristics three years later (Raikkonen, Matthews, & Salomon, 2003).

In sum, the link between anti-social behaviour and poor health may be partly explained by closely related mental health conditions and personality traits. This research, of course, raises the question of what comes first: Does anti-social behaviour precede the development of co-morbid conditions, such as depression, and poor physical health? Or does anti-social behaviour mediate the relationship between personality traits, such as hostility, and poor health? Future research is required to isolate the independent contribution of anti-social behaviour to poor health and test whether gender plays a role in altering these relationships.

4. Social Inequalities May Underlie the Development of Both Anti-Social Behaviour and Poor Health

Social disparities in health are well documented (Kramer, Seguin, Lydon, & Goulet, 2000; Starfield, Riley, Witt, & Robertson, 2002; Winkleby, Jatulis, Frank, & Fortmann, 1992). Thus, it is likely that low socio-economic status and related risk factors (e.g., low parental education, poor housing conditions, food insecurity, and limited access to medical care) underlie life-course trajectories of *both* poor physical health and anti-social behaviour. For example, we know that children growing up in deprivation go on to experience poor adult health, including cardiovascular disease, obesity, and related problems (Galobardes, Smith, & Lynch, 2006; Lawlor, Ronalds, Macintyre, Clark, & Leon, 2006; Melchior, Moffitt, Milne, Poulton, & Caspi, 2007; Poulton et al., 2002). Due to the fact that socio-economic status is one of the most robust predictors of mortality and overall well-being, it should account for at least a portion of the relationship between anti-social behaviour and poor health.

Adopting this type of common-risk-factor approach challenges the claim that anti-social behaviour leads to poor health, or vice versa, and, instead, raises the possibility that both anti-social behaviour and poor health are caused by a set of common predictors. Indeed, most studies suggest that the processes mediating the link between low socio-economic status in childhood and health outcomes are multifactorial, with anti-social behaviour and low socio-economic status each predicting a portion of the variance in poor adult health (Farrington, 1995; Shepherd et al., 2004; Melchior et al., 2007). Again, more research is required to understand whether socio-economic status has a differential influence on health among high-risk girls and, in particular, to explore how gender-specific vulnerabilities and strengths can be leveraged to support girls growing up within deprived contexts (Leadbeater & Way, 2007).

Although the precise mechanisms that link childhood anti-social behaviour to poor physical health are still unknown, research has converged on a number of take-home points:

- The association between anti-social behaviour early in life and poor adult physical health has been documented across a number of longitudinal cohort studies and holds after controlling for a wide range of individual, family, and other potentially confounding factors.
- The link between anti-social behaviour and poor health has been consistently reported for both males and females. However, there are reasons to believe that the physical health consequences for anti-social girls growing up in risky families may be more severe due to higher rates of victimization and the greater tendency for girls to internalize stressful life events.
- More research is required to: (a) identify the precise mechanisms that connect early behavioural problems and poor health, and (b) test whether the pathways from childhood anti-social behaviour to poor heath are gender specific. In particular, we know very little about the likelihood of childhood injury, risk taking, and/or engagement of health-promoting behaviours among high-risk girls.
- Finally, it is clear that the costs of early-onset and persistent anti-social behaviour need to be recalibrated to account for a wide range of medical and health-care expenses. This will be especially true as current cohorts (who are now primarily in their 30s and 40s) are followed further across the lifespan where age-related disease endpoints and health consequences can be more reliably assessed.

WHAT CAN BE DONE TO PROMOTE POSITIVE PHYSICAL HEALTH OUTCOMES OF CHILDREN WHO EXHIBIT SIGNS OF ANTI-SOCIAL BEHAVIOUR AND AGGRESSION EARLY IN LIFE?

The possibility that anti-social behaviour is an early marker or causal factor in poor physical health raises the intriguing possibility of designing prevention and intervention strategies that could influence both anti-social behaviour and health. Targeted prevention efforts across developmental stages would be ideal, as the untreated consequences of both anti-social behaviour and poor physical health are costly and are unlikely to be remedied via a single dose of prevention. Such strategies would require the co-operation of psychologists, pediatricians, and educators to promote the well-being of the "whole child." This type of multidisciplinary approach is challenging as it requires the movement of health-care providers across professional boundaries. However, these steps are necessary as it is no longer feasible to treat the mental or physical health of the child in isolation— multi-systemic and integrated approaches to child and adolescent health are required.

While a focus on physical health risks among children at risk for anti-social and aggressive behaviour is an important public health priority, there is also a need to refocus our attention on the physical health of young persons more generally. For the first time in recent history, we are entering into a period where life expectancy of the population may drop because adolescents and young adults are beginning to exhibit signs of chronic diseases. Arguably, joining forces across medicine, psychology, and education will be required to reverse current trends in child and adolescent health. Psychologists, pediatricians, educators, parents, *and children* all have a role to play in physical and mental health promotion.

NOTE
Address correspondence to: Candice L. Odgers (candice.odgers@duke.edu), Center for Child and Family Policy, Sanford School of Public Policy and Department of Psychology and Neuroscience, 218 Rubenstein Hall, Duke University, Durham, NC 27708.

REFERENCES
Bardone, A.M., Moffitt, T.E., Caspi, A., Dickson, N., Stanton, W.R., & Silva, P.A. (1998). Adult physical health outcomes of adolescent girls with conduct disorder, depression, and anxiety. *Journal of the American Academy of Child and Adolescent Psychiatry, 37,* 594–601.

Bongers, I.L., Koot, H.M., van der Ende, J., & Verhulst, F.C. (2004). Developmental trajectories of externalizing behaviors in childhood and adolescence. *Child Development, 75,* 1523–1537.

Borowsky, I.W., Mozayeny, S., Stuenkel, K., & Ireland, M. (2004). Effects of a primary care-based intervention on violent behavior and injury in children. *Pediatrics, 114,* e392–399.

Brehaut, J.C., Miller, A., Raina, P., & McGrail, K.M. (2003). Childhood behavior disorders and injuries among children and youth: A population-based study. *Pediatrics, 111,* 262–269.

Broidy, L.M., Nagin, D.S., Tremblay, R.E., Bates, J.E., Brame, B., Dodge, K.A.,...Vitaro, F. (2003). Developmental trajectories of childhood disruptive behaviors and adolescent delinquency: A six-site, cross-national study. *Developmental Psychology, 39,* 222–245.

Cauffman, E., Feldman, S.S., Waterman, J., & Steiner, H. (1998). Posttraumatic stress disorder among female juvenile offenders. *Journal of the American Academy of Child and Adolescent Psychiatry, 37,* 1209–1216.

Cauffman, E., & Steinberg, L. (2000). (Im)maturity of judgment in adolescence: Why adolescents may be less culpable than adults. *Behavioral Sciences and the Law, 18,* 741–760.

Cohen, S. (2004). Social relationships and health. *American Psychologist, 59,* 676–684.

Coté, S., Tremblay, R.E., Nagin, D.S., Zoccolillo, M., & Vitaro, F. (2002). Childhood behavioral profiles leading to adolescent conduct disorder: Risk trajectories for boys and girls. *Journal of the American Academy of Child and Adolescent Psychiatry, 41,* 1086–1094.

Coté, S., Zoccolillo, M., Tremblay, R.E., Nagin, D., & Vitaro, F. (2001). Predicting girls' conduct disorder in adolescence from childhood trajectories of disruptive behaviors. *Journal of the American Academy of Child and Adolescent Psychiatry, 40,* 678–684.

Danese, A., Pariante, C.M., Caspi, A., Taylor, A., & Poulton, R. (2007). Childhood maltreatment predicts adult inflammation in a life-course study. *Proceedings of the National Academy of Sciences of the United States of America, 104,* 1319–1324.

De Genna, N.M., Stack, D.M., Serbin, L.A., Ledingham, J.E., & Schwartzman, A.E. (2006). From risky behavior to health risk: Continuity across two generations. *Journal of Developmental and Behavioral Pediatrics, 27,* 297–309.

De Vogli, R., Chandola, T., & Marmot, M.G. (2007). Negative aspects of close relationships and heart disease. *Archives of Internal Medicine, 167,* 1951–1957.

DiScala, C., Lescohier, I., Barthel, M., & Li, G.H. (1998). Injuries to children with attention deficit hyperactivity disorder. *Pediatrics, 102,* 1415–1421.

Dobkin, P.L., Tremblay, R.E., & McDuff, P. (1997). Can childhood behavioral characteristics predict adolescent boys' health? A nine-year longitudinal study. *Journal of Health Psychology, 2,* 445–456.

Elliot, D.S. (1993). Health-enhancing and health-compromising lifestyles. In S.G. Millstein, A.C. Petersen, & E.O. Nightingale (Eds.), *Promoting the health* of adolescents: New directions for the twenty-first century (pp. 119–145). New York: Oxford University Press.

Farrington, D.P. (1995). Crime and physical health: Illnesses, injuries, accidents and offending in the Cambridge Study. *Criminal Behaviour and Mental Health*, 5, 261–278.

Felitti, V.J., Anda, R.F., Nordenberg, D., Williamson, D.F., Spitz, A.M., Edwards, V.,...Marks, J. S. (1998). Relationship of childhood abuse and household dysfunction to many of the leading causes of death in adults: The Adverse Childhood Experiences (ACE) study. *American Journal of Preventive Medicine*, 14, 245–258.

Fergusson, D.M., & Horwood, J.L. (2002). Male and female offending trajectories. *Development and Psychopathology*, 14, 159–177.

Fergusson, D.M., Horwood, J.L., & Ridder, E.M. (2005). Show me the child at seven: The consequences of conduct problems in childhood for psychosocial functioning in adulthood. *Journal of Child Psychology and Psychiatry*, 46, 837–849.

Fontaine, N., Carbonneau, R., Barker, E., Vitaro, F., Hébert, M., Côté, S.M.,...Tremblay, R.E. (2008). Girls' hyperactivity and physical aggression during childhood predict adjustment in early adulthood: A 15-year longitudinal study. *Archives of General Psychiatry*, 65, 320–328.

Galobardes, B., Smith, G.D., & Lynch, J.W. (2006). Systematic review of the influence of childhood socioeconomic circumstances on risk for cardiovascular disease in adulthood. *Annals of Epidemiology*, 16, 91–104.

Gorman-Smith, D., & Loeber, R. (2005). Are developmental pathways in disruptive behaviors the same for girls and boys? *Journal of Child and Family Studies*, 14, 15–27.

Gump, B.B., Matthews, K.A., & Raikkonen, K. (1999). Modeling relationships among socioeconomic status, hostility, cardiovascular reactivity, and left ventricular mass in African American and White children. *Health Psychology*, 18, 140–150.

Gunnar, M., & Quevedo, K. (2007). The neurobiology of stress and development. *Annual Review of Psychology*, 58, 145–173.

Hay, D.F. (2007). The gradual emergence of sex differences in aggression: alternative hypotheses. *Psychological Medicine*, 37, 1527–1537.

Hipwell, A.E., Loeber, R., Stouthamer-Loeber, M., Keenan, K., White, H.R., & Krone-Man, L. (2002). Characteristics of girls with early onset disruptive and antisocial behaviour. *Criminal Behaviour and Mental Health*, 12, 99–118.

Keenan, K., Loeber, R., & Green, S. (1999). Conduct disorder in girls: A review of the literature. *Clinical Child and Family Psychology Review*, 2, 3–19.

Keenan, K., Stouthamer-Loeber, M., & Loeber, R. (2005). Developmental approaches to studying conduct problems in girls. In D.J. Pepler, K.C. Madsen, C. Webster & K.S. Levene (Eds.), *The development and treatment of girlhood aggression* (pp. 29–46). Mahwah, NJ: Lawrence Erlbaum Associates.

Kim-Cohen, J., Caspi, A., Moffitt, T.E., Harrington, H., Milne, B.J., & Poulton, R. (2003). Prior juvenile diagnoses in adults with mental disorder: Developmental follow-back of a prospective-longitudinal cohort. *Archives of General Psychiatry, 60,* 709–717.

Knox, S.S., Weidner, G., Adelman, A., Stoney, C.M., & Ellison, C. (2004). Hostility and physiological risk in the National Heart, Lung, and Blood Institute Family Heart Study. *Archives of Internal Medicine, 164,* 2442–2448.

Kramer, M.S., Seguin, L., Lydon, J., & Goulet, L. (2000). Socio-economic disparities in pregnancy outcome: Why do the poor fare so poorly? *Paediatric and Perinatal Epidemiology, 14,* 194–210.

Kratzer, L., & Hodgins, S. (1997). Adult outcomes of child conduct problems: A cohort study. *Journal of Abnormal Child Psychology, 25,* 65–81.

Kratzer, L., & Hodgins, S. (1999). A typology of offenders: A test of Moffitt's theory among males and females from childhood to age 30. *Criminal Behaviour and Mental Health, 9,* 57–73.

Lahey, B.B., Van Hulle, C.A., Waldman, I.D., Rodgers, J.L., D'Onofrio, B.M., Pedlow, S.,...Keenan, K. (2006). Testing descriptive hypotheses regarding sex differences in the development of conduct problems and delinquency. *Journal of Abnormal Child Psychology, 34,* 737–755.

Lalloo, R., & Sheiham, A. (2003). Risk factors for childhood major and minor head and other injuries in a nationally representative sample. *International Journal of the Care of the Injured, 34,* 261–266.

Lawlor, D.A., Ronalds, G., Macintyre, S., Clark, H., & Leon, D.A. (2006). Family socioeconomic position at birth and future cardiovascular disease risk: Findings from the Aberdeen children of the 1950s cohort study. *American Journal of Public Health, 96,* 1271–1277.

Leadbeater, B.J.R., & Way, N. (2007). *Urban girls revisited: Building strengths.* New York: New York University Press.

Leibson, C.L., Katusic, S.K., Barbaresi, W.J., Ransom, J., & O'Brien, P.C. (2001). Use and costs of medical care for children and adolescents with and without attention-deficit/hyperactivity disorder. *Journal of the American Medical Association, 285,* 60–66.

Melchior, M., Moffitt, T.E., Milne, B.J., Poulton, R., & Caspi, A. (2007). Why do children from socioeconomically disadvantaged families suffer from poor health when they reach adulthood? A life-course study. *American Journal of Epidemiology, 166,* 966–974.

Messer, J., Goodman, R., Rowe, R., Meltzer, H., & Maughan, B. (2006). Preadolescent conduct problems in girls and boys. *Journal of the American Academy of Child and Adolescent Psychiatry, 45,* 184–191.

Miller, T.Q., Smith, T.W., Turner, C.W., Guijarro, M.L., & Hallet, A.J. (1996). A meta-analytic review of research on hostility and physical health. *Psychological Bulletin, 119,* 322–348.

Millstein, S.G., Petersen, A.C., & Nightingale, E.O. (Eds.). (1993). *Promoting the health of adolescents: New directions for the twenty-first century.* New York: Oxford University Press.

Moffitt, T.E. (1993). Adolescence-limited and life-course-persistent antisocial behavior: A developmental taxonomy. *Psychological Review, 100,* 674–701.

Moffitt, T.E. (1994). Natural histories of delinquency. In E. Wietekamp & H.J. Kerner (Eds.), *Cross-national longitudinal research on human development and criminal behaviour* (pp. 3–61). Dordrecht: Kluwer Academic Press.

Moffitt, T.E. (2006). Life-course-persistent and adolescent-limited antisocial behavior. In D. Cicchetti & D.J. Cohen (Eds.), *Developmental psychopathology, Vol. 3: Risk, disorder, and adaptation* (pp. 570–598). New York: John Wiley and Sons.

Moffitt, T.E., Caspi, A., Harrington, H., & Milne, B.J. (2002). Males on the life-course-persistent and adolescence-limited antisocial pathways: Follow-up at age 26 years. *Development and Psychopathology, 14,* 179–207.

Moffitt, T.E., Caspi, A., Rutter, M., & Silva, P.A. (2001). *Sex differences in antisocial behaviour: Conduct disorder, delinquency, and violence in the Dunedin Longitudinal Study.* New York: Cambridge University Press.

Moretti, M.M., Holland, R., & McKay, S. (2001). Self-other representations and relational and overt aggression in adolescent girls and boys. *Behavioral Sciences and the Law, 19,* 109–126.

Moretti, M.M., Odgers, C.L., & Jackson, M.A. (2004). *Girls and aggression: Contributing factors and intervention principles.* New York: Kluwer Academic/Plenum.

Odgers, C.L., Caspi, A., Broadbent, J.M., Dickson, N.P., Hancox, R., Harrington, H.,…Moffitt, T.E. (2007). Conduct problem subtypes in males predict differential health burden. *Archives of General Psychiatry, 64,* 476–484.

Odgers, C.L., Caspi, A., Nagin, D., Piquero, A.R., Slutske, W.S., Milne, B.,…Moffitt, T.E. (2008). Is it important to prevent early exposure to drugs and alcohol among adolescents? *Psychological Science, 19*(10), 1037–1044.

Odgers, C.L., Moffitt, T.E., Broadbent, J.M., Dickson, N., Hancox, R.J., Harrington, H.,…Caspi, A. (2008). Female and male antisocial trajectories: From childhood origins to adult outcomes. *Development and Psychopathology, 20,* 673–716.

Odgers, C.L., & Moretti, M.M. (2002). Aggressive and antisocial girls: Research update and challenges. *International Journal of Forensic and Mental Health, 2,* 17–33.

Pajer, K.A. (1998). What happens to "bad" girls? A review of the adult outcomes of antisocial adolescent girls. *American Journal of Psychiatry, 155,* 862–870.

Pajer, K.A. (2007). Cardiovascular disease risk factors in adolescents: Do negative emotions and hypothalamic-pituitary-adrenal axis function play a role? *Current Opinion in Pediatrics, 19,* 559–564.

Pajer, K.A., & Gardner, W.P. (2004). Adolescent antisocial girls: Do they have more health problems? *Pediatric Research, 55,* 5A–A.

Pajer, K.A., Kazmi, A., Gardner, W.P., & Wang, Y. (2007). Female conduct disorder: Health status in young adulthood. *Journal of Adolescent Health, 40*(1), 84.e1–84.e7.

Pajer, K., Leininger, L., & Lourie, A. (2011). Physical health in adolescent girls with antisocial behaviour. In M. Kerr, H. Stattin, C.M. Rutger, E. Engels, G. Overbeek, & A. Andershed (Eds.), *Understanding Girls' Problem Behavior* (pp. 69–92). Chichester, UK: John Wiley and Sons. doi: 10.1002/9780470977453.ch3

Pajer, K., Stouthamer-Loeber, M., Gardner, W., & Loeber, R. (2006). Women with antisocial behaviour: Long-term health disability and help-seeking for emotional problems. *Criminal Behaviour and Mental Health, 16,* 29–42.

Pepler, D.J., & Craig, W.M. (2005). Aggressive girls on troubled trajectories: A developmental perspective. In D.J. Pepler, K.C. Madsen, C. Webster, & K.S. Levene (Eds.), *The development and treatment of girlhood aggression* (pp. 3–28). Mahwah, NJ: Lawrence Erlbaum Associates.

Pepler, D., Jiang, D.P., Craig, W., & Connolly, J. (2008). Developmental trajectories of bullying and associated factors. *Child Development, 79,* 325–338.

Pepler, D.J., Madsen, K.C., Webster, C., & Levene, K.S. (2005). *The development and treatment of girlhood aggression.* Mahwah, NJ: Lawrence Erlbaum Associates.

Pine, D.S., Cohen, P., Brook, J., & Coplan, J.D. (1997). Psychiatric symptoms in adolescence as predictors of obesity in early adulthood: A longitudinal study. *American Journal of Public Health, 87,* 1303–1310.

Piquero, A.R., Gibson, C.L., Daigle, L., Leeper-Piquero, N., & Tibbetts, S.G. (2007). Are life-course persistent offenders at risk for adverse health outcomes? *Journal of Research in Crime and Delinquency, 44,* 185–207.

Poulton, R., Caspi, A., Milne, B.J., Thomson, W.M., Taylor, A., Sears, M.R., & Moffit, T.E. (2002). Association between children's experience of socioeconomic disadvantage and adult health: A life-course study. *Lancet, 360,* 1640–1645.

Putallaz, M., & Bierman, K.L. (2004). *Aggression, antisocial behavior, and violence among girls: A developmental perspective.* New York: Guilford Press.

Quinn, P.O. (2005). Treating adolescent girls and women with ADHD: Gender-specific issues. *Journal of Clinical Psychology, 61,* 579–587.

Raikkonen, K., Matthews, K.A., & Salomon, K. (2003). Hostility predicts metabolic syndrome risk factors in children and adolescents. *Health Psychology, 22,* 279–286.

Raikkonen, K., Matthews, K.A., Sutton-Tyrrell, K., & Kuller, L.H. (2004). Trait anger and the metabolic syndrome predict progression of carotid atherosclerosis in healthy middle-aged women. *Psychosomatic Medicine, 66,* 903–908.

Ramrakha, S., Bell, M.L., Paul, C., Dickson, N., Moffitt, T.E., & Caspi, A. (2007). Childhood behavior problems linked to sexual risk taking in young adulthood: A birth cohort study. *Journal of the American Academy of Child and Adolescent Psychiatry, 46,* 1272–1279.

Ravaja, N., Keltikangas-Jarvinen, L., & Keskivaara, P. (1996). Type A factors as predictors of changes in the metabolic syndrome precursors in adolescents and young adults: A 3-year follow-up study. *Health Psychology, 15,* 18–29.

Repetti, R.L., Taylor, S.E., & Seeman, T.E. (2002). Risky families: Family social environments and the mental and physical health of offspring. *Psychological Bulletin, 128,* 330–366.

Robins, L., & Rutter, M. (Eds.). (1990). *Straight and deviant pathways from childhood to adulthood.* New York: Cambridge University Press.

Sabuncuoglu, O. (2007). Traumatic dental injuries and attention-deficit/hyperactivity disorder: Is there a link? *Dental Traumatology, 23*, 137–142.

Schaeffer, C.M., Petras, H., Ialongo, N., Masyn, K.E., Hubbard, S., Poduska, J., Kellam, S. (2006). A comparison of girls' and boys' aggressive-disruptive behavior trajectories across elementary school: Prediction to young adult antisocial outcomes. *Journal of Consulting and Clinical Psychology, 74*, 500–510.

Schwebel, D.C., Speltz, M.L., Jones, K., & Bardina, P. (2002). Unintentional injury in preschool boys with and without early onset of disruptive behavior. *Journal of Pediatric Psychology, 27*, 727–737.

Serbin, L.A., Stack, D.M., De Genna, N., Grunzeweig, N., Temcheff, C.E., Schwartzman, A.E., & Ledingham, J. (2004). When aggressive girls become mothers: Problems in parenting, health, and development across two generations. In M. Putallaz & K.L. Bierman (Eds.), *Aggression, antisocial behavior, and violence among girls: A developmental perspective* (pp. 262–285). New York: Guilford Press.

Shepherd, J., & Farrington, D. (2003). The impact of antisocial lifestyle on health: Family, school, and police interventions can reduce health risks. *British Medical Journal, 326*, 834–835.

Shepherd, J., Farrington, D., & Potts, J. (2002). Relations between offending, injury and illness. *Journal of the Royal Society of Medicine, 95*, 539–544.

Shepherd, J., Farrington, D., & Potts, J. (2004). Impact of antisocial lifestyle on health. *Journal of Public Health, 26*, 347–352.

Simon, G.E., Von Korff, M., Saunders, K., Miglioretti, D.L., Crane, P.K., van Belle, G., & Kessler, R.C. (2006). Association between obesity and psychiatric disorders in the US adult population. *Archives of General Psychiatry, 63*, 824–830.

Starfield, B., Riley, A.W., Witt, W.P., & Robertson, J. (2002). Social class gradients in health during adolescence. *Journal of Epidemiology and Community Health, 56*, 354–361.

Temcheff, C.E., Serbin, L.A., Martin-Storey, A., Stack, D.M., Hodgins, S., Ledingham, J., & Schwartzman, A.E. (2008). Continuity and pathways from aggression in childhood to family violence in adulthood: A 30-year longitudinal study. *Journal of Family Violence, 23*, 231–242.

Tremblay, R. (2002). Prevention of injury by early socialization of aggressive behavior. *Injury Prevention, 8*, iv17–iv21.

White, N.A., & Piquero, A.R. (2004). A preliminary empirical test of Silverthorn and Frick's delayed-onset pathway in girls using an urban, African-American, US-based sample. *Criminal Behaviour and Mental Health, 14*, 291–309.

Whooley, M.A. (2006). Depression and cardiovascular disease: Healing the broken-hearted. *Journal of the American Medical Association, 295*, 2874–2881.

Wickrama, K.A.S., Lorenz, F.O., Wallace, L.E., Peiris, L., Conger, R.D., & Elder, G.H. (2001). Family influence on physical health during the middle years: The case of onset of hypertension. *Journal of Marriage and the Family, 63*, 527–539.

Wiesner, M., Kim, H.K., & Capaldi, D.M. (2005). Developmental trajectories of offending: Validation and prediction to young adult alcohol use, drug use, and depressive symptoms. *Development and Psychopathology, 17*, 251–270.

Winkleby, M.A., Jatulis, D.E., Frank, E., & Fortmann, S.P. (1992). Socioeconomic status and health: How education, income, and occupation contribute to risk factors for cardiovascular disease. *American Journal of Public Health, 82*, 816–820.

Wolfe, D.A. (2006). Preventing violence in relationships: Psychological science addressing complex social issues. *Canadian Psychology/Psychologie canadienne, 47*, 44–50.

CHAPTER THREE

THE DEVELOPMENT OF GIRLS' AGGRESSION IN DIFFERENT STAGES

COMMENTARY BY
M. STOUTHAMER-LOEBER

ON
DIFFERENT PATHS TO AGGRESSION FOR GIRLS AND BOYS
D.F. HAY, L. MUNDY, AND K. HUDSON

AND
ADULT HEALTH OUTCOMES OF GIRLS WITH ANTI-SOCIAL BEHAVIOUR PROBLEMS
C.L. ODGERS

Chapters 1 and 2 both examine the development of aggression in different phases of girls' development. Whereas the first chapter deals with early development, the second considers development into adulthood. Both review the related literature and have substantial reference lists that can be used for further reading.

In the past, studies on girls have lagged in comparison to studies on boys. This was certainly the case in the area of aggression. The reason may have been that boys have a higher prevalence of aggression; however, the prevalence of aggression or of anti-social behaviour in girls is not negligible. In Chapter 2, Candice Odgers reviews some studies showing percentages of girls with persistent disruptive or anti-social behaviours ranging from 3.5% to 11%. The higher percentages were found in studies with older girls. Considering the harm that anti-social behaviour inflicts on society, this group of girls is worth studying further in the hope that more light may be shed on prevention and intervention strategies.

In what follows, I will first review the two chapters and then make some general comments.

The first chapter, by Dale Hay, Lisa Mundy, and Kathryn Hudson, poses questions about how boys and girls begin to develop differences in aggression after they start out with similar levels of aggression. In other words, why do fewer girls than boys persist in aggressive behaviour? The authors propose that relatively small sex differences that are biologically based, such as differences in temperament and rate of maturation, become amplified over time in the context of the socializing influence of parents and peers. They consider four areas of inquiry:

1. *The role of temperament.* Evidence is brought to bear on the greater capacity of girls at an early age for self-regulation, attention, activity, and emotion. At least in maternal reports girls are seen as better able to regulate themselves. It is noted that no differences have been found between boys and girls with regard to emotional negativity.
2. *The potential vulnerability of males, compared with females, to perinatal and postnatal risks.* Although the findings are not uniform, boys seem to have more perinatal and postnatal risk and possibly acquire more neurobiological deficits connected to the development of aggressive behaviours. An example is the effect of smoking during pregnancy. Some studies report a greater effect on boys. However, the findings are not consistent. Hay and colleagues pose the possibility of interplay between genetics and prenatal insults.
3. *Female precocity and male developmental delay.* Female precocity may have several beneficial effects with regard to lowering the prevalence of aggression. Higher self-regulation may help girls desist from aggression. In addition, girls' higher verbal skills make it possible for them to resolve conflicts at a verbal level rather than resorting to physical aggression. Also, these verbal skills make girls easier for parents and teachers to deal with. This is not to say that girls' verbal skills cannot be used to harm others. A fair amount of literature has accumulated about the harm of covert aggression, in which girls seem to have the edge over boys.
4. *Gender segregation.* Apart from neurobiological differences, girls and boys are actively socialized into "sex-appropriate" roles. These roles are encouraged by adults in the child's environment, but also and

particularly by same-sex peer groups. In these groups heavy social-ization occurs and non-conforming children may be rejected, as is sometimes the case with the minority of physically aggressive girls. If they do not conform, girls may seek association with boys. In that case, the influence of female socialization is further reduced.

Hay and colleagues present data from the South London Child Development Study to show that highly aggressive girls may have "fallen off" the typical female pathway due to prenatal insults, maturational delay, or poor peer relationships. The data show, for instance, that girls who have incurred prenatal risks may not have the maturational advantage that girls in general have. Although the results are intriguing, the number of girls who qualified as highly aggressive was small (13); therefore, replication of the findings is necessary.

The second chapter, by Candice Odgers, focuses on a later period in girls' development and links adult relationship violence, occurring within families or with romantic partners, and poor health to early behaviour problems. Odgers uses the distinction developed by Moffitt (1993—see References in Chapter 2) between life-course-persistent and adolescent-limited anti-social youth. Whereas children in the life-course-persistent pathway are characterized by social, familial, and neuro-developmental deficits, those in the adolescent-limited pathway are expected to give a relatively normative response to the role-less years between biological maturation and access to the privileges of adulthood. Those on the adolescent-limited pathway are also expected to make a fairly normal transition to adulthood, provided they have not been trapped into substance dependence or have incurred a criminal record. It should be kept in mind, however, that there is not a specific age at which the two pathways diverge and so the division is somewhat artificial.

A smaller number of girls, compared to boys, follow the life-course-persistent pathway, possibly due to girls' lower rate of nervous system dysfunction and its associated problems. However, as stated earlier, and reviewed in Odgers' chapter, the number of girls on the life-course-persistent pathway is not negligible. These girls may be at risk for physical and psychological aggression towards others, including their romantic partners, in adulthood. A wide range of poor health outcomes is also predicted for this life-course-persistent group. Odgers presents the following four theories for the association between their anti-social behaviour and poor physical health:

1. Risky family and relationship contexts, characterized by high levels of adversity, conflict, and risk of child maltreatment and neglect,

may produce disruptions in the stress-response system and interact with genetic vulnerabilities. This may impede psychosocial development and indicate the greater likelihood of aggression and poor health behaviour.

2. Anti-social children may engage in more health-risk behaviours, including alcohol and drug abuse, dangerous driving, unprotected sex, fewer medical checkups, and a poor diet.

3. Mental health conditions such as hostility, negative affect, and depression often experienced by anti-social males and females may confer greater physiological vulnerability, thus explaining at least in part the link between anti-social behaviour and poor physical health.

4. Social inequalities may underlie both anti-social behaviours, such as problem aggression and poor health. Although more research is required on this common-risk-factor approach, some factors that could be listed here are mentioned in the previous two explanations, such as family adversity and poor diet. Social inequalities may have shaped the parents' lives even before their child's conception. The prenatal and postnatal health of the baby may be influenced by the same forces. Circumstances such as low education of parents, single parenthood, unemployment, dependence on social welfare, and crime may have then continued during childhood, with the added contexts of poor neighbourhoods and inferior schools where role models for a different, more healthy lifestyle may have been lacking. The value of such factors is that they may be possible entry points for prevention and intervention.

The chapters by Hay et al. and Odgers emphasize research showing both gender differences as well as differences within the female gender. Research on gender differences can point to potentially different factors related to male and female development. Most important though is to find factors influencing different developments within gender. This type of research has been done extensively for boys, but is only slowly starting for girls. The reason seems to be that, until recently, research on anti-social behaviour in boys had a greater perceived urgency due to the greater prevalence of this behaviour in boys and its potential for delinquency. Related to the issue of prevalence is the fact that a large sample is needed in studies of girls to provide enough data for analyses. We are now emerging from the era where anti-social problems in girls were seen as similar in origin and appearance to those in boys, but just less common. We have come to a stage now where problems in girls can be studied in their own right rather than in reference to those problems in boys. Both chapters summarize important areas of research on female development of anti-social behaviour. They lay out research that has already been undertaken (some needing further replication), and also present theories explaining the results as well as pointers to a host of issues requiring further examination. Clearly, the two chapters show that this is an exciting and rewarding field of research.

CHAPTER FOUR

SOME KEY ISSUES IN THE EARLY DEVELOPMENT OF AGGRESSION IN GIRLS

ROLF LOEBER, MAGDA STOUTHAMER-LOEBER,
ALISON E. HIPWELL, JEFFREY D. BURKE,
AND DEENA R. BATTISTA

After decades of focusing on boys, girls' disruptive and delinquent behaviour is increasingly featured in scientific publications (Chesney-Lind, 1997; Moffitt, Caspi, Rutter, & Silva, 2001; Moretti, Odgers, & Jackson, 2004; Pepler, Madsen, Webster, & Levene, 2005; Putallaz & Bierman, 2004; Zahn et al., 2007). However, most of the studies on girls concern adolescence, with few dealing with the preadolescent years (e.g., Hipwell et al., 2002; Tiet & Huizinga, 2002), and with only a handful of community-based studies conducted on sizeable samples of girls (e.g., Costello et al., 1996; Hipwell et al., 2002; McConaughy, Stanger, & Achenbach, 1992).

The lack of studies of girls during preadolescence is somewhat understandable because many problems among girls such as delinquency, substance use, and depression typically emerge after that period (Moffitt et al., 2001). The preadolescent period (defined here as ages 5–12) is one in which some girls already display a variety of problem behaviours, including disruptive behaviour and depressed mood (Loeber, Pardini, Stouthamer-Loeber, Hipwell, & Sembower, 2009). It is plausible that some of the beginnings of adolescent problem behaviour are laid down during the preadolescent period.

There are several major gaps in knowledge of girls' problem behaviour during the preadolescent period that warrant closer attention. For example, how prevalent are diagnoses of disruptive behaviour disorder by the end of the preadolescent period? Are disruptive behaviours at that time highly intercorrelated or can they be distinguished into different subtypes? And how stable are these types of disruptive behaviours? Anger is another important emotion in girls and boys, and it can become manifest independent of disruptive and delinquent behaviour (Averill, 1983; Cavell & Malcolm, 2007). For instance, although there is some evidence of developmental pathways in disruptive and delinquent behaviours in girls (Gorman-Smith & Loeber, 2005), it is unclear whether there is a developmental pathway leading to girls' recurrent anger at a young age. In addition, scientists have long been aware of the need to understand the etiology of comorbid conditions, such as oppositional problems, conduct problems, and depression (e.g., Angold, Costello, & Erkanli, 1999). The developmental interplay between the emotional aspects of oppositional behaviour (rather than conduct problems) and depressed mood has been demonstrated in boys (Burke, Loeber, Lahey, & Rathouz, 2005) but still remains to be investigated in girls. Some conduct-problem girls will become depressed. What is the developmental ordering between conduct problems and depression? Does depression precede conduct problems or do conduct problems precede depression as is the case in boys (Burke et al., 2005; Nock, Kazdin, Hiripi, & Kessler, 2007)? Does the developmental sequence of conduct problems and depression depend on the presence of oppositional problems?

We will address the above issues in this chapter. Because of space limitations we cannot present a full review of all relevant studies; instead, we will present a selection of what we consider the most relevant ones together with data from the Pittsburgh Girls Study, an ongoing longitudinal study on a community sample of girls from middle childhood to adolescence (Hipwell et al., 2002).

THE PITTSBURGH GIRLS STUDY

The Pittsburgh Girls Study (PGS) is a multiple-cohort, longitudinal study on the development of Oppositional Defiant Disorder (ODD), Conduct Disorder (CD), and Major Depressive Disorder (MDD) and their comorbid conditions in a community sample of 2,451 inner-city African American and Caucasian girls. The study began in 1998 with a one-year preparatory phase followed by an enumeration of 103,238 Pittsburgh households in order to locate girls ages 5, 6, 7, and 8 years old who, with a parent, could be enrolled into four age cohorts. For the enumeration, city neighbourhoods were divided in 23 "disadvantaged" (> 25% of families living in poverty) and 66 "non-disadvantaged" neighbourhoods using information on household poverty from the 1990 US Census (see Hipwell et al., 2002). The goal was to enumerate all households in the disadvantaged neighbourhoods, and 50% of the remainder, in order to increase the prevalence of CD in the sample (Costello et al., 1996). Of 2,876 girls who were eligible, 2,451 agreed to participate (85.2%). We started wave 10 in August 2008. Approximately half of the sample is African American (53.0%), 41.2% is Caucasian, and most of the remaining girls are of mixed ethnicity. When weights are applied to correct for the over-sampling of disadvantaged neighbourhoods, the racial distribution in these neighbourhoods is similar to that reported in the 2000 US Census for girls aged 5–8 (45.6% were African American according to the Census, compared with 43.9% in the weighted PGS sample). Across the cohorts, 56% to 61% of the parents were cohabiting with a husband or partner in wave 1, about 48% of the parents had completed 12 or fewer years of formal education, and 39% of the sample was receiving public assistance. The assessments consist of separate, structured face-to-face interviews with the child and the parent using a laptop computer, and a self-administered questionnaire booklet for the parent and the teacher. In addition, the interviewers rate their impressions of the child, the parent, and the neighbourhood. Over six years, the average participation rate has been 94.5%. Teacher data has been collected yearly by questionnaire booklets, with an average retention rate of 86.3%.

How Prevalent Are Diagnoses in Girls at Age 12?

At age 12 years, the weighted prevalence of CD assessed by best estimate (using parent and child report) was 5.4%. It should be noted, however, that African American girls were significantly more likely to meet criteria of CD (8.3%) compared with Caucasian girls (2.3%) ($X^2 = 20.08$, df = 1, p < .001). The weighted prevalence of ODD at age 12 years, as assessed by parent report, was slightly higher than CD at 7.6%. In contrast to CD, rates did not differ by racial/ethnic group. The best-estimate (using parent and child report) weighted prevalence of MDD at age 12 was 6.7%. Similar to CD, African American girls were significantly more likely to meet criteria for MDD (9.6%) compared with Caucasian girls (4.0%) ($X^2 = 13.68$, df = 1, p < .001). At this age, 1.1% of girls report clinically significant suicidal ideation, with an additional 8.1% reporting occasional or vague thoughts about death or suicide. Furthermore, 1.5% of girls met criteria for both CD and MDD at age 12, whereas 2.4% met criteria for both CD and ODD and 1.6% met criteria for both ODD and MDD.

Are There Distinct and Stable Categories of Disruptive Behaviour in Preadolescent Girls?

Studies have concentrated on adolescent-onset of disruptive behaviour in girls (e.g., Silverthorn & Frick, 1999) but have neglected early-onset cases. This is curious, because we know that an early onset of delinquency in girls (before age 13) raises the odds of later serious delinquent behaviour by a factor of two or three (Loeber & Farrington, 2001). An additional issue in need of investigation is whether there are empirical distinctions between categories of girls' disruptive behaviours (such as relational aggression, oppositional defiant problems, conduct problems, and callous-unemotional problems) and attention-deficit hyperactivity.

In the next set of analyses, we used four data waves covering ages 5–12 years (Loeber et al., 2009). Examples of common symptoms of conduct problems at age 12 were: stealing without confrontation (8.3%), lost temper (10.9%), and destroying property (8.0%).

Factor analyses resulted in five factors when parents were the informants and four factors when teachers were the informants. In the case of parents as informants (mostly mothers), we found the following factors: oppositional/conduct problems, relational aggression, callous-unemotional problems, inattention, and hyperactivity-impulsivity. Note that no distinct factors

TABLE 4.1   DIFFERENT FACTORS/CATEGORIES OF DISRUPTIVE BEHAVIOURS AND THEIR EXEMPLARS

Factor/Category	Exemplars
Oppositional/conduct problems	Loses temper, argues with adults, defies or refuses deliberately, annoys, blames others, touchy or easily annoyed, angry or resentful, vindictive, bullies, starts physical fights, engages in serious violence or cruelty
Relational aggression	Excludes to get even, spreads rumors, tries to get others to stop liking, lies about peers, ignores others
Callous/unemotional problems	Does not keep promises, unconcerned about school work, does not feel bad when something wrong is done, not concerned about feelings of others, does not show feelings, does not keep the same friends
Inattention	Makes careless mistakes, has difficulty paying attention, does not listen, fails to finish, disorganized, avoids mental effort, loses things, easily distracted or forgetful
Hyperactivity/impulsivity	Blurts out answers, has difficulty waiting turn, interrupts activities, runs or climbs, has difficulty playing quietly, "driven by motor," talks excessively

of oppositional behaviour and conduct problems were found. Table 4.1 summarizes examples of the behaviours which loaded onto each of the factors. Separate analyses were done on teacher ratings, which resulted in four factors that were somewhat parallel to the parent factors: oppositional/ conduct problems combined with callous-unemotional problems (a single factor), relational aggression, hyperactivity-impulsivity, and inattention.

The parent factors were quite stable with age. For example, the intraclass correlations (ICC) from age 10 to 11 were very similar across the different factors: oppositional/conduct problems (ICC = .83), callous-unemotional problems (.81), relational aggression (.76), hyperactivity-impulsivity (.81), and inattention (.80). The stability of the different factors appeared to increase with age. For each factor, the intraclass correlation was lowest between ages 5 and 6 and gradually increased in magnitude with age. The stability of teacher factors, with the exception of relational aggression, was as high as that for parent factors, but no distinct age trends were discernable (Loeber et al., 2009).

Against this backdrop of increasing stability with age, we found that certain behaviours decreased and others increased with age. Specifically, with increasing age girls were rated as lower on hyperactive/impulsive symptoms and on callous-unemotional behaviours. In contrast, they were rated as more oppositional (but only according to teachers, not parents) and more relationally aggressive at an older age (Keenan, Hipwell, Duax, Stouthamer-Loeber, & Loeber, 2004; Loeber et al., 2009), but there were no developmental changes for conduct problems.

In summary, the results indicate that it is useful to distinguish between different forms of disruptive child behaviour at a young age, but the distinctions are somewhat clearer when parents, compared to teachers, are the informants. The stabilities of the parent- and teacher-based factors were comparable—with an exception for indirect aggression, which showed higher stability when based on parent, compared to teacher, ratings, perhaps as a function of parents' greater opportunities for observation.

IS THERE A DEVELOPMENTAL PATHWAY INVOLVING ANGRY EMOTIONALITY?

The factor analysis on disruptive behaviour did not include a measure of anger. The main reason for this is that anger is not a specific symptom of disruptive behaviour (Averill, 1983), although anger may be expressed in conjunction with other disruptive symptoms such as temper tantrums, physical aggression, and indirect aggression. Also, anger is not specific to disruptive behaviour and often takes place in reaction to aversive events or stimuli, usually of a social nature (e.g., being denigrated or ignored by others, fearing the loss of a loved one, etc.).

Relatively little is known about the developmental nature of anger in young girls, with most of the studies dealing with adolescent girls (Armstead & Clark, 2002; Reyes, Meininger, Liehr, Chan, & Mueller, 2003) and the development of conflict (e.g., Dunn, 2001), and fewer dealing with anger in younger girls (e.g., Nichols, Graber, Brooks-Gunn, & Botvin, 2006). Researchers have proposed different severity levels of anger, such as annoyance (Averill, 1983), to which we add irritability, with anger being the most serious expression. Some have proposed that women differ from men in that women, although biologically capable of expressing anger, often are inhibited from doing so (e.g., Averill, 1983). However, we pose that even if anger is more often inhibited in girls and women, an accumulation of inhibited angry cognitions and emotions fills a reservoir of negative emotion that eventually is likely to overflow. Such a release of overt anger is related, but not limited, to intermittent explosive disorder "characterized by discrete episodes of failure to resist aggressive impulses resulting in serious assaults or destruction of property" (American Psychiatric Association, 1994, p. 609). This diagnosis mostly applies to adults, but we think, at a less serious level, it can also be observed at younger ages.

There is an ongoing debate about the developmental period in which the transition between emotional states and subsequent anger takes place (e.g., Bierman, 2007). Keenan and Shaw (2003) proposed a dual stage escalation model for boys and girls in the preschool period. Of the two hypothesized pathways, the *pathway to reactive anti-social behaviour* started with irritable behaviour during infancy. The authors postulated that toddlers displaying persistent irritability are at risk of developing emotional difficulties and oppositional behaviours (low frustration tolerance, overactivity, and being demanding), which in turn set the stage for the development of disruptive, angry behaviours in the preschool period.

We postulate that the etiology of anger can take place at different developmental ages and, thus, is not limited to the preschool period. In other words, we hypothesize that the development of anger can be traced in preadolescence (defined as ages 5 to 12) as well as at later ages. We also ask whether anger in preadolescent girls emerges without behavioural or emotional precursors or whether there is a developmental pathway from an emotional state to anger over time—that is, are most of the girls who show repeated anger prone to display this emotional state earlier in life?

The first step in the identification of developmental pathways is to examine the onset of behaviours over time (Loeber, Wung, et al., 1993). Only when categories of behaviour have distinct onset graphs is it worth examining whether individuals' behavioural development of anger is hetero-

FIGURE 4.1   DEVELOPMENT OF IRRITABILITY AND ANGER IN PREADOLESCENT GIRLS

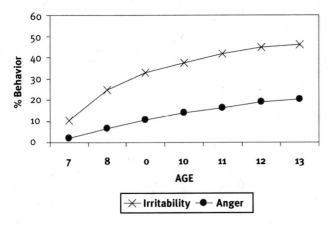

Note: **Irritability:** lose temper, annoy, blame; **Anger:** spiteful, vindictive, anger, resentful

typic and occurs in a systematic manner. We plotted the development of different emotional states between ages 7 and 13, and then examined whether the graphs of certain emotional states were different from other emotional states. The results showed that the DSM-IV symptoms of "losing temper," "annoying others," and "blaming others" had similar onset graphs, while "spiteful behaviour," "vindictive behaviour," "anger," and "resentful behaviour" formed another cluster of onset graphs. For that reason, we made two developmental constructs: one was labelled irritability (composed of losing temper, annoying others, and blaming others), and the other was labelled anger (composed of spiteful behaviour, vindictive behaviour, anger, and resentful behaviour). Figure 4.1 shows that the onset of irritability increased from about 10% to 46% between ages 7 and 13. In contrast, a lower percentage of girls showed the onset of anger, from 2% at age 7 to 20% at age 13.

The next question is whether there is a developmental pathway and to test whether the majority of those who displayed anger often had gone through an earlier stage of persistent irritable behaviour. This is represented in the pathway model of Figure 4.2. The results show that 88.8% of those girls who displayed recurrent anger had gone through an earlier phase of highly irritable behaviour. The reverse, irritable girls who have gone through an earlier period of anger, was much less common (3.0%). In short, irritability appears as a behavioural precursor to the onset of angry emotionality in a subsample of irritable girls, but it is unclear why some girls and not others make the transition from irritability to angry emotionality.

FIGURE 4.2   NEGATIVE AFFECT PATHWAY IN PREADOLESCENT GIRLS

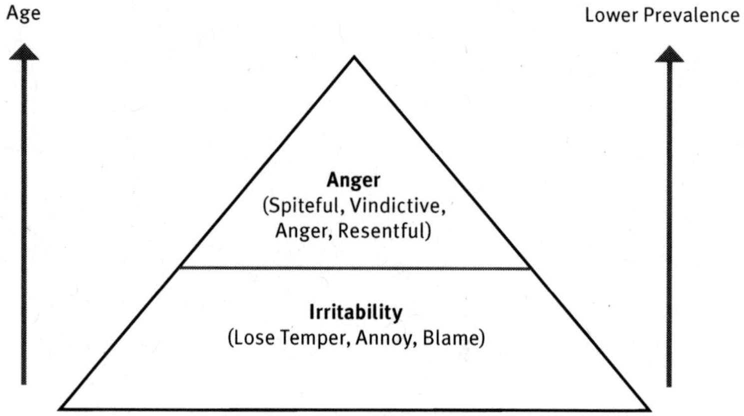

Age   Lower Prevalence

Anger
(Spiteful, Vindictive,
Anger, Resentful)

Irritability
(Lose Temper, Annoy, Blame)

It is still too early to compute the probability of irritable girls advancing to anger, because the risk for such a transition is likely to extend beyond the measurements available for these analyses.

In summary, the results show an increase in irritability and anger with age. Based on a shorter longitudinal study than the PGS, Nichols et al. (2006) also reported that anger increased between grades 6 and 7. We demonstrated that this increase can be traced back to an earlier age. In addition, we identified a pathway from irritable behaviours to anger during preadolescence. It should be noted that many girls made the transition from irritability to anger prior to puberty, and it remains to be seen to what extent puberty affects the transition further.

WHAT IS THE ROLE OF ANGRY EMOTIONALITY AND OPPOSITIONAL BEHAVIOUR IN THE ETIOLOGY OF CONDUCT PROBLEMS AND DEPRESSED MOOD?

Oppositional symptoms often emerge prior to the onset of Conduct Disorder and delinquency in boys (Loeber, Keenan, et al., 1993; Loeber, Wung, et al., 1993) and girls (Gorman-Smith & Loeber, 2005). However, for a proportion of girls, oppositional symptoms may not lead to conduct problems. Could it be that oppositional behaviour is related to the emergence of depression? Among a clinical sample of boys, oppositional symptoms predicted later depression, whereas symptoms of CD (here called conduct problems) did not (Burke et al., 2005). In subsequent analyses, a specific dimension of negative affect among oppositional symptoms in particular appeared to explain the direct links to later depression (Burke, 2012). If this finding held for girls, these symptoms could be an early marker in childhood, years before the onset of depressive disorder.

This issue was examined using parental reports from the PGS of symptom severity from the Child Symptom Inventory–4 (Gadow & Sprafkin, 2002) for the symptoms of ODD, CD, Attention Deficit Hyperactivity Disorder (ADHD), and depression. The Screen for Child Anxiety Related Emotional Disorders (SCARED)–Parent Version (Birmaher et al., 1997) was used to assess anxiety disorder symptoms. Demographic factors included race, parental educational level, single parenthood, and whether the family was on public assistance. (In Year 1, ODD symptom interviews included only lifetime and past-two-month windows, and were thus not included. The subsequent assessment waves queried past-year symptom severity scores and served as the basis for the present analyses.)

Factor Analysis

Factor analyses of symptom severity scores were conducted separately in Years 2 (girls aged 6–9 years), 3 (7–10 years), and 4 (8–11 years). In each year, items loaded onto factors in a consistent fashion: losing temper, arguing, and defying loaded onto one factor (Oppositional Behaviour); being touchy, angry, and spiteful loaded onto a second factor (Negative Affect); and annoying and blaming others loaded onto a third factor (Antagonism). The factors of Negative Affect and Oppositional Behaviour are consistent with the factors identified in the Developmental Trends Study (Burke, 2012), but Antagonism was not identified among the clinical sample of boys as a separate factor.

For the following transitional marginal regression analyses, we created constructs in accord with the factor analyses described above by summing the symptom severity scores from the CSI-4 for the items within each factor. In these models, the outcomes of Years 3, 4, and 5 (Time t + 1) were predicted by scores at Years 2, 3, and 4 (Time t), accounting for correlated error within the panel data. Each model included the measure of the outcome variable of the preceding wave. For further discussion of similar statistical models, see Burke et al. (2005).

Oppositional Symptom Dimensions Predicting Depression

Predicting depression symptom severity at Time t + 1, the Time t predictors of Oppositional Behaviour and Antagonism were not significant, and were removed from the model. In addition, the covariates of public assistance, parental low education level, and race were not significant and were also removed from the model, yielding the final model of predictors of depression as shown in Table 4.2.

TABLE 4.2   DIMENSIONS OF OPPOSITIONAL SYMPTOMS PREDICTING DEPRESSION SYMPTOM SEVERITY AT TIME T + 1

	b	se	p	95% Confidence Interval
Depression	.079	.003	.001	.072 – .086
Negative Affect	.027	.005	<.001	.016 – .038
ADHD	.008	.001	<.001	.001 – .010
Anxiety	.009	.001	<.001	.007 – .011
Single Parenthood	.056	.014	<.001	.027 – .085
Age	.035	.005	<.001	.025 – .044
constant	.356	.053	<.001	.251 – .459

Note: b = unstandardized regression coefficient. All predictors, excluding Age, are measured at Time t

Oppositional Symptom Dimensions Predicting Conduct Problems

In predicting conduct problem symptom severity at Time t + 1, depression, anxiety, and parental low education level were removed from the model. In testing for interactions among the variables remaining in the model, a significant interaction was found between race and Negative Affect. Probing this interaction revealed that Negative Affective severity scores were predictive of conduct problems for Caucasian girls (b = .101, se = .03, p = .002, 95% CI = .038 – .164), but not for African American girls (b = .037, se = .023, p = .110, 95% CI = -.008 – .082). The final model of predictors is shown in Table 4.3.

TABLE 4.3   DIMENSIONS OF OPPOSITIONAL BEHAVIOUR PREDICTING CD SYMPTOM SEVERITY AT TIME T+1

	b	se	p	95% Confidence Interval
CD	0.232	.017	<.001	.199 – .266
Oppositional Behaviour	0.066	.016	<.001	.035 – .096
Antagonism	0.195	.023	<.001	.150 – .241
Negative Affect	0.151	.028	<.001	.096 – .205
Race	1.06	.170	<.001	.730 – 1.40
Negative Affect * Race	−.151	.030	<.001	−.210 – -.091
ADHD	.021	.003	<.001	.015 – .028
Single Parenthood	.223	.042	<.001	.141 – .307
Public Assistance	.179	.044	<.001	.093 – .265
Age	−.004	.013	0.78	−.029 – .022
constant	−2.95	.194	<.001	−3.33 – -2.57

Note: b = unstandardized regression coefficient. All predictors, excluding Age and Race, are measured at Time t

FIGURE 4.3   ODD SYMPTOMS AND THEIR RELATION TO CONDUCT PROBLEMS AND DEPRESSION

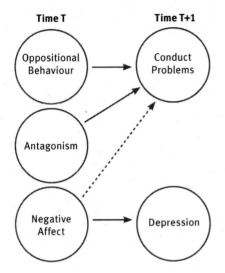

The dotted line indicates that the effect of Negative Affect on Conduct Problems is significant only for Caucasian girls

Thus, consistent with the findings from a clinical sample of boys (Burke, 2012), the Negative Affect dimension of ODD symptoms, consisting of the items angry, spiteful, and touchy significantly predicts later depression. On the other hand, the remaining dimensions of ODD symptoms, along with conduct problems, do not predict depression, but do predict later conduct problems (see Figure 4.3). Unlike those previous findings, for some children (namely Caucasian girls), Negative Affect symptoms predicted later depression as well. Nevertheless, these findings support the role of Negative Affect symptoms of ODD as a potential marker in early childhood for later depression.

WHAT IS THE TEMPORAL ORDER BETWEEN CONDUCT PROBLEMS AND DEPRESSED MOOD?

Beginning in adolescence, there is a rapid increase in the rate of depression among girls (Ge, Conger, Lorenz, & Simons, 1994; Hankin et al., 1998). While depression is the disorder that is most likely to co-occur with CD, especially during adolescence (Offord, Alder, & Boyle, 1986), a number of questions about the nature of the relation between these two forms of psychopathology remain. For example, what is the most common pattern of temporal ordering of depression and conduct symptoms? Data from the Dunedin Longitudinal Study (Moffitt et al., 2001) indicate that depression typically emerges between ages 15 and 21, which is later than the typical onset of Conduct Disorder in girls.

Depressed mood was assessed by parent report on 11 items. Seven items (e.g., lack of interest, feelings of worthlessness or guilt) were rated on a four-point scale ranging from "never" to "very often" whereas four items (e.g., appetite, sleep) were scored as either "yes" or "no". All 11 items were summed to create a depressed mood severity score. Conduct problems were assessed by parent report on 13 items (e.g., physical cruelty to animals, forced sexual activity) rated on a four-point scale ranging from "never" to "very often". All 13 items were summed to create a conduct problems severity score. Before addressing temporal ordering, we examined the year-to-year stability of depressed mood and conduct problems. The stability (ICC) for depressed mood ranged from .49 to .60 between ages 8 and 12, and the two-year stability between ages 8 and 11 from .45 to .50 (D. Battista, personal communication, 2008). Thus, depressed mood was moderately stable during the preadolescent years. This stability was slightly higher for conduct problems compared to depressed mood. The stability (ICC) for conduct problems ranged from .60 to .67 between ages 8 and 12, and the two-year stability between ages 8 and 11 from .58 to .66 (D. Battista, personal communication, 2008).

What then is the temporal precedence of depressed mood and conduct problems in preadolescent girls, and does it make a difference if oppositional behaviour is also present? Hipwell, Stepp, Feng, Burke, Battista, Loeber, & Keenan (2011) examined this question in a cross-lagged path model using data from the PGS. Analyses focused on the severity of conduct problems at ages 8, 9, 10, and 11 to predict depressed mood at ages 9, 10, 11, and 12 respectively (with race and poverty included as time-invariant covariates). The model fit was acceptable. There were significant paths from conduct problems at ages 8, 9, and 10 to depressed mood at ages 9, 10, and 11 respectively. There was also a significant path from depressed mood at age 9 to conduct problems at age 10, and depressed mood at age 11 predicted conduct problems at age 12. In other words, depressed mood predicted conduct problems in only two waves, and these two waves were not consecutive. Thus, findings revealed that conduct problems more often preceded depressed mood than vice versa. Although there was also some evidence for a bidirectional sequence with some prediction from depressed mood to conduct problems, this pattern was not consistent across all waves and no systematic temporal change could be identified among the girls during this developmental period.

Given the association between oppositional behaviour and depression, Hipwell et al. (2011) also tested a model that included oppositional behaviours as a time-varying covariate of conduct problems (with race and poverty again included as time-invariant covariates as in the previous models). In this model, the cross-lagged associations between conduct problems and depression were estimated after accounting for the effects of concurrent oppositional behaviour on conduct problems. The model fit was again acceptable. Oppositional behaviours were significantly associated with conduct problems at each age. The results showed that the addition of oppositional behaviours did not account for the previously observed significant paths from conduct problems at ages 8, 9, and 10 to depressed mood at ages 9, 10, and 11 respectively. However, by accounting for oppositional behaviours in the model, the paths from depressed mood to subsequent conduct problems became negligible. Thus, the majority of the evidence indicates that, when oppositional behaviour is taken into account, conduct problems in preadolescent girls more often predict depressed mood than the reverse.

In summary, we found that conduct problems typically preceded depressed mood in preadolescent girls. The results agree with those reported by Moffitt et al. (2001), who also reported that in adolescent girls it is more common for conduct problems to precede depression than the reverse. The fact that our result in the PGS of conduct problems preceding depression in preadolescent girls is most distinct when oppositional behaviour is taken into account may indicate that some emotional aspects of oppositional behaviour are key for the developmental transition between oppositional behaviour, depressed mood, and conduct problems. This, however, still needs to be investigated.

SOME UNRESOLVED QUESTIONS

There are several unresolved questions that can be addressed in future research:

Much of the data presented here deal with the preadolescent years. It is unclear whether the present findings are also applicable to adolescence and adulthood, particularly late-onset forms of violence (against family members and partners).

In addition, it not clear whether emotionally reactive girls, when confronted with problems in social relations, are more likely to experience depression (e.g., Strayer, 1986) or whether depression results from excessive control or inhibition of negative emotions such as anger (Bromberger & Matthews, 1996; Saarni,1984; Underwood, Hurley, Johanson, & Mosley, 1999).

Relatively little is known about the development of anger at a young age. We assume that feelings of persistent anger can apply to anti-social behaviour but that persistent anger without anti-social behaviour is not uncommon in girls and women. Anger can be related to fears of social and achievement evaluation and tends to increase during adolescence (Westenberg, Drewes, Goedhart, Siebelink, & Treffers, 2004). Similarly, irritability in girls tends to increase during adolescence as well, which is a time when the correlation between irritability and hostile rumination also tends to increase in girls (Caprara, Paciello, Gerbino, & Cugini, 2007).

Anger can also be related to depression (caused by, e.g., jealousy, being discounted as a person, feeling trapped in social relationships, fear of loss of loved ones). Most of the empirical knowledge about the linkage between non-anti-social anger and depression is from studies on adult women, but we need to know more about how this may develop during childhood. However, differences exist between girls and boys in their recall of past wrongs, rumination (Bybee, 1998; Lyubomirsky, Caldwell, & Nolen-Hoeksema, 1998), and, possibly, more persistent resentment.

Further, it is critical to know more about the possible impact of the social environment (parents, peers) on moulding conduct problems and angry and depressed emotionality at a young age, and how this interacts with girls' temperament and biological makeup.

ACKNOWLEDGMENTS
Special thanks go to Kate Keenan, Helene Raskin White, and Jennifer Wilson. We are also much indebted to the staff of the Pittsburgh Girls Study for their dedication and hard work in conducting the study, and to the participant families. The study was financed by grants from the National Institute of Mental Health (MH 056630) and the National Institute on Drug Abuse (DA012237).

NOTE
Corresponding author: Rolf Loeber, Ph.D. ,WPIC, 3811 O'Hara St., Pittsburgh, PA 15206, loeberr@upmc.edu.

REFERENCES
American Psychiatric Association. (1994). *Diagnostic and statistical manual of mental disorders.* Washington, DC: Author.
Angold, A., Costello, E.J., & Erkanli, A. (1999). Comorbidity. *Journal of Child Psychology and Psychiatry, 40,* 57–87.

Armstead, C.A., & Clark, R. (2002). Assessment of self-reported anger expression in pre- and early adolescent African Americans: Psychometric considerations. *Journal of Adolescence, 25*, 365–371.

Averill, J.R. (1983). Studies on anger and aggression: Implications for theories of emotion. *American Psychologist, 38*, 1145–1160.

Bierman, K. (2007). Anger and aggression: A developmental perspective. In T.A. Cavell, & K.T. Malcolm (Eds.), *Anger, aggression, and interventions for interpersonal violence* (pp. 215–238). Mahwah, NJ: Lawrence Erlbaum.

Birmaher, B., Khetarpal, S., Brent, D., Cully, M., Balach, L., Kaufman, J., & Neer, S.M. (1997). The Screen for Child Anxiety Related Emotional Disorders (SCARED): Scale construction and psychometric characteristics. *Journal of the American Academy of Child and Adolescent Psychiatry, 36*, 545–553.

Bromberger, J.T., & Matthews, K.A. (1996). A longitudinal study of the effects of pessimism, trait anxiety, and life stress on depressive symptoms in middle-aged women. *Psychology and Aging, 11*, 207–213.

Burke, J.D. (2012). An affective dimension within ODD symptoms among boys: Personality and psychopathology outcomes into early adulthood. *Journal of Child Psychology and Psychiatry, 53*(11), 1176–1883.

Burke, J.D., Loeber, R., Lahey, B.B., & Rathouz, P.J. (2005). Developmental transitions among affective and behavioural disorders in adolescent boys. *Journal of Child Psychology and Psychiatry, 46*, 1200–1210.

Bybee, J. (1998). The emergence of gender differences in guilt during adolescence. In J. Byee (Ed.), *Guilt and children* (pp. 114–125). New York: Academic Press.

Caprara, G.V., Paciello, M., Gerbino, M., & Cugini, C. (2007). Individual differences conducive to aggression and violence: Trajectories and correlates of irritability and hostile rumination through adolescence. *Aggressive Behavior, 33*, 359–374.

Cavell, T.A., & Malcolm, K.T. (2007). Introduction: The anger-aggression relation. In T.A. Cavell, & K.T. Malcolm (Eds.), *Anger, aggression, and interventions for interpersonal violence* (pp. xv–xxxi). Mahwah, NJ: Lawrence Erlbaum.

Chesney-Lind, M. (1997). *The female offender.* Thousand Oaks, CA: Sage.

Costello, E.J., Angold, A., Burns, B.J., Stangl, D.K., Tweed, D.L., Erkanli, A., & Worthman, C.M. (1996). The Great Smokey Mountains Study of Youth: Goals, design, methods, and the prevalence of DSM-III-R disorders. *Archives of General Psychiatry, 53*, 1129–1136.

Dunn, J. (2001). The development of children's conflict and prosocial behaviour: Lessons from research on social understanding and gender. In J. Hill, & B. Maughan (Eds.), *Conduct disorders in childhood and adolescence* (pp. 49–66). Cambridge: Cambridge University Press.

Gadow, K.D., & Sprafkin, J. (2002). *Child Symptom Inventory 4: Screening and norms manual.* Stony Brook, NY: Checkmate Plus.

Ge, X., Conger, R.D., Lorenz, F.O., & Simons, R.L. (1994). Parents' stressful life events and adolescent depressed mood. *Journal of Health and Social Behavior, 35*, 28–44.

Gorman-Smith, D., & Loeber, R. (2005). Are developmental pathways in disruptive behaviors the same for girls and boys? *Journal of Child and Family Studies, 14,* 15–27.

Hankin, B.L., Abramson, L.Y., Moffitt, T.E., Silva, P.A., McGee, R., & Angell, K.E. (1998). Development of depression from preadolescence to young adulthood: Emerging gender differences in a 10-year longitudinal study. *Journal of Abnormal Psychology, 107,* 128–140.

Hipwell, A.E., Loeber, R., Stouthamer-Loeber, M., Keenan, K., White H.R., & Kroneman, L. (2002). Characteristic of girls with early-onset disruptive and antisocial behaviour. *Criminal Behaviour and Mental Health, 12,* 99–118.

Hipwell, A.E., Stepp, S., Feng, X., Burke, J., Battista, D.R., Loeber, R., & Keenan, K. (2011). Impact of oppositional defiant disorder dimensions on the temporal ordering of conduct problems and depression across childhood and adolescence in girls. *Journal of Child Psychology and Psychiatry, 52*(10), 1099–1108.

Keenan, K., Hipwell, A., Duax, J., Stouthamer-Loeber, M., & Loeber, R. (2004). Phenomenology of depression in young girls. *Journal of the American Academy of Child and Adolescent Psychiatry, 43,* 1098–1106.

Keenan, K., & Shaw, D.D. (2003). Development of conduct problems during the preschool years. In B.B. Lahey, T.E. Moffitt, & A. Caspi (Eds.), *Causes of conduct disorder and juvenile delinquency* (pp. 153–181). New York: Guilford.

Loeber, R., & Farrington, D.P. (2001). *Child delinquents: Development, intervention and service Needs.* Thousand Oaks, CA: Sage.

Loeber, R., Keenan, K., Lahey, B.B., Green, S.M., & Thomas, C. (1993). Evidence for developmentally based diagnosis of oppositional defiant disorder and conduct disorder. *Journal of Abnormal Child Psychology, 21,* 377–410.

Loeber, R., Pardini, D., Stouthamer-Loeber, M., Hipwell, A.E., & Sembower, M. (2009). Are there stable factors in girls' externalizing behaviors in middle childhood? *Journal of Abnormal Child Psychology, 37*(6), 777–791.

Loeber, R., Wung, P., Keenan, K., Giroux, B., Stouthamer-Loeber, M., van Kammen, W.B., & Maughan, B. (1993). Developmental pathways in disruptive child behaviour. *Development and Psychopathology, 5,* 101–132.

Lyubomirsky, S., Caldwell, N.D., & Nolen-Hoeksema, S. (1998). Effects of ruminative and distracting responses to depressed mood on retrieval of autobiographical memories. *Journal of Personality and Social Psychology, 75,* 166–177.

McConaughy, S.H., Stanger, C., & Achenbach, T. (1992). Three-year course of behavioral/emotional problems in a national sample of 4 to 16-year-olds: I. Agreement among informants. *Journal of the American Academy of Child and Adolescent Psychiatry, 31,* 932–940.

Moffitt, T.E., Caspi, A., Rutter, M., & Silva, P.A. (2001). *Sex differences in antisocial behaviour: Conduct disorder, delinquency and violence in the Dunedin Longitudinal Study.* New York: Cambridge University Press.

Moretti, M.M., Odgers, C.L., & Jackson, M.A. (2004). *Girls and aggression: Contributing factors and intervention principles.* New York: Kluwer Academic/ Plenum.

Nichols, T.R., Graber, J.A., Brooks-Gunn, J., & Botvin, G.J. (2006). Sex differences in overt aggression and delinquency among urban minority middle
school students. *Applied Developmental Psychology*, *27*, 78–91.

Nock, M.K., Kazdin, A.E., Hiripi, E., & Kessler, R.C. (2007). Lifetime prevalence,
correlates, and persistence of oppositional defiant disorder: Results from the
National Comorbidity Survey Replication. *Journal of Child Psychology and
Psychiatry*, *48*, 703–713.

Offord, D.R., Alder, R.J., & Boyle, M.H. (1986). Prevalence and sociodemo-
graphic correlates of conduct disorder. *American Journal of Social Psychiatry*,
6, 272–278.

Pepler, D.J., Madsen, K.C., Webster, C., & Levene, K.S. (2005). *The development
and treatment of girlhood aggression*. Mahwah, NJ: Erlbaum.

Putallaz, M., & Bierman, K.L. (2004). *Aggression, antisocial behavior and violence
amongst girls*. New York: Guilford.

Reyes, L.R., Meininger, J.C., Liehr, P., Chan. W., & Mueller, W.H. (2003). Anger
in adolescents: Sex, ethnicity, age differences, and psychometric properties.
Nursing Research, *52*, 2–11.

Saarni, C. (1984). An observational study of children's attempts to monitor their
expressive behavior. *Child Development*, *55*, 1504–1513.

Silverthorn, P., & Frick, P.J. (1999). Developmental pathways to antisocial behaviour: The delayed-onset pathway in girls. *Development and Psychopathology*,
11(1), 101–126.

Strayer, J. (1986). Children's attributions regarding the situational determinants
of emotions in self and others. *Developmental Psychology*, *17*, 649–654.

Tiet, Q.Q., & Huizinga, D. (2002). Dimensions of the construct of resilience
and adaptation among inner-city youth. *Journal of Adolescent Research*, *17*,
260–276.

Underwood, M.K., Hurley, J.C., Johanson, C.A., & Mosley, J.E. (1999). An experimental, observational investigation of children's responses to peer provocation: Developmental and gender differences in middle childhood. *Child
Development*, *70*, 1428–1446.

Westenberg, P.M., Drewes, M.J., Goedhart, A.W., Siebelink, B.M., & Treffers,
P.D.A. (2004). A developmental analysis of self-reported fears in late child-
hood through mid-adolescence: Social-evaluative fears on the rise? *Journal of
Child Psychology and Psychiatry*, *45*, 481–495.

Zahn, M.A., Steffensmeier, D., Feld, B.C., Morash, M., Chesney-Lind, M., Miller,
J., Brumbaugh, S. (2007). *Violence and teenage girls*. Washington, DC: Office
of Juvenile Justice and Delinquency Prevention.

CHAPTER FIVE

WEBS OF STRENGTH AND RESISTANCE: HEARING ABORIGINAL ADOLESCENT GIRLS TELLING THEIR STORIES

SUSAN D. DION

FACULTY OF EDUCATION, YORK UNIVERSITY

INTRODUCTION

"It sounds to me like you are just being nosy about our lives." A young Anishnabe adolescent girl spoke these words during a community meeting. The meeting, held in northern Ontario, was the first phase of a research project titled *Talking Back: Aboriginal Girls Telling Their Stories.*[1] The goal of this qualitative research was to advance our understanding of the lived experiences of adolescent Aboriginal girls including the stresses and risks associated with the occurrence of "aggressive" behaviour. The purpose of the meeting was to introduce the project to members of the community, to address their comments and questions, and to draw on their knowledge and expertise to inform our research practice. While the meetings were successful with much lively discussion, expressions of interest and support, suggestions with regard to recruitment and ideas on how to protect the girls' anonymity, I found these words particularly significant. In her statement, I heard this young woman reminding me that my request for her participation brought with it a series of responsibilities. As a researcher I was responsible for recognizing the girls as authorities on their lives, for paying attention to what they were asking me to hear, and for taking action in ways that would be respectful of what I might learn from listening to their stories. Additionally, the statement carried a cautionary message, reminding me of the animosity and distrust that permeates the speaking-listening relationship between Aboriginal people and newcomers, between "academic" researchers (historically non-Aboriginal) and Aboriginal people, between adults and adolescents. Really, I asked myself, why would adolescent Aboriginal girls speak to researchers at all? But speak to us they did, compelling me to take seriously my responsibilities as a researcher.

As an Aboriginal woman, teacher, and researcher I recognize research encounters as significant sites for the production and reproduction of dominant ways of knowing. I agree with Linda Tuhiwai Smith (1999) who explains, "research is not an innocent or distant academic exercise but an activity that has something at stake and that occurs in a set of political and social conditions" (p. 5). Conscious of the oppressive ways in which research activity was done on, and done to, Aboriginal people, the *Talking Back* project was informed by decolonizing, feminist, and critical methodologies. Rather than uncovering the researchers' truths about Aboriginal girls, our aim, working in collaboration with the community, was to learn from how the girls represent their own lived experiences, and from the truths they tell about their own lives. As Smith (1999) writes, "Representation of indigenous peoples by indigenous people is about countering the dominant society's image of indigenous peoples, their lifestyles and belief systems. It is also about proposing solutions to the real-life dilemmas that indigenous communities confront and trying to capture the complexities of being indigenous" (p. 151). We invited the girls to speak with us and, in spite of the risks, many accepted our invitation. In doing so the girls made a significant contribution to self-representation.

Having told the girls that we wanted to hear their stories, the challenge for me became one of respectful and reliable listening. I spent time immersed in their transcripts listening and listening and listening again for an indication of what the girls might be asking me to hear and asking myself what meanings I might make from what I was hearing. In this chapter I share the girls' stories with the hope of communicating what they themselves had to say about the complexities of their lives and the place aggression occupies in their day-to-day experiences. Wanting to provide space for the girls to speak for themselves, I include extended quotes from their interviews. In response to the questions we ask, the girls describe their lived experiences, including their experience of being adolescent girls, what it is like for them to live within the residue of the colonial legacy, what they know and do not know about the anger they feel, and most importantly where they locate solace. For me, the stories they tell reflect and provoke questions about what their aggressive behaviours accomplish, their need to find and/or create spaces within which they can experience and express their agency, the possibilities offered and the limitations imposed by the social-political context within which they are living, and their own awareness of what is required to improve the material reality of their lives.

This study originated at a time when there was increasing attention to girlhood aggression in the media, popular culture, academic theorizing, and research. The literature that emerged during the 1990s contributed to the construction of a discourse on "aggressive girls" that in many ways served to pathologize them. Drawing on the work of critical feminist scholarship (Chesney-Lind & Eliason, 2006; Currie, Kelly, & Pomerantz, 2007; Gonick, 2004; Ringrose, 2006), I develop a contextual definition of aggression as a strategy rather than an essential trait and reflect how the girls take up and make use of aggression for a range of purposes. Rather than pathologizing or criminalizing their aggressive acts, I work at seeing what the girls want to accomplish with their aggression and hear their expressions of anger and frustration as a communicative act, an act of resistance, an act of self-protection, an active search for attention to that which is unbearable in their lives. I am not advocating for, nor supporting, their use of aggression; my aim is to de-essentialize anger and aggression and to understand how and why the girls use it. As a responsible researcher I must listen and respond with an awareness of and an appreciation for their needs and the social-political contexts within which they are living.

PROJECT DESCRIPTION
The request for this research came from Dilico Anishinabek Family Care (Dilico). Dilico is a multi-service agency that, in accordance with Anishnabe values, traditions, and beliefs, provides a wide range of child welfare, treatment, and health services.[2] The *Talking Back* project was initiated by staff members who were concerned by what they observed as "increasing incidents of aggression" among Aboriginal adolescent girls in the communities they serve. Family members, community members, and the girls themselves identified the use of aggression as a problem and expressed a desire to accomplish change in their ways of knowing about and responding to its use. The project was a partnership between researchers, clinicians, community members, and the girls. The research team included three Toronto-based academic researchers and four community-based members of the Dilico staff.[3] We interviewed 40 girls between the ages of 12 and 18. Girls were invited to participate in the project by members of the community and were interviewed by Aboriginal women.[4] Our questions, developed in collaboration with women from the community,[5] addressed

four topics: People in Your Life, Self, School, and Home. Our project involved listening to First Nations girls to explore both the conditions of risk in their lives and the protective processes that enable the girls to cope with adversity. Drawing on their stories, we hoped to improve our understanding of their day-to-day lived experiences of violence as both victims and perpetrators, with the goal of improving existing and developing new prevention and intervention programs for them. The project was not about us as outsiders helping Aboriginal girls. It was about working with, alongside, and for Aboriginal girls, their families, and their communities as they and we struggled to make sense of and learn from their experiences.

As much as the research team members had a shared interest in the work of the project, we each occupied our own positions and each of us had our own specific objectives and our own interpretations. For example, the directors and staff at Dilico were immersed in the life of the communities where the girls live. They had intimate knowledge of the girls' strengths and the challenges the girls confront. They were looking for and were in need of specific and practical results that would inform the delivery of services to the girls and their communities. The academics on the project had an interest in knowledge construction specifically as it relates to girlhood aggression. As an Aboriginal woman/teacher/researcher, I was particularly concerned with questions of representation. I worked with a conscious awareness of the ways in which negative constructions of Aboriginal woman have contributed to our experiences of oppression. I have written this chapter conscious of my role as interpreter and re-presenter of the girls' voices.

I have focused on the stories of four girls who participated in the project. The case study approach has allowed for a detailed telling of each girl's story creating the possibility for readers to hear individual voices. When I received the first set of transcribed interviews, a subset of nine, I read through all of them and chose four based on the depth and clarity of the girl's responses. This paper was shared with members of the research team as well as with the women's advisory committee.[6]

HEARING THEIR STORIES
There is very little in the literature about Aboriginal adolescent girls and much of what there is describes the extent to which and the multiple ways in which Aboriginal girls are susceptible to violence, poverty, and abuse (see, e.g., Downe, 2006). In the *Talking Back* interviews, while the girls did not ignore their experiences of poverty and violence, I hear them telling an alternative story, a story that rejects the discourses that position them

as either pitiful victims of oppression, heroic survivors of an oppressive past, or angry girls living a violent present. I hear their desire to be seen and to be recognized as young women doing the work of the adolescent, that is, cultivating a sense of themselves in relationship with their families, friends, communities, and culture. Within Aboriginal ways of being, a sense of self and the individual is formed within a sense of responsibility to community and within relationships (Anderson, 2000, p. 50). In spite of the violence of colonialism, the significance of coming to know the self in relationship with community surfaces in the girls' stories.

Alice
Alice is 12 years old and recognizes herself as a strong student. In response to the question, "Can you tell me something that you're really good at?" Alice responds, "Learning; I won an academic award at school." She describes herself as "shy from people" and tells us that she enjoys taking care of young children. She lives with her mother, father, two siblings, and a cousin in a home without hydro. As Alice says, this means that "Well, [we] have no hot water, we can't take a shower and all that. But I, like, get really down and it makes me mad sometimes." What makes her really sad is thinking about her cousin who "killed herself, she OD'd." Alice lives in a remote community but wishes that she could live in Thunder Bay where many of her friends have moved. She is happy just hanging out with her friends, talking and laughing with them. Like many adolescent girls, her friends are important to her. As she says of one of them: "Like we're there for each other [mumble]. And we tell everything about each other…We like never, I don't know, we just like talk and talk about life and all that and like understanding each other. I'll tell her when I'm happy and all of that."

Britt
Seventeen-year-old Britt sees herself as happy and funny. She does not consider herself a successful student, but she likes being at school because it is a place where she can be around people and make them laugh. She is a "tough" girl; nothing makes her sad except when she argues with her best friend. She is protective of both her younger siblings and her parents. She tells us about getting into a fight at school when someone was going to beat up her little cousin who was too small to protect herself. One day she would like to be a paramedic, but she worries about whether or not she will graduate from high school because her grades are not good. She skips a lot of school because she finds it difficult to pay attention. Britt is currently boarding with a family in Thunder Bay so that she can attend high school. She is, in part, relieved to be away from home on the reserve where people

are always arguing. She admires her mother who, as Britt explains, "knows right from wrong." When asked to expand she says, "No, I don't like talking about my parents."

Casey

Thirteen-year-old Casey describes herself as funny. She likes to be with her friends at school, where she is part of a "new" group; in the past she was "hanging with a 'bad' group." Casey is living with a foster family and tells us that thinking about her mom makes her sad and afraid. Her mother is in a treatment program because she has a "drinking problem" and is unable to take care of Casey and her brother. When we ask her to describe the best thing that ever happened to her, Casey responds, "I don't know. It feels like everything in my life has gone wrong." She feels as if she is often blamed for things that go wrong that are not her fault. In response to our question, "What do you wish for?" she says, "I wish that I could get through one day when my foster mother wasn't blaming me for something I didn't do." She tends to throw things when she is angry and ends up breaking things. When we ask about how she deals with her anger, Casey responds, "Sometimes when I am at home and I can't go to my friend's house, I usually just go to my room and start crying. And I accidentally broke this clock last time, and it was really expensive."

Donna

Fifteen-year-old Donna presents herself as a strong, perceptive girl. She thinks of herself as stubborn and tells us that she is a typical teenage girl who likes to watch movies, play cards, go for walks, and hang out with her friends. She is observant and is learning to ignore what people say about her behind her back and rather to believe in herself. Donna describes her community as a place where "there's nothing to do. You have nothing for, like

TABLE 5.1   THE GIRLS' AGES, COMMUNITY, FAMILY, AND CLINICAL STATUS

	Age	Community	Family Status	Clinical Status
Alice	12	Remote	Lives with parents	Non-clinical (Aggressive)
Britt	17	Remote/Urban	Boarding	Clinical (Aggressive)
Casey	13	Urban	Foster care	Non-clinical (Non-aggressive/self-harm)
Donna	15	Remote	Lives with mother	Clinical (Non-aggressive)

teenagers my age, to do. People don't get along, there's always lots of fighting, families don't get along." She has a big family who provide her with a lot of support. She does not know her father but tells us, "My mother is my best friend. She is like my protector. She's always been there for me."

In multiple ways the girls ask us to hear their stories of "normal" adolescence. They tell us that they are typical teenage girls who enjoy hanging out with their friends; they talk about boys, play cards, and watch movies. As Alice explains, "I'm happy when I get to be with my family and friends." Donna says, "I am a teenager and teenagers always think that nobody understands what they are saying." They are busy accomplishing the *work of the adolescent*; that is, cultivating a sense of themselves as independent beings, in relationship with their families, communities, and culture. They are searching for a place of belonging; they are in need of love, care, and acceptance; they want to be able to make a contribution; and they want opportunities to learn and to be challenged.

THE COLONIAL LEGACY: WHAT IT IS LIKE FOR THEM
While the girls "insist" that we recognize the ordinariness of their lives, they are at the same time acutely observant of the ways in which the legacy of colonialism impacts them. The girls live day to day amid the residue of colonialism including loss, family disruption, poverty, racism, small communities that are isolated from one another, and an education system that reflects the colonizer and colonial history, language, and culture. We asked the girls a series of questions that created the space for them to tell "what it is like for us."

Alice describes the worst thing that ever happened to her:

> *Alice*: When they would argue my mom would try pushing him but she knew when … that dad wouldn't hurt her. He was just pushing her trying to get her away. He didn't want to hurt her, but he must have got mad and he tried hitting her, but I jumped in front of her and told him to hit me first and he backed off.

Alice also talks about her community:

> *Jan* (a member of the research team): When someone asks, "Where are you from?" how do you feel about telling him or her that you are from the reserve?
> *Alice*: I don't know. Sometimes, like, I just … it's weird saying that I'm from the reserve.
> *Jan*: Why do you think it is weird saying that?

Alice: I don't know. [Mumble]. I don't know. Sounds like a junk here.

Jan: "Junk here." So you're not too proud of it sometimes?

Alice: Not too proud.

Jan: Okay.

Alice: Then again I really care that I'm from here. But sometimes it's like I'm not proud of it and a lot of times I am proud of it.

Jan: What kind of things do you think you're proud of?

Alice: Well, people in Thunder Bay just think that the reserve...they think that it's a really dumb place and all that. But...and then they say that there are good people from here. There are some people that can jog really well.

Similar to Alice, Britt expresses her feelings about living on the reserve. When Jan asks her to complete the sentence "I wish that I could ..." she responds:

Britt: Move away.

Jan: Okay, so you wish that you could move away. Is there somewhere specific where you want to move to?

Britt: No.

Jan: Just anywhere?

Britt: Yeah.

Jan: Is it because you don't like it here, or ...?

Britt: Yeah.

Casey is sad because she can't be with her mother and worries:

Casey: I don't know, whenever I am not with my mom I feel that she is going to get hurt because, like when I used to live with her, um, her boyfriends would always really hurt her. I don't know, I don't exactly like all her boyfriends, they are all really mean. And always drunk. And I am afraid that...it's gonna happen.

Donna offers these observations about her community:

Donna: The community likes to do a lot of fighting. They cannot get along. Like [they] have band meetings and stuff. But like band meetings are like their chance to like fight and let's talk about each other and say bad things about each other and stuff. Like I think our reserve has so much potential to do stuff, but people can't get along so there's nothing that can get done.

There is something familiar in the girls' descriptions. I recognize the ways in which poverty, violence, fear, and loss permeate reserve life. As an adult who has the privilege of education, I understand that the socio-economic conditions are an outcome of colonization. The girls' descriptions cause me to question what Aboriginal students in Ontario public schools learn about the history of colonialism. Do the girls know why things are the way that they are? Are they developing the knowledge, skills, and understanding that would enable them to work for change? In her critique of public education Marie Battiste (1998) argues, "We cannot continue to allow Aboriginal students to be given a fragmented existence in a curriculum that does not mirror them, nor should they be denied understanding the historical context that has created that fragmentation" (p. 24).

In what ways does this knowing and not knowing inform the girls' identity formation? To what extent do they blame themselves and to what extent are they confused, frustrated, and angered by the conditions of their lives? Alice's words reflect a sense of confusion; she is both proud and not proud. And while confusion is an expected state of being for the adolescent, the relationship between one's sense of self and one's understanding of what it means to be Aboriginal offers particular challenges. In both public and private realms, Aboriginal identity is formed in relationship with community and culture. In Canada there is no escaping the negative representations and the oppressive living conditions confronted by the vast majority of Aboriginal people and their families and communities. Within this context developing a positive sense of self can be a daunting task.

ANGER AND FRUSTRATION

We did not ask the girls directly about their participation in acts of aggression; we did however ask them, "What makes you angry and what do you do when you get angry?"

Boys at school bother Alice and that makes her angry:

> *Jan*: So what do you do when they bother you?
> *Alice*: I don't know, I just get mad, chase after them, and some-
> 'times I just ignore them and just talk to my mom about it.

Following up, Jan asks Alice to complete the following sentence: "I can never make my family understand why ..."

> *Alice*: Like why I get angry so much.
> *Jan*: Okay. Why do you get angry so much?
> *Alice*: I don't know.

Britt tells us that what makes her angry is:

> *Britt*: Seeing drunks.
> *Jan*: So you don't like it when you see drunks. How do you deal with your anger, like when you get upset and mad, what do you do?
> *Britt*: Punch the wall.
> *Jan*: You punch the wall? Is there a reason? How often do you do that?
> *Britt*: Once a month, yeah.
> *Jan*: Like is it a specific thing that bothers you a lot or is it somebody or... or do you hit anything that you get angry at?
> *Britt*: Anything.

Casey gets angry when:

> *Casey*: Um, when people blame things on me when I didn't do it.
> *Jan*: Does that happen a lot? Can you give me examples?
> *Casey*: Okay, my foster mom, this was this week, my foster mom found these needles in the garage and she thought that I... that they were mine, but they weren't. And she was yelling at me so I went to my friend's house.

And in response to questions about what makes her angry, Donna says:

> *Donna*: When I hear people talking about my family. Or when I hear people talking nasty about Native people I get really angry with that.
> *Amy*: Do you notice that that happens a lot around you?
> *Donna*: Yeah, just lately in my school. There was a big thing where these White kids were like really nagging on Natives, like dirty Indians and bla bla whatever. They almost closed school that one day because they thought there was gonna be a big brawl between the Whites and the Native people. It's pretty cool now, like we've been going good, but there is still certain people like to—mumble dirty Indian. And some people just look and they get really mad.

The girls tell us what makes them angry and about some of their coping strategies. Informed by their emerging awareness of inequity based on race, class, and gender, they are able to identify what is unfair and exhibit a willingness to take action in response. As Aboriginal adolescents and as Aboriginal girls, they are having to confront their positions of empowerment and disempowerment. They find ways to respond within the constraints imposed by the contexts within which they live, including the extent to which they are required to discipline and regulate their expression of strong feelings of anger.

SOLACE

These girls are not paralyzed by the conditions of their day-to-day lives. They actively search out and cultivate experiences and relationships that affirm their sense of themselves as worthy beings, that is, as beings worthy of care and concern from significant others in their lives—significant others who will protect them from harm, provide them with guidance, and offer them space within which to explore their developing sense of self and of themselves in their world. The girls identify sources of solace and inspiration that are available to them. All four of the girls talk about writing as a strategy for responding to their anger. They look to their mothers, grandmothers, sisters, and cousins for guidance. They identify people in their lives who have survived difficult times themselves as mentors and sources of support. They enjoy and work hard at their Ojibwa language classes and locate strength in attending powwows.

Jan asks the girls about their favourite school subjects:

> *Jan*: Do you have a favourite school subject?
> *Alice*: English—poetry.
> *Jan*: Any reason? Why is it your favourite?
> *Alice*: I just like writing poems. Sometimes I write poems about life and like when I get mad I'll write poems.

And with Britt, Jan asks:

> *Jan*: Do you have a favourite school subject?
> *Britt*: Yeah.
> *Jan*: What is your favourite school subject?
> *Britt*: English.
> *Jan*: Interesting. What do you enjoy the most about your favourite school subject?
> *Britt*: Writing.
> *Jan*: The writing part. Is there a specific reason or you just ...? Do you like writing all the time?
> *Britt*: Yeah, I just like writing, anything.
> *Jan*: Do you write poems, or songs?
> *Britt*: Lots of stuff.
> *Jan*: Do you just write? When do you do this, like at school, at home?
> *Britt*: At school, at home, weekends. Pretty much every day.

We ask about the girls' significant relationships:

> *Jan*: Tell me about one person that you like to spend time with.
> *Britt*: My granny.
> *Jan*: Do you have a lot of time to spend with her?
> *Britt*: No. Just during the summer.
> *Jan*: Why did you choose this person, your granny?
> *Britt*: Because I am always happy around her.
> *Jan*: Finish the next [sentence] for me: The person that I most admire is …
> *Britt*: My granny.
> *Jan*: Why do you admire her so much?
> *Britt*: She teaches me lots of stuff.
> *Jan*: What types of stuff does she teach you?
> *Britt*: How to speak Ojibwa.
> *Jan*: She speaks Ojibwa.
> *Britt*: Yeah, I can a little bit.
> *Jan*: Is there any other reason why you admire your grandmother so much?
> *Britt*: No, she keeps me happy.

Casey tells about her memories of spending time with her grandmother:

> *Jan*: Finish the next [sentence] for me: When I was seven, I remember I would always…
> *Casey*: Seven, see my grandma.
> *Jan*: Okay. Do you remember, why would you choose your grandma?
> *Casey*: She used to always mostly take care of us, me and my brother and my sisters. And she would always come and take us out to McDonald's or go to powwows.

With Amy, another member of the research team, Donna describes her relationship with her grandmother:

> *Amy*: So what types of things did you and your grandma do?
> *Donna*: She babysat me for the first 10 years of my life. We would play cards, go for a walk, and sit outside and [have] picnics and we would talk.
> *Amy*: So you said earlier that you looked at your grandma as a role model. And what types of things did she show you?
> *Donna*: Well she was just a strong woman, and she had lots of pride in whatever she did and was really wise.

The girls speak with favour and pride about their opportunities to access the Ojibwa language and other sources of traditional knowledge:

Jan: The best thing my family ever did for me was...
Casey: Uh, taking me to the powwows.
Jan: What do you enjoy about powwows?
Casey: I like seeing other Aboriginal people, like, coming together. The other people coming.
Jan: Do you go to powwows often?
Casey: With my family. Mostly.

The girls demonstrate the capacity to identify and locate strategies to cope with the various sources of stress in their lives. They use writing as a tool to work through their feelings and turn to friends for support. Experiencing love, happiness, and care in relationship with their grandmothers, the girls highly respect these women who provide guidance and teaching through which they learn to understand themselves and their place in the world. The girls' stories affirm what Kim Anderson (2000) heard from adult woman she interviewed. In her book *A Recognition of Being: Reconstructing Native Womanhood*, Anderson notes that, drawing on the position women occupied in traditional societies, grandmothers act with authority, power, and wisdom. Caregiving, contributing to economic decision-making, taking up leadership roles in the political life of the community, acting as keepers and teachers of traditional wisdom, strong women offer girls support and demonstrate what is possible for them. Similar to the adult women Anderson interviewed, the girls describe the significance of grandmothers in their learning about community interdependency, survival, and resistance.

DISCUSSION: WHAT I HEAR IN THE GIRLS' STORIES

Thinking about the context in which the girls are living, I am reminded of the work of Stoh:lo writer and scholar Lee Maracle (1996), who said, "We did not create this history, we had no say in any of the conditions into which we were born (nor did our ancestors), yet we are saddled with the responsibility for altering these conditions and re-building our nations" (p. x). Listening to the girls' interviews, I am overwhelmed by their need to be ever vigilant. They do not let down their guard; they are always working at and responding to their own feelings and to those of others. The girls are involved in a constant state of emotionally laden identity-work, navigating contradictory feelings of shame and pride, affirmation and denial, fear and comfort, love and profound loss. Confusion, uncertainty, and struggle are present in their lives as they participate in surviving, recuperating, and rebuilding themselves, their families, communities, and nation.

We did not ask the girls specific questions about their own experiences as witnesses or as survivors of violence nor did we ask them to provide details of their participation in acts of aggression. We know that three of the four girls are survivors of violence, that all of the girls have witnessed violence in their families, and that at the time of interviewing three of the four girls were identified as "aggressive." We did not ask the girls to speak to the violence in their lives because we started the project well aware of the depth to which violence pervades the lives of Aboriginal women and girls. The pervasiveness and intensity of violence in their lives has been extensively documented. Sexual assault, physical abuse, domestic violence, incest, childhood sexual abuse, emotional abuse, and homicide are documented at significantly higher levels among Aboriginal girls and women than the rest of the Canadian population. According to Statistics Canada, Aboriginal women are at risk of more "severe and potentially life-threatening forms of violence" than non-Aboriginal women, and up to 75% of victims of sex crimes in Aboriginal communities are female under 18 years of age (Correctional Service of Canada cited in McIvor & Nahanee, 1998, p. 65).

Additionally and just as significant as our knowledge of the violence in the lives of Aboriginal girls is our awareness of the work Aboriginal women are doing in their communities to nurture children, reclaim traditional knowledge, and accomplish change. As Maracle (1999) explains, "We, as Native women, are in the process of rediscovering and reclaiming our separate body of knowledge. I have felt the burden of having to drive through darkened tunnels of memory and magic to reclaim the internal world of women" (p. 14). Laguna Pueblo-Sioux scholar Paula Gunn Allen (1992) writes, "We survive, and we do more than survive. We bond, we care, we fight, we teach, we nurse, we bear, we feed, we earn, we laugh, we love, we hang in there, no matter what" (p. 190).

Knowing that while the girls live with violence they also live with stories of resistance, I ask to what extent are the girls confronted with difficult and contradictory demands. To what extent are they "charged" with a decolonizing project? What does it mean to take up this project, living the colonial legacy but living in the absence of any real knowledge and understanding of the complex social, political, and historical context that created the conditions that they are living? While recognizing the human capacities for resistance to domination and for self-creation, Michel Foucault reminds us that there are social and political limits to the exercise of those capacities. He identifies and differentiates between technologies of power, which impact the conduct of individuals and submit them to certain ends

or domination, and technologies of the self, which he defines as allowing "individuals to effect a certain number of operations on their own
bodies and souls, thoughts, conduct and way of being, so as to transform
themselves in order to attain a certain state of happiness, purity, wisdom"
(Foucault, 1988, p. 18).

What are the technologies of power that determine the "conduct" of
the girls, and what are the technologies of the self that the girls take up?
What are the operations that they are conducting on themselves so as to
transform themselves in order to attain a certain state of happiness? Are
the girls presenting themselves as "tough" and "in control" of their lives
because they think that is what they are expected to do? Are they struggling with competing discourses—one that tells them they are meant to
be "in control" and "tough," that they are to be strong, proud Aboriginal
girls, and another that derives from or is constructed out of the residues
of colonialism that has them living lives of shame, poverty, violence, and
abuse? I recognize these discourses as possible resources rather than strict
limitations for girls' agency and power, yet they are problematic. The girls
work to perform, they have a desire to be "strong Aboriginal girls," they
recognize the need to be "empowered," but what does that look like? How
do we define empowered and strong? How do we articulate it to the girls?
Where are the girls expected to learn how to perform as strong adolescent
Aboriginal girls or young women? And how do they accomplish that given
the realities of their day-to-day lives? What are the strategies available to
the girls within the existing power relations—what is possible and what is
permissible? In what ways might the girls be engaged in a struggle to assert
control over their lives—claiming the right to defend themselves?

The girls' stories reflect a profound sense of responsibility. They are taking up the challenge to protect, to defend, to learn their languages and ceremonies, to survive, to transform, and to become young women. Thinking
about possible links between their expressions of anger and frustration and
their active participation in aggressive behaviour, I find myself asking what
does their aggression accomplish? I am certain that it accomplishes protection, that it has value as expression, and that it may be a performance of the
strong Aboriginal girl, giving them status within the competitive hierarchy
of youth cultures and deriving from a demand that we pay attention. It may
be that the girls are telling us that the conditions in which they are living
are unacceptable and that they refuse to take it anymore.

Critical feminist scholar Lyn Mikel Brown (1998) argues that "a sex-
ist, masculinist and racist culture shapes and constrains girls' capacities
to easily express emotions such as anger and aggression" (p. 413). Others,
including Gonick (2004), Ringrose (2006), and Chesney-Lind and Eliason

(2006), argue that discourses of girlhood aggression and "girlfighting" (see, e.g., Wiseman, 2002; Simmons, 2002) decontextualize girls' emotional expression from the larger cultural and social world of school and family relationships. As a result, the "'universalization' and 'normalization' of girl meanness elides complex differences among girls and vastly different familial, community and educational contexts under which femininity, aggression and violence are to be constituted and regulated" (Ringrose, 2006, p. 407). Aboriginal girls confront multiple demands; they work to explore and express their femininity within a context that is often unsafe, a context that demands strength but within which expressions of aggression put them at risk of being positioned as "violent girls." Chesney-Lind and Eliason (2006) argue that the "mean girl" discourse is reflective of girls' powerlessness. They also argue that, not permitted direct aggression, white middle-class girls in particular are said to resort to "relational aggression" as a way of establishing power while maintaining their positions within the protected sphere of traditional femininity. Threatened by images and stories of girlhood aggression, the creation and maintenance of a mean girl discourse serves to shelter white middle-class girls who are positioned against the in-your-face violence associated with masculinized and racialized girls (Chesney-Lind & Eliason, 2006). My hearing of what the girls told us in the *Talking Back* project draws attention to the issues informing their aggression, including colonialism, patriarchy, and systems of race and class privilege. Recognizing the girls' use of aggression as a strategy for surviving and responding to the violence in their lives, I ask: To what extent are the girls making use of aggression because "it works"? In what ways does it work or not work? What are the consequences for these girls and how might interested and invested adults intervene? What alternatives are available? How might interventions be applied in ways that will allow the girls to accomplish their objectives? And what possibilities exist to alleviate conditions that drive their need to rely on aggression?

CONCLUSION

"It is the children who will have to learn to claw, dig, scratch in unison if we are to get out of this deep shaft" (Maracle, 1996, p. 12).

The girls who participated in the *Talking Back* project spoke clearly and described in detail the sources of stress and places of solace in their lives. They talked about their desire to be "ordinary" and about the anger, frustration, and fear that is a normalized aspect of their day-to-day lives. Drawing on interviews with four girls who participated in the project, I argue that the girls use aggression as a strategy that allows them to survive, respond to, and meet specific needs within the contexts of their lives. Rather than pathologizing their use of aggression, it is important to think about what it is the girls want to accomplish and to provide them with alternative strategies to meet their needs. While it is useful to investigate and learn from their shared experiences, it is equally important to recognize their individual subjectivities.

Aboriginal people know that to decolonize ourselves and actively resist colonial paradigms is a complex and daunting task: those of us working in support of decolonization also know that if we are to succeed we must involve our children and youth. The girls who participated in the *Talking Back* project made a significant contribution to the work. Understanding and responding to their stories requires a series of actions.

The girls identify writing as a tool for working through their anger. Introducing them to Aboriginal women's writing would provide opportunities to expand their understanding of colonialism, the history of their communities, and how it came to be that Aboriginal people occupy the positions that they do.

Participation in aggressive behaviour allows the girls to explore and express anger and frustration. They explained that talking with their friends is an alternative strategy. Creating opportunities for girls to gather and to explore their feelings of anger and frustration with each other in supportive contexts might alleviate their reliance on aggression.

While the girls expressed negative attitudes about formal schooling, they reported strong motivation for learning their indigenous language, the meaning and practice of ceremonies, and traditional knowledge. Integrating Aboriginal content in the secondary school curriculum and allowing students to earn high school credits for their learning would legitimize Aboriginal ways of knowing and have the potential to reduce Aboriginal students' experiences of alienation within school contexts.

Building on the positive relationships girls have with their grandmothers, it is important to create and support opportunities for nurturing strong relationships between and across generations of women. These positive relationships would be of service to the whole of the community.

The girls are conscious of the violence and injustice that permeates their communities. They need and want opportunities to be involved in activist work contributing to accomplishing change for themselves, their families, and their nations.

Much of the existing literature on girlhood aggression has a focus on white middle-class girls. It is important to consider how the "mean girls" discourse informs research practices with Aboriginal girls, including the questions we ask, our methods, our interpretations and findings. Additionally, we need to think about the ways in which the discourse may be impacting how the girls see themselves. Building on the work of the *Talking Back* project we need further research to explore the intricacies of and motivations for aggression. That is, we need to know more about what the girls themselves have to say about how they use aggression, and what they are working to accomplish with their acts of aggression.

Keeping in mind the admonishment I heard at the start of this project, I have worked conscious of my responsibilities as a researcher and would like to express my deep appreciation to the research team and most especially to the girls who accepted a risk and shared their stories in the hope of advancing our understanding of Aboriginal adolescent girls and improving the day-to-day lived experiences of girls like themselves.[7]

NOTES

1 In the spring of 2003, the *Talking Back* project team received a Research Development Initiative Grant from the Social Sciences and Humanities Council. The project was a partnership between researchers, clinicians, community members, and First Nations girls. Our goal was to develop an innovative research program with adolescent girls from the 13 First Nations of the Robertson Superior Treaty Area.

2 "Dilico Ojibway Child and Family Services" was incorporated on July 23, 1986. Dilico's mandate was to develop and implement a child welfare system to strengthen, maintain, and support Anishnabek children and families. Its offices are situated in five locations, including Fort William, Armstrong, Longlac, Nipigon, and Mobert. Dilico is governed by representatives from the following First Nations: Fort William, Ginoogaming, Gull Bay, Lake Nipigon, Long Lake #58, Michipicoten, Pays Plat, Pic Mobert, Pic River, Red Rock, Rocky Bay, Sandpoint, and Whitesand.

3 Dr. Kirsten C. Madsen, Sheridan Institute of Technology and Advanced Learning, was the principal investigator; Dr. Debra Pepler, Psychology, Faculty of Health, York University, and Dr. Susan D. Dion, Faculty of Education, York University, were co-investigators. We worked closely with three women from the community, including Debbie Sault, Amanda Shebobman, and Destany Johns. Debbie and Amanda completed the majority of the interviews. Destany transcribed the interviews. Diane Wickman, a director at Dilico, was an active participant in the completion of the project.

4 Community partners who were recognized as Aboriginal women actively involved in the community completed the majority of the interviews. However, if participants knew both interviewers personally, I completed the interviews; this occurred in less than five cases.

5 The research team worked in collaboration with a woman's advisory committee. Women known to be active members of First Nations communities who had an interest in the experiences of Aboriginal girls were invited to join the committee.

6 Members of the woman's advisory committee expressed their approval of the paper. Their comments included "you've got it right" and "keep going." At least

one member felt that I had not described, in sufficient detail, the violence and aggression that permeates the girls' lives. Their responses brought to my attention the differences in our relationship to the project.

7 Additionally I express sincere appreciation to Krista Johnson for her exceptional skills as a research assistant; her work contributed to the strength of this paper. I would also like to express thanks to Dr. Carla Rice for her careful reading and helpful comments on the paper.

REFERENCES

Allen, P.G. (1992). *The sacred hoop: Recovering the feminine in American Indian traditions*. Boston, MA: Beacon Press.

Anderson, K. (2000). *A recognition of being: Reconstructing native womanhood*. Toronto: Second Story Press.

Battiste, M. (1998). Enabling the autumn seed: Toward a decolonized approach to aboriginal knowledge, language, and education. *Canadian Journal of Native Education, 22*(1), 16–27.

Brown, L.M. (1998). *Raising their voices: The politics of girls' anger*. Cambridge, MA: Harvard University Press.

Chesney-Lind, M., & Eliason, M. (2006). From invisible to incorrigible: The demonization of marginalized women and girls. *Crime, Media, Culture: An International Journal, 2*(1), 29–47.

Currie, D.H., Kelly, D.M., & Pomerantz, S. (2007). "The power to squash people": Understanding girls' relational aggression. *British Journal of Sociology of Education, 28*(1), 23–37.

Downe, P.J. (2006). Aboriginal girls in Canada: Living histories of dislocation, exploitation and strength. In Y. Jiwani, C. Steenbergen, & C. Mitchell (Eds.), *Girlhood: Redefining the limits* (pp. 1–15). Montreal: Black Rose Books.

Foucault, M. (1988). In L.H. Martin, H. Gutman, & P.H. Hutton (Eds.), *Technologies of the self: A seminar with Michel Foucault*. Boston: University of Massachusetts.

Gonick, M. (2004). The "mean girl" crisis: Problematizing representations of girls' friendships. *Feminism and Psychology, 14*(3), 395–400.

Maracle, L. (1996). *I am woman: A native perspective on sociology and feminism*. Vancouver: Press Gang Publishers.

Maracle, L. (1999). *Sojourners and sundogs*. Vancouver: Press Gang Publishers.

Mazzarella, S.R., & Pecora, N.O. (2001). *Growing up girls: Popular culture and the construction of identity*. New York: Peter Lang.

McIvor, S.D., & Nahanee, T.A. (1998). Aboriginal women: Invisible victims of violence. In K. Bonnycastle & G.S. Rigakos (Eds.), *Unsettling truths: Battered women, policy, politics, and contemporary research in Canada* (pp. 63–69). Vancouver: Collective Press.

Reinharz, S. (1992). *Feminist methods in social research*. New York: Oxford University Press.

Ringrose, J. (2006). A new universal mean girl: Examining the discursive construction and social regulation of a new feminine pathology. *Feminism and Psychology*, *16*(4), 405–424.

Simmons, R. (2002). *Odd girl out: The hidden culture of aggression in girls*. New York: Harcourt.

Smith, L.T. (1999). *Decolonizing methodologies: Research and indigenous peoples*. New York: St. Martin's Press.

Wiseman, R. (2002). *Queen bees and wannabees: Helping your daughter survive cliques, gossip, boyfriends and other realities of adolescence*. New York: Crown.

CHAPTER SIX

THE ROLE OF ANGER IN AGGRESSION

COMMENTARY BY

WENDY M. CRAIG

DEPARTMENT OF PSYCHOLOGY, QUEEN'S UNIVERSITY

ON

SOME KEY ISSUES IN THE EARLY DEVELOPMENT OF AGGRESSION IN GIRLS

R. LOEBER, M. STOUTHAMER-LOEBER, A.E. HIPWELL, J.D. BURKE, AND D.R. BATTISTA

AND

WEBS OF STRENGTH AND RESISTANCE: HEARING ABORIGINAL ADOLESCENT GIRLS TELLING THEIR STORIES

S.D. DION

The two preceding chapters contributed by Rolf Loeber and colleagues, and Susan Dion, describe different methods and have different foci, but convey similar messages. Both chapters highlight three important ideas related to girls' aggression and anger: (a) the individual mechanisms that underlie girls' aggression transcend cultural contexts; (b) different relationships can act as protective or risk factors; and (c) anger and depression may have an important role in the development of aggressive behaviour. From a developmental-contextual perspective, these two chapters indicate that both girls' own dysregulation, as well as the stressful relationships (e.g., with family and peers) and contexts (historical) in which they live, contribute to their aggressive problems. Consequently, identifying and intervening to support these girls early in their development may substantially reduce the likelihood that they will develop conduct disorders and delinquency problems. Girls who develop aggressive behaviour patterns will become the young mothers of tomorrow and the grandmothers of future generations. By supporting these girls' individual development trajectories and relationships, we can disrupt the cycle of troubled relationships and aggressive behaviour problems to prevent its continuation into the next generations.

Both of the chapters highlight the role of emotional regulation, or lack of emotional regulation, as a critical mechanism in the development of aggressive behaviour problems. Loeber and colleagues conducted longitudinal research in Pittsburgh over a six-year period on an inner city sample of African American and Caucasian youth to understand the role of anger in the development of depression and aggression. They identified the developmental pathways of two constructs—irritability (composed of losing one's temper, annoying others, and blaming others) and anger (composed of spiteful behaviour, vindictive behaviour, anger, and resentful behaviour). The prevalence of irritability increased in girls from 20% at age 7 to 46% at age 13. Anger also increased with age, but at a lower rate than irritability, from 2% at age 7 to 20% at age 13. Furthermore, irritability preceded the onset of anger for a subsample of irritable girls. Thus, it appears that the development of anger from high levels of irritability may place girls at risk later for developing conduct problems and depression. Dion describes a similar pattern from anger to aggression based primarily on her interviews with four Aboriginal girls who were living in both rural and urban communities in varying living arrangements (living with parents, boarding, foster care, living with mother). These girls spoke about how their aggression serves as an outlet for their anger, which arises from many different stressors in their lives. Thus, for these girls, the underlying mechanism of their aggression is anger and stress.

The Aboriginal girls that Dion interviewed identified a range of stressful triggers for their anger such as: boys, seeing drunks, getting blamed for things they did not do, and the negative stereotyping that they experience as Aboriginals. Dion suggests that these triggers reflect the complex and stressful issues that the girls face in their lives, such as poverty, the colonial legacy, racism, and community isolation. Some of these triggers may be unique to the Aboriginal population, given the significance and the impact of colonialism. In other words, these girls' anger triggers their aggression as an adaptive mechanism to cope with the complexity of the relationships, communities, and country in which they live. In both the Pittsburgh inner-city and the Aboriginal samples, anger appears to underlie girls' aggression, and their aggression provides an outlet for the anger. Thus, the mechanism for the aggressive behaviour is similar in these two very distinct samples of female youth. The triggers for the anger, however, and the prevention and intervention strategies to address these potential developmental problems of these two groups may be quite distinct. These chapters highlight a dilemma in these girls' lives: their abilities to regulate their emotions may limit these girls' abilities to engage in and maintain positive relationships which may serve as a protective function in their lives. At the same time, the relationships in which they live on a day-to-day basis may create a context in which these girls' aggressive behaviours are sustained and potentially exacerbated.

Both Loeber and colleagues and Dion also consider the nature and role of relationship contexts in which at-risk girls are growing up. Children's development is continually shaped through interactions between their own behaviours and the contexts in which they develop. Children with aggressive behaviour problems approach relationships with a disadvantage in their capacity to form and maintain healthy relationships. A recent longitudinal transactional analysis of maternal negativity and child externalizing behavior indicated that children and mothers influenced each other's behaviours, with the impact of children's aggressive behaviours on mothers' negativity over time being stronger with age than the reciprocal effect (Zadeh, Jenkins, & Pepler, 2010). Considering the family contexts of the girls studied by Loeber and colleagues and Dion, it becomes clear that early identification of and support for families that are struggling with general stresses, as well as the specific stresses of raising children, may be able to interrupt the dance of child and parental negativity. If parents slip into negativity in their efforts to raise an increasingly difficult child, then the parents' behaviours will in turn exacerbate the girls' behaviour problems as they try to cope with the stresses in their lives.

For girls who grow up in highly stressful family environments, other relationships may become a source of comfort and protection, but they can also be an additional source of stress. The Aboriginal girls in Dion's research related how they look to their families for support and sometimes find it, particularly in relationships with their grandmothers. Although the girls spoke of actively seeking out healthy and positive relationships, even their relationships with friends could be at the same time positive and negative. School was also described in ambivalent terms by the girls. They recognized the protective role of school, but they were disappointed with their education that did not provide them with knowledge about their own culture, indigenous language, ceremonies, and traditional knowledge. At this point, schools do not provide girls with a sense of identity as Aboriginal, making it difficult for them to develop a positive view of themselves. The tensions at school highlight another dilemma for girls who are troubled—the one place where they might be safe is also a place where they might not belong because of their dysregulation, anger, and aggression. As described in the Chapter 1 by Dale Hay and colleagues, girls who are dysregulated and aggressive are notably out of step with their peers and, therefore, more likely to be rejected. These difficult experiences in the peer group may, in turn, be alienating and lead to increasing anger and depressive symptoms.

Chapters 4 and 5 provide critical insights into the development of aggression from two very different perspectives: that of a large, comprehensive longitudinal study and that of a small, intense qualitative analysis of girls' voices and reports of their own experiences. The authors point to the underlying role of dysregulation, irritability, and anger in the development of girls' aggression. Rather than seeing aggression as a problem in and of itself, the authors challenge us to consider aggression as a symptom of the girls' attempts to cope with their internal dysregulation and the dysregulation and unpredictability in their relationships. The Aboriginal girls use their voices to challenge us to recognize that they rely on aggression as a strategy that allows them to survive, respond, and meet specific needs within the contexts of their lives—not as something to pathologize. The research also provides guidance for early identification and prevention of conduct problems and depression. Those girls who are persistently irritable are at risk for developing emotional difficulties and oppositional behaviour. This developmental pathway is similar to that of boys for whom the negative affect dimension of oppositional symptoms predicted later depression. If we can intervene early to disrupt these troubled and troubling developmental pathways, we can provide youth with positive relationship experiences that promote their capacities to regulate and understand their emotions and behaviours and the resilience to cope more positively with highly stressful relationship contexts in their lives both currently and into the future.

REFERENCE

Zadeh, Z., Jenkins, J., & Pepler D. (2010). A transactional analysis of maternal negativity and child externalizing behavior. *International Journal of Behavioral Development, 34*(3), 218–228.

CHAPTER SEVEN

USING EVIDENCE TO REDUCE THE BULLYING BEHAVIOUR EXPERIENCED BY GIRLS

DONNA CROSS, THERESE SHAW, HELEN MONKS,
STACEY WATERS, AND LEANNE LESTER

To find out a girl's faults, praise her to her girl friends.
—*Benjamin Franklin*

INTRODUCTION

Bullying is a deliberate form of aggressive behaviour that is repeated over time, intended to cause harm, and involves an imbalance of power (Aalsma & Brown, 2008; Dodge, Coie, Pettit, & Price, 1990; Nansel et al., 2001; Smith, 2000). Approximately 10% of Australian school students report being bullied every few weeks or more often, with almost one half reporting they were bullied at least once during the last term at school (Cross et al., 2009). Similar to other research, Australian boys report they are more likely to be bullied and to bully others on a regular basis than girls (Cross et al., 2009; Ladd, 2005; Nansel, Overpeck, Haynie, Ruan, & Scheidt, 2003; Nansel et al., 2001; Rigby & Slee, 1991). Australian girls and boys also report bullying differently, with girls more likely to experience indirect bullying, but less direct physical and verbal bullying than boys, especially in primary school (Cross et al., 2009; Owens, Daly, & Slee, 2005). Similar to Pepler, Craig, Yuile, and Connolly's (2004) research, Australian boys and girls may also differ in terms of the effects of bullying on their health, well-being, and development (Cross et al., 2009).

This chapter discusses the experiences and effects of gender similarities and differences in bullying behaviour, and uses available evidence to examine how school-based interventions may need to be tailored to adequately protect both boys and girls equally from bullying. Data collected from two Australian group randomized intervention research projects, one focusing on elementary school students and the other on secondary school students, conducted by the Western Australian Child Health Promotion Research Centre (CHPRC) at Edith Cowan University from 2002 to 2006, are used to highlight key differences in the effects of two similar bullying prevention interventions on the bullying experiences of girls and boys. This chapter concludes with recommendations for school-based policy and practice, to help address the factors associated with girls' bullying experiences and to enable girls to take positive action to reduce potential harm from bullying behaviour.

TYPES OF BULLYING/AGGRESSION USED BY SCHOOL-AGE GIRLS

Aggression is traditionally viewed as a male phenomenon, with males often regarded as the more aggressive gender (Owens, Shute, & Slee, 2000). However, rates of aggression between boys and girls may be more similar than different when all forms of aggression including verbal (e.g., yelling, teasing, insulting); and indirect (e.g., spreading secrets or stories, gossiping, excluding) are considered (Chesney-Lind, Morash, & Irwin, 2007; Cross et al., 2009). Whereas direct physical and verbal aggression appear more common among boys, indirect aggression is more common among girls (Crick & Grotpeter, 1995; Fekkes, Pijpers, & Verloove-Vanhorick, 2005; Galen & Underwood, 1997; Nansel et al., 2001; Owens, 1996; Owens et al., 2005; Whitney & Smith, 1993). Given that the more covert or social forms of aggression typically have a lower probability of detection, girls may be incorrectly considered to be less aggressive (Leckie, 1998; Pepler et al., 2004). This difference may occur because girls may want to hurt their peers but are socialized to be less overtly aggressive, and as such they find more indirect ways to express this aggression (Owens et al., 2005).

Covert or indirect bullying has the potential to result in social and psychological harms at least equivalent to those experienced through physical bullying (Archer & Coyne, 2005; Duncan & Owen-Smith, 2006; Galen & Underwood, 1997; Lancelotta & Vaughn, 1989; Prinstein, 2001). Girls are also more likely than boys to remember and to report more negative thoughts and feelings following experiences of indirect aggression. While a longitudinal study (Murray-Close, Ostrov, & Crick, 2007) found no difference between the genders' internalizing and externalising symptoms following an indirect bullying experience, other research has found that girls generally internalize problems and emotions associated with relationally aggressive behaviour (Garber & Flynn, 2001; Hammen & Rudolph, 1996; Nolen-Hoeksema & Girgus, 1994) leading to depression and anxiety, whereas boys are more likely to externalize problems, resulting in physically aggressive, delinquent, and impulsive conduct (Kiesner, 2002; Masten et al., 2005).

Gender Differences in Bystander Behaviour
Gender differences have also been found in the bystander roles students take in bullying situations. Boys appear more likely to be an assistant to or reinforcer of the student who bullies, while girls appear more likely to defend the student being bullied or withdraw from the bullying situation (Goosens, Olthof, & Dekker, 2006; Salmivalli, Lappalainen, & Lagerspetz, 1998). Salmivalli et al. (1998; Salmivalli, Kaukiainen, Voeten, & Sinisammal, 2004) also found that class context and the bystander behaviour of their current peers had a greater effect on girls' bystander behaviour in bullying situations than it did on boys' bystander behaviour.

Gender Differences in Social Skills
Gender differences in bullying and bystander behaviours may be explained by the intensity, exclusivity, and reciprocity disparities in the ways boys and girls socialize or structure their friendship groups (Daniels-Beirness, 1988). Generally boys' friendships are more extensive in size, and they are more open to newcomers joining their group (Daniels-Beirness, 1988). In contrast, girls' friendships are likely to be less inclusive, characterised by closeness, intimacy, and high levels of self-disclosure (Daniels-Beirness, 1988; Leckie, 1998). Unlike boys, their fewer but stronger friendships allow girls to develop closer friendships and have greater comfort disclosing personal information with their friends (Eder & Hallinan, 1978). This may explain why girls appear to have superior social understanding, perspective taking, and empathy skills, and are more compliant and prosocial, compared to boys (Bosacki & Astington, 1999). Taken together these differences in socialization suggest reasons why girls may at a younger age be more vulnerable and more likely to perpetrate indirect bullying than boys.

Gender Differences in Disclosure of Bullying
Girls also appear to be significantly more likely than boys to report being bullied and to believe that telling adults or peers about bullying will help (Cowie, 2000; Hunter, Boyle, & Warden, 2004; Newman, Murray, & Lussier,

2001; Unnever & Cornell, 2004). Self-disclosure to peers may be easier for girls than boys because they have fewer but more intimate friendships (Eder & Hallinan, 1978; Leckie, 1998), whereas boys are often socialized to believe that they should handle bullying problems on their own (Kochenderfer-Ladd & Skinner, 2002). The effects of gender on the decision to report bullying may also be influenced, however, by the type of bullying experienced. In Paquette's study (Paquette & Underwood, 1999), while girls were more likely than boys to disclose being the target of social aggression, both girls and boys were equally likely to tell someone if they were physically bullied.

Gender Differences in Bullying Interventions
Given the potential for gender differences in bullying experiences, it is important to consider how well school-based interventions can accommodate these differences when taking action to prevent or manage bullying. Several researchers encourage adults to intervene cautiously in bullying interactions involving girls, as some adolescent girls report that an adult intervention can make the bullying worse and more covert, making it even more difficult for adults to address (Owens et al., 2000; Underwood, 2004).

Interestingly it also appears that girls and boys respond differently to bullying interventions. For instance, several peer support interventions to reduce bullying were found to have differential effectiveness with male and female participants. The ChildLine in Partnership with Schools' peer support schemes found that secondary school boys received the program less favourably than did staff and girls (Smith & Watson, 2004). Secondary school girls were more likely than secondary school boys to believe that the peer support scheme was a good idea and was helping to stop bullying in their school. Similarly, they were more likely than the boys to report that the program helped them personally. Cowie (2000), who had difficulty recruiting boys as peer supporters, found that as peer supporters boys dropped out more than girls and that boys did not use the peer supporters as much as the girls did.

A "befriending intervention" designed to influence participant roles in bullying found that boys showed more of a decrease in bullying and outsider roles compared with girls, but less of an increase in reinforcer and assistant roles (Menesini, Codecasa, Benelli, & Cowie, 2003). Similarly, a study conducted by Salmivalli (2001) showed that a school-based, peer-led intervention was more effective in reducing reported levels of bullying and increasing willingness to address bullying problems among girls than boys, with boys showing an increase in pro-bullying attitudes. Girls also provided a more positive evaluation of the intervention's effectiveness and benefits, compared to boys (Salmivalli, 2001).

It appears that parent support for girls may provide a buffer against internalized distress due to bullying (Davidson & Demaray, 2007). For boys, teacher, classmate, and school social support was found to moderate the relationship between victimization and internalizing distress from bullying (Davidson & Demaray, 2007). This research suggests that social support may work differently for girls and boys, and that it may be beneficial to use parent support when planning interventions for girls aimed at reducing internalizing distress from victimization (Davidson & Demaray, 2007).

There may also be gender differences with regard to long-term effects of anti-bullying interventions. A review of outcomes from the Sheffield project found that there was a long-term reduction in bullying among boys, but not among girls (Eslea & Smith, 1998). It was suggested that this may be because the intervention did not address indirect bullying, which is more commonly reported among girls, but instead focused on "typical" male bullying behaviour, leading to the program's greater success among boys (Eslea & Smith, 1998).

While existing research offers some clues for effective policy and practice to prevent or reduce social aggression in girls (Underwood, 2004), there still exists much conjecture and a paucity of quality empirical research to identify the active intervention "ingredients" for positive change for girls in school-based bullying prevention interventions. The following list provides a summary of the current "promising" research recommendations to prevent or effectively manage girls' bullying behaviour.

School-based intervention strategies for girls need to:

- Specifically target indirect bullying (Eslea & Smith, 1998).
- Engage the social support of parents (Davidson & Demaray, 2007).
- Address social skills and peer support (Salmivalli, 2001), using girls' high levels of social intelligence, close relationships, and cohesive groups to engage peers in resolving conflict (Letendre, 2007; Owens et al., 2000).
- Recognize the high value girls place on relationships and the anxiety that is created when relationships are threatened (Letendre, 2007).
- Help them feel they belong and engage in activities that increase their sense of group acceptance, so they do not feel they need to exclude others to confirm their own acceptance (Adler & Adler, 1995; Pepler et al., 2004)
- Provide meaningful activities during school breaks so they have less time to be involved in indirect aggression (Larson, Wilson, Brown, Furstenberg, & Verma, 2002; Owens et al., 2000).
- Focus on increasing feelings of empathy (Pepler et al., 2004).

- Encourage girls to not tolerate or condone aggression, including indirect aggression (Putallaz, Kupersmidt, Coie, McKnight, & Grimes, 2004).
- De-escalate or manage conflict in socially positive ways when responding to others' aggressive acts by using direct forms of communication, defending themselves appropriately, changing their behaviour or finding a compromise, or using self-deprecating humour rather than only ignoring the behaviour (Letendre, 2007; Putallaz et al., 2004; Underwood, 2004).

The research behind this summary of recommendations provides some evidence in support of gender-specific interventions for bullying, and suggests some promising school-based strategies that build on girls' social strengths while also addressing their specific needs. Although many of these strategies have not been empirically tested, evidence does support the need to tailor school-based programs for girls by: (a) specifically addressing indirect forms of bullying and aggression, (b) actively engaging parents, and (c) building empathy, social competence, and addressing positive conflict resolution, including peer-led and peer-support programs.

Two Australian research projects, one targeting elementary school students (*Friendly Schools Friendly Families*) and the other secondary school students (*Supportive Schools Project*), were developed using the available gender-based evidence suggesting specific school intervention strategies needed to reduce bullying behaviour among both boys and girls. In developmentally appropriate form these strategies were included in both programs to equally reduce the bullying behaviour experienced by boys and girls. We hypothesized that if we integrated this specific gender evidence into the design of our school-based program we would observe no differential intervention effects among male and female participants; however, our findings, as follows, showed otherwise.

THE FRIENDLY SCHOOLS FRIENDLY FAMILIES ELEMENTARY SCHOOL BULLYING PREVENTION PROJECT

The Friendly Schools Friendly Families (FSFF) project was a prospective group randomized controlled trial which tracked a cohort of 1,295 grade 4 (ages 8–9) and 1,257 grade 6 (ages 10–11) students over two school years (2002–2003). These students were recruited using active-passive consent from 20 randomly selected government elementary schools in the Perth metropolitan area (Cross et al., 2003; Cross et al., 2010). The student cohort received one of three levels of intervention: high, moderate, or low (for comparison). Both the high and moderate intervention conditions included whole-school, classroom, and selective and indicated bullying management strategies as described below. The high intervention group also received more intense family engagement activities.

Moderate and High Intervention

Whole-school activities aimed to: (a) build a positive social climate, positive relations, and connectedness between students, school staff, and parents, (b) provide effective policies and common understandings and practices to prevent and effectively manage and reduce current overt and covert bullying, and (c) build school capacity support for implementation through assessment of organizational structures, resources, skills, and commitment levels.

Developmentally appropriate *classroom activities* for *all* grade levels (not only the FSFF study cohorts) in the school aimed to develop common understandings about the nature of direct and indirect bullying, and facilitated students' empathy building between peers and social skill development, including assertiveness and social decision making. The activities encouraged teachers to establish positive interactions with students using role play, stories, role modelling, skills training, and observational learning. All staff received a two-hour, in-school training session to consolidate their understandings about bullying and enhance their understanding of ways to systemically prevent and manage bullying, to develop students' social skills and their role in teaching the learning activities.

Selective and indicated bullying management activities aimed to support victimized students, to help modify the behaviour of students who bully others, and to facilitate school links with local health professionals with specialist skills. Key school staff were trained to use problem-solving, restorative approaches to prevent and manage bullying incidents, including use of the Method of Shared Concern (Pikas, 2002).

High Intervention Only

Family level activities aimed to enhance parents' or carers' awareness, attitudes, and self-efficacy to help their children develop social skills and to prevent or cope with bullying. These activities were also designed to build the relationship between the participating schools and families, and to increase families' awareness of the schools' efforts to reduce bullying. The high intervention schools received an additional three-hour school project team training session in each study year to increase their capacity to engage parents, and a series of targeted awareness-raising and skill-building activities for parents and their families.

The "comparison" schools received a "low dose" standard bullying intervention accessible to most schools.

Two behavioural outcomes were used to measure the FSFF intervention impact: student self-report of (a) "how often they were bullied last term at school" ("bullied frequently" was defined as being bullied every few weeks or more often), and (b) "how often they bullied others last term at school" ("bullying others frequently" was defined as bullying others every few weeks or more often). These outcomes were measured using two items adapted from the Revised Olweus Bully/Victim Questionnaire (Olweus, 1996) and the Australian Peer Relations Assessment Questionnaire (PRAQ) (Rigby, 1997). Each item was assessed for reliability using weighted Kappa statistics. Frequency of being bullied ($\kappa_w = 0.54$) and frequency of bullying others ($\kappa_w = 0.41$) had "moderate" agreement (Altman, 1991). A list of seven direct and indirect bullying behaviours was also provided to students to measure the nature of the bullying they perpetrated or experienced. Direct forms of bullying included being physically bullied, being teased in hurtful ways, being called mean and hurtful names, having money or other things taken or broken, and being threatened; indirect forms included being hurtfully ignored, excluded, or left out and having nasty lies or rumours spread to others.

These outcome data were analyzed in Stata and MLwiN using multi-level random coefficients models to account for school level clustering and repeated measures. Differential intervention effects were assessed by testing for significant gender by group interactions at each post-intervention measurement. These models controlled for the baseline measure of the outcome and school size.

Friendly Schools Friendly Families Project Results

Differential intervention impact on the likelihood of being bullied frequently or bullying others frequently was assessed by comparing differences between the high, moderate, and low study conditions for girls and for boys at each post-test (the end of each school year).

No differential intervention effects were found by gender between the high, moderate, and low intervention groups in the grade 4 cohort for being bullied frequently or frequently bullying others at each of the three post-test measurements.

However, data collected from the grade 6 cohort after one year of intervention found differences in being bullied frequently for girls and boys between the study conditions (LR $\chi^2(2, n = 1135) = 6.3, p = .042$). Specifically, girls in the low intervention group were 2.2 times (95% CI 1.3; 3.9) more likely to report being bullied frequently than girls in the high intervention group. Girls in the moderate intervention group were also slightly more likely to be bullied frequently than those in the high intervention, but the difference was not statistically significant (OR = 1.7, 95% CI 0.9; 3.1).

In comparison, boys in each of the study conditions had similar odds of being bullied regularly. These differential gender effects found at the first post-test measurement were not evident at the second post-test (i.e., a year later when the students were in grade 7).

To determine which types of bullying the intervention had differential impact for girls and boys at the first post-test, the study conditions were compared for seven different types of bullying (described previously). Significant differences were found between the study conditions for girls, that were not present for boys, for "being called mean and hurtful names lots of times" (LR $\chi^2(2, n = 1141) = 8.3, p = .016$) and "being made afraid they would be hurt lots of times" (LR $\chi^2(2, n = 1131) = 7.9, p = .019$). However, the number of students who were frequently made afraid they would be hurt was very low and hence this latter result needs to be interpreted with caution. Girls in the low intervention group at the first post-test were 2.8 times (95% CI 1.2; 6.7) more likely, and girls in the moderate intervention group were 3.1 times (95% CI 1.2; 7.8) more likely to be called mean and hurtful names frequently than girls in the high intervention group. In comparison, the likelihood of being bullied frequently in this way was similar for boys in each of the study conditions.

In terms of bullying others frequently, as was the case for the grade 4 cohort, no differential effects were observed at the first or the second post-test measurements.

These results suggest that while most program effects were equivalent for boys and girls, the FSFF high intervention appears to have been more effective at reducing the proportion of grade 6 (age 11) girls who report they are being bullied frequently following one year of implementation. The major difference between the high and moderate intervention was the level of parent engagement in the program. Hence, similar to research by Davidson and Demaray (2007) it could be concluded from these analyses that engaging the whole school and especially the social support of parents as part of a whole-of-school bullying prevention program (high intervention) compared to low intervention (standard low dose bullying prevention program) appears to have differentially reduced the amount of frequent bullying, particularly hurtful name-calling, reported by girls and boys in grade 6.

THE SUPPORTIVE SCHOOLS SECONDARY BULLYING PREVENTION PROJECT
The Supportive Schools Project (SSP), another Australian group randomized controlled trial conducted by the authors designed to reduce bullying among secondary school students, also found differential gender-related effects but for perpetration of bullying rather than victimization.

The SSP project was very similar in design to the FSFF trial but tracked a cohort of 3,317 grade 8 students from 2005 to 2006 (Waters, Epstein, Cross, & Hall, 2008). It aimed to enhance the capacity of secondary schools to implement a whole-school bullying reduction intervention (including strategies to help students transition to secondary school) and compare this intervention using a prospective group randomized trial to the standard behaviour management practices currently used in Western Australian secondary schools. The SSP project comprised two study conditions, a high and a low intervention. However, unlike the FSFF program, the SSP intervention did not involve all students in the recruited secondary schools in classroom teaching and learning activities. The SSP whole-of-school strategies to address school ethos, policy, organization, and social change were provided using the same whole-school manual used for the FSFF program. However, the SSP schools received more active support via four hours of coaching in each study year to help them assess their policy and practice strengths and needs and to fast track their implementation of whole-school change. Also, other than two information sheets and eight brief newsletter items, the contact and engagement with SSP parents was much less than for the FSFF program. The classroom activities offered to the SSP study cohort focused on specific skill building to address different types of bullying, actions that can be taken as bystanders, and strategies to encourage students to build a social norm that advocates against bullying in the school. Unlike FSFF, very little emphasis was provided in the classroom activities on social skill development, assertiveness, and conflict resolution skills.

The "bullied frequently" and "bullying others frequently" outcome variables and the list of bullying behaviours, as described previously for the FSFF project, were used as outcome variables in the SSP project. The SSP data were analysed in the same way as the FSFF data, in Stata and MLwiN using multi-level random coefficients models accounting for school level clustering and repeated measures.

Supportive Schools Project Results
While no differential intervention effects were found in the SSP grade 8 students for being bullied regularly (i.e., differences between the comparison and intervention groups were similar for girls and boys at each of the two post-test measurements), a significant study condition by gender interaction was found following one year of program implementation (LR $\chi^2(1, n = 3076) = 6.6, p = .011$). At the end of grade 8, the boys in the comparison group were twice as likely to report having bullied others frequently than those in the high intervention group (OR=2.0, 95% CI 1.32; 3.15), while

no differences between the study conditions were observed for girls (OR = 0.8, 95% CI 0.35; 2.02). Boys in the comparison group were almost twice as likely to have made fun of or teased another student(s) (OR = 1.8, 95% CI 1.16; 2.88), to have called another student(s) mean and hurtful names (OR = 1.9, 95% CI 1.19; 3.11), to have ignored another student(s), not let them join in, or left them out on purpose (OR = 1.6, 95% CI 1.03; 2.56), and to have hit, kicked, or pushed another student(s) around (OR = 2.0, 95% CI 1.21; 3.23). In comparison the odds of these behaviours occurring did not differ significantly between the intervention and comparison groups for girls.

Hence, the SSP intervention "worked better" for grade 8 boys, reducing the reported prevalence of boys' frequently bullying others, but similar effects were not seen for the girls; whereas the FSFF intervention "worked better" for grade 6 girls, reducing the reported prevalence of girls being bullied frequently, with no similar effects found in boys.

What may have contributed to the differential effects in SSP and FSFF?

Our FSFF data suggest that after one year of intervention, when an intense family engagement component is added to a whole-of-school intervention, the proportion of bullying (especially hurtful name-calling) experienced by girls, but not boys, decreases. In contrast, we found in our SSP secondary bullying prevention study that the intervention didn't differentially reduce victimization in girls or boys, but instead reduced the perpetration of bullying by boys (but not girls) after one year of intervention. While both the FSFF and SSP interventions were similar there were three major differences other than the age groups targeted: the FSFF program had greater parent engagement and the learning activities had greater student reach (beyond the study cohort) and included social skill development.

Parent/Carer Engagement

The SSP's family engagement component focused on ways to help students transition from elementary to secondary school and to a much lesser extent (compared to FSFF) on building the relationship between the school and parents/carers, involving them in school-based decision making, and enhancing their self-efficacy to help their children to develop social skills. It may be, as found by Davidson and Demaray (2007), that higher levels of parent/carer support and engagement are necessary to help girls (but not necessarily boys) to avoid or deal more effectively with bullying.

Classroom Teaching and Learning

The FSFF project's moderate and high intervention provided every grade 1 to 7 student with teaching and learning activities related to bullying prevention and social skill development, whereas in the SSP project only the study cohort (grade 8) students received classroom teaching and learning. Accordingly, if the classroom activities were helpful, the whole school population in FSFF was developing common understandings, empathy building, and skills to prevent or manage bullying. Given bullying is not always perpetrated by students who are the same age as the students they bully, it may be that in the FSFF study girls were more likely than the boys to have been victimized by students older and/or younger than them, which may consequently, as a result of the high intervention, have contributed to lower levels of frequent victimization in girls, rather than boys. To reduce victimization it is logical that all potential perpetrators in a school need to receive the intervention. However, as was the case in SSP when the intervention was only delivered to the study cohort, the greatest effects would be expected in those whose behaviours can be most affected (i.e., the perpetrators). It may not be surprising therefore that only perpetration not victimization was reduced in the SSP. But why was this decrease only in boys? Similar to the findings of Eslea and Smith (1998), this differential effect may be because the intervention emphasized overt (typically more common in boys) rather than covert bullying behaviours. Of the 10 learning activities implemented in the first year of the SSP, when this differential effect was observed, seven activities focused on mainly overt bullying behaviours.

The FSFF classroom teaching and learning activities also focused more directly than did the SSP on developing positive relationships, social skills, empathy building, and peer support programs, which is suggested as being important to reduce bullying in girls (Letendre, 2007; Owens et al., 2000; Salmivalli, 2001), and may help to explain why girls benefited more from the FSFF intervention than did the boys.

Age of Students

Given the seemingly different effects on bullying behaviour from relatively similar whole-school interventions on 11-year-old and 13-year-old boys and girls in the FSFF and SSP studies, it is difficult to determine whether the gender differences observed were developmental or related to the intervention design and implementation. Longitudinal studies are needed to untangle the temporal sequence of bullying behaviours and to identify an optimal developmental window(s) in boys and girls to address bullying. This information will help policy makers and practitioners to identify the most advantageous times to deliver bullying prevention and management interventions to boys and girls.

CONCLUSION

The paucity of quality research purposely testing the differential effects of bullying prevention interventions for boys and girls makes it difficult to determine what gender-specific policy and practices need to be implemented in schools. Most current research in this area was not designed to specifically test the effectiveness of bullying prevention and management strategies with girls and/or boys, but instead is based on conjecture following differential findings.

Taken together, however, these findings along with previous research suggest that to enhance intervention effectiveness for girls, programs need to include parent/carer engagement, peer support and specific covert bullying, and social skill based teaching and learning that builds on their socialization strengths and gender role characteristics.

Importantly, however, because girls report they experience more harm and internalize their bullying experiences more so than do boys, girls may constitute a priority population for future research into bullying behaviours and interventions.

REFERENCES

Aalsma, M.C., & Brown, J.R. (2008). What is bullying? *Journal of Adolescent Health, 43*(2), 101–102.

Adler, P.A., & Adler, P. (1995). Dynamics of inclusion and exclusion in school cliques. *Social Psychology Quarterly, 58*, 145–162.

Altman, D.G. (1991). *Practical statistics for medical research.* London: Chapman and Hall.

Archer, J., & Coyne, S.M. (2005). An integrated review of indirect, relational, and social aggression. *Personality and Social Psychology Review, 9*(3), 212–230.

Bosacki, S., & Astington, J.W. (1999). Theory of mind in preadolescence: Relations between social understanding and social competence. *Social Development, 8*(2), 237–255.

Chesney-Lind, M., Morash, M., & Irwin, K. (2007). Policing girlhood? Relational aggression and violence prevention. *Youth Violence and Juvenile Justice, 5*(3), 328–345.

Cowie, H. (2000). Bystanding or standing by: Gender issues in coping with bullying in English schools. *Aggressive Behavior, 26*, 85–97.

Crick, N.R., & Grotpeter, J.K. (1995). Relational aggression, gender, and social-psychological adjustment. *Child Development, 66*(3), 710–722.

Cross, D., Hall, M., Erceg, E., Pintabona, Y., Hamilton, G., & Roberts, C. (2003). The Friendly Schools Project: An empirically grounded school bullying prevention program. *Australian Journal of Guidance and Counselling, 13*(1), 36–46.

Cross, D., Shaw, T., Hearn, L., Epstein, M., Monks, H., Lester, L., & Thomas, L. (2009). *Australian Covert Bullying Prevalence Study (ACBPS)* (Research Report ISBN No. 978-0-7298-0675-6). Perth, Australia: Child Health Promotion Research Centre, Edith Cowan University.

Cross, D., Hall, M., Shaw, T., Pintabona, Y., Erceg, E., Hamilton, G.,...Lester, L. (2011). Three-year results of the Friendly Schools whole-of-school intervention on children's bullying behaviour. *British Educational Research Journal, 37*(1), 105–129.

Daniels-Beirness, T. (1988). Measuring peer status in boys and girls: A problem of apples and oranges? In B.H. Schneider, G. Attili, J. Nadel, & R. Weissberg (Eds.), *Social competence in developmental perspective* (pp. 107–120). Les Arcs, France: Kluwer Academic Publishers.

Davidson, L.M., & Demaray, M.K. (2007). Social support as a moderator between victimization and internalizing-externalizing distress from bullying. *School Psychology Review, 36*(3), 383–405.

Dodge, K.A., Coie, J.D., Pettit, G.S., & Price, J.M. (1990). Peer status and aggression in boys' groups: Developmental and contextual analyses. *Child Development, 61*, 1289–1309.

Duncan, L., & Owen-Smith, A. (2006). Powerlessness and the use of indirect aggression in friendships. *Sex Roles, 55*, 493–502.

Eder, D., & Hallinan, M.T. (1978). Sex differences in children's friendships. *American Sociological Review, 43*, 237–250.

Eslea, M., & Smith, P.K. (1998). The long-term effectiveness of anti-bullying work in primary schools. *Educational Research, 40*(2), 203–218.

Fekkes, M., Pijpers, F., & Verloove-Vanhorick, S.P. (2005). Bullying: Who does what, when and where? Involvement of children, teachers and parents in bullying behaviour. *Health Education Research, 20*(1), 81–91.

Galen, B.R., & Underwood, M.K. (1997). A developmental investigation of social aggression among children. *Developmental Psychology, 33*, 589–600.

Garber, J., & Flynn, C. (2001). Vulnerability to depression in childhood and adolescence. In R. Ingram & J. Price (Eds.), *Vulnerability to psychopathology: Risk across the lifespan* (pp. 189–247). New York: Guildford Press.

Goosens, F.A., Olthof, T., & Dekker, P.H. (2006). New participant role scales: Comparison between various criteria and assigning roles and indications for their validity. *Aggressive Behavior, 32*, 343–357.

Hammen, C., & Rudolph, K. (1996). Childhood depression. In E. Mash & R. Barkley (Eds.), *Childhood Psychopathology* (pp. 153–195). New York: Guildford Press.

Hunter, S.C., Boyle, J.M.E., & Warden, D. (2004). Help seeking amongst child and adolescent victims of peer-aggression and bullying: The influence of school-stage, gender, victimization, appraisal, and emotion. *British Journal of Educational Psychology, 74*, 375–390.

Kiesner, J. (2002). Depressive symptoms in early adolescence: Their relations with classroom problem behavior and peer status. *Journal of Research on Adolescence, 12*, 463–478.

Kochenderfer-Ladd, B., & Skinner, K. (2002). Children's coping strategies: Moderators of the effects of peer victimization? *Developmental Psychology, 38*, 267–278.

Ladd, G.W. (2005). *Children's peer relations and social competence.* New Haven: Yale University Press.

Lancelotta, G.X., & Vaughn, S. (1989). Relations between types of aggression and sociometric status: Peer and teacher perceptions. *Journal of Educational Psychology, 81*(1), 86–90.

Larson, R.W., Wilson, S., Brown, B.B., Furstenberg, F.F., & Verma, S. (2002). Changes in adolescents' interpersonal competence: Are they being prepared for adult relationships in the 21st century? *Journal of Research on Adolescence, 12*, 31–68.

Leckie, B. (1998, April). *Girls, bullying behaviours and peer relationships: The double edged sword of exclusion and rejection.* Paper presented at the Annual Conference of the Australian Association for Research in Education, Brisbane, Australia.

Letendre, J. (2007). "Sugar and spice but not always nice": Gender socialization and its impact on development and maintenance of aggression in adolescent girls. *Child and Adolescent Social Work Journal, 24*(4), 353–368.

Masten, A.S., Roisman, G.I., Long, J.D., Burt, K.B., Obradovic, J., Riley, J.R.,... Tellegen, A. (2005). Developmental cascades: Linking academic achievement, externalizing, and internalizing problems over 20 years. *Developmental Psychology, 41*, 733–746.

Menesini, E., Codecasa, E., Benelli, B., & Cowie, H. (2003). Enhancing children's responsibility to take action against bullying: Evaluation of a befriending intervention in Italian middle schools. *Aggressive Behavior, 29*, 1–14.

Murray-Close, D., Ostrov, J.M., & Crick, N.R. (2007). A short-term longitudinal study of growth of relational aggression during middle childhood: Associations with gender, friendship intimacy, and internalizing problems. *Development and Psychopathology, 19*, 187–203.

Nansel, T., Overpeck, M., Haynie, D., Ruan, J., & Scheidt, P.C. (2003). Relationships between bullying and violence among US youth. *Archives of Pediatric and Adolescent Medicine, 157*(4), 348–353.

Nansel, T., Overpeck, M., Pilla, R., Ruan, W.J., Simons-Morton, B., & Scheidt, P. (2001). Bullying behaviours among US youth: Prevalence and association with psychosocial adjustment. *Journal of the American Medical Association, 285*(16), 2094–2100.

Newman, R.S., Murray, B., & Lussier, C. (2001). Confrontation with aggressive peers at school: Students' reluctance to seek help from the teacher. *Journal of Educational Psychology, 93*(2), 398–410.

Nolen-Hoeksema, S., & Girgus, J. (1994). The emergence of gender differences in depression during adolescence. *Psychological Bulletin, 115*, 424–443.

Olweus, D. (1996). *The Revised Olweus Bully/Victim Questionnaire.* Bergen, Norway: Research Centre for Health Promotion, University of Bergen.

Owens, L. (1996). Sticks and stones and sugar and spice: Girls' and boys' aggression in schools. *Australian Journal of Guidance and Counselling, 6*, 45–55.

Owens, L., Daly, A., & Slee, P. (2005). Sex and age differences in victimization and conflict resolution among adolescents in a South Australian school. *Aggressive Behavior, 31*, 1–12.

Owens, L., Shute, R., & Slee, P. (2000). "Guess what I just heard!": Indirect aggression among teenage girls in Australia. *Aggressive Behavior, 26*, 67–83.

Paquette, J.A., & Underwood, M.K. (1999). Gender differences in young adolescents' experiences of peer victimization: Social and physical aggression. *Merrill-Palmer Quarterly, 45*(2), 242–266.

Pepler, D., Craig, W., Yuile, A., & Connolly, J. (2004). Girls who bully: A developmental and relational perspective. In M. Putallaz & K.L. Bierman (Eds.), *Aggression, antisocial behavior, and violence among girls: A developmental perspective* (pp. 90–109). New York: Guilford Press.

Pikas, A. (2002). New developments of the Shared Concern method. *School Psychology International, 23*(3), 307–326.

Prinstein, M.J. (2001). Overt and relational aggression in adolescents: Social-psychological adjustment of aggressors and victims. *Journal of Clinical Child Psychology, 30*(4), 479–491.

Putallaz, M., Kupersmidt, J.B., Coie, J.D., McKnight, K., & Grimes, C.L. (2004). A behavioral analysis of girls' aggression and victimization. In M. Putallaz & K.L. Bierman (Eds.), *Aggression, antisocial behavior, and violence among girls: A developmental perspective* (pp. 110–134). New York: Guilford Press.

Rigby, K. (1997). *The Peer Relations Assessment Questionnaires (PRAQ)*. Victoria, Australia: Professional Reading Guide for Educational Administrators.

Rigby, K., & Slee, P.T. (1991). Bullying among Australian school children: Reported behavior and attitudes toward victims. *Journal of Social Psychology, 131*(5), 615–627.

Salmivalli, C. (2001). Peer-led intervention campaign against school bullying: Who considered it useful, who benefited? *Educational Research, 43*(3), 263–278.

Salmivalli, C., Kaukiainen, A., Voeten, M., & Sinisammal, M. (2004). Targeting the group as a whole: The Finnish anti-bullying intervention. In K. Rigby , P.K. Smith, & D. Pepler (Eds.), *Bullying in schools: How successful can interventions be?* (pp. 251–273). Cambridge: Cambridge University Press.

Salmivalli, C., Lappalainen, M., & Lagerspetz, K.M.J. (1998). Stability and change of behaviour in connection with bullying in schools: A two-year follow-up. *Aggressive Behavior, 24*, 205–218.

Smith, P.K. (2000). Bullying in schools: Lessons from two decades of research. *Aggressive Behavior, 26*, 1–9.

Smith, P.K., & Watson, D. (2004). *An evaluation of the ChildLine in Partnership with Schools (CHIPS) Programme*. London: Unit for School and Family Studies, Goldsmiths College.

Underwood, M.K. (2004). Glares of contempt, eye rolls of disgust and turning away to exclude: Non-verbal forms of social aggression among girls. *Feminism and Psychology, 14*, 371–375.

Unnever, J., & Cornell, D.G. (2004). Middle school victims of bullying: Who reports being bullied? *Aggressive Behavior, 30*, 373–388.

Waters, S., Epstein, M., Cross, D., & Hall, M. (2008). *A randomised control trial to reduce bullying and other aggressive behaviours in secondary schools: Final report to Healthway.* Perth, Australia: Child Health Promotion Research Centre, Edith Cowan University.

Whitney, I., & Smith, P.K. (1993). A survey of the nature and extent of bullying in junior/middle and secondary schools. *Educational Research, 35*(1), 3–25.

CHAPTER EIGHT

MATCHING THE PREVENTION OF INTERPERSONAL AGGRESSION TO CRITICAL DEVELOPMENTAL AND CONTEXTUAL TRANSITIONS IN MIDDLE SCHOOL

BONNIE LEADBEATER

Middle school students experience rapid changes in social, cognitive, and emotional development that are influenced by the new salience and intimacy of peer friendships and by desires for group membership and popularity. Simultaneously, moves to new school contexts and disruptions to their social networks create additional challenges for this age group. Yet few bullying prevention programs exist that are sensitive to these developmental and contextual changes. After explicating some of these changes and the research relating them to concerns about interpersonal aggression, I outline the ingredients that may determine developmentally sensitive prevention programs for reducing interpersonal aggression in middle school students. I discuss developmentally appropriate, ecologically valid strategies for reducing peer aggression and victimization that target personal, peer, and contextual concerns.

In contrast to physical or verbal types of interpersonal aggression (hitting, shoving, pushing, threatening), the distinctions among the types of non-physical (indirect, relational, or social aggression) have been the subject of considerable debate among researchers (Archer, 2004; Björkqvist, Lagerspetz, & Kaukiainen, 1992; Coyne, Archer, & Eslea, 2006; Underwood,

2003; Underwood, Galen, & Paquette, 2001; Xie, R.B. Cairns & Cairns, 2005). However, it is likely that, in practice, both types of interpersonal aggression should be understood as multi-dimensional and changing in response to factors such as children's social sophistication, status, and goals as well as in response to differences in the contextual norms, challenges, and sanctions that they experience. In this paper, I use the broad term *interpersonal aggression* to refer to all types of bullying and aggression that target peers and I use *social aggression* to refer to non-physical (but not necessarily non-confrontational or covert) aggression. I am interested in how what we know about the function of all types of interpersonal aggression in peer relationships can inform developmentally appropriate prevention efforts in middle school.

There is substantial evidence indicating that physical types of aggression decline over the early school grades. By the end of grade three, less than 3% of children show persistently high levels of aggression (Archer, 2004; Nagin & Tremblay, 1999; NICHD Early Child Care Research Network, 2004; Vaillancourt, Brendgen, Boivin, & Tremblay, 2003). However, this small figure stands in contrast to the equally convincing evidence of persistence in bullying behaviours in middle school students. Research with nationally representative samples in the United States (Nansel, Haynie, & Simons-Morton, 2003; Nansel et al., 2001) found that a total of 29.9% of children reported moderate or frequent involvement in bullying, as a bully (13.0%), one who was bullied (10.6%), or both (6.3%), and the frequency of bullying was higher among sixth- through eighth-grade students than among ninth- and tenth-grade students. With more selected samples, rates are even higher. For example, 31% of middle school students in one Maryland county were bullied more than three times in the previous year (Haynie et al., 2001). In research with European American and African American students in a southeastern metropolitan area, Unnever and Cornell (2004) found that 36% of middle school students reported being bullied.

Reviewing the available cross-sectional evidence, Vaillancourt and Hymel (2004) suggest that social manipulation and ostracism (e.g., alienation, rumours, and social rejection) increase as children move from middle childhood into adolescence. Longitudinal studies of the trajectories of social, relational, or indirect aggression are rare but also suggest that the use of social aggression increases in early adolescence for both boys and girls (Björkqvist et al., 1992; Harachi et al., 2006; Leadbeater, Hoglund, & Woods, 2003; Salmivalli & Kaukiainen, 2004). A three-year longitudinal study of mothers' reports for children aged 4 to 11 years (using data from the Canadian National Longitudinal Survey of Children and Youth), did not support the idea that forms of aggression change from direct physical to more indirect social aggression forms (Vaillancourt et al., 2003).

In this chapter, I argue that key developmental transitions influence middle school students' sensitivities to and use of interpersonal aggression. These include heightened identity-related concerns about popularity, group membership, and social status, as well as changes in the quality of intimacy of peer friendships and increases in perspective-taking abilities and consequence-based reasoning (predicting what will happen in the future). Peer-group membership becomes central to the affirmation of identity and regulation of self-esteem. Indeed, the developmental tasks of this age group fuel a sense of urgency to be affirmed in peer relationships. These developmental changes usher in opportunities for growth, but they also create vulnerability to victimization and occasions for aggression. Competencies gained in early adolescence interact with friendship and peer-group norms, as well as social norms delineated by family, classroom, school, neighbourhood, and community cultures. Hence, I argue that the match (or mismatch) of adolescents' needs for recognition by significant others, intimacy in friendships, and group membership with the norms and responsiveness of peers, teachers, and other family and non-family adults in middle school settings can influence levels of aggression and victimization.

The transition from an elementary to a middle school context both expands the population of potential network members and disrupts childhood playgroups. Transitions in this age group create a critical opportunity for young people to learn about how to sustain healthy friendships, manage social aggression, and solve peer conflicts. It is at this critical transition that interventions may be both most needed and effective in reducing bullying. Beyond promoting social skills of individuals, interventions for bullying may need to promote prosocial leadership, social responsibility, and group, classroom, school, neighbourhood, and family norms that reject interpersonal aggression.

IDENTITY DEVELOPMENT IS A TWO-WAY STREET

Popular beliefs hold that youth who bully or who are bullied have low self-esteem and are trying to build themselves up by putting others down or dominating them. However, struggling with issues of self-esteem in the face of an uncertain sense of self or self-identity is a concern of *every* middle school student. According to Erikson (1975), the question of identity emerges from an earlier period of tension between industry and inferiority as children begin to sort out for themselves and for others the answer to the question "What can I do well?" The question of identity that emerges in early adolescence is more than this childhood search for personal talents, beliefs, and skills. Identity development is, rather, an *interpersonal* question of "Who am I?" and "Who can I be for others who are significant to me?" This bidirectional co-construction of identity has been largely lost in descriptions of identity as a personal search. Erickson (1975) described identity as "a subjective sense as well as an observable quality of personal sameness and continuity, *paired* with some belief in the sameness and continuity of some shared world image" (p. 18). It is a finding not only of self but also of communality with others. In other words, a sense of who-I-really-am emerges only gradually as young people *both* try on possible selves *and* monitor the reception to these possible selves by important others in their social networks (Oyserman, 2007; Oyserman, Bybee, & Terry, 2006). Young adolescents' answer to the identity question "Who am I?" is deeply rooted in the response of significant others to the question "With whom do I belong?" Thus, interactions with peers are central to emerging definitions of possible selves. This quest for self-definition in interactions with peers intensifies the meaning and significance of belonging to a group, being popular, sharing group solidarity and norms, and establishing in-group and out-group members. The capacity to understand others' views of the self is also advanced by several other transitions in this life stage, including changes in the quality of intimacy of friendships and gains in social cognitive skills such as perspective taking and thinking about the future.

INTIMACY IN FRIENDSHIPS

Sullivan (1953) describes this shift in interpersonal intimacy as moving from a focus in childhood on what they can do to enhance their own prestige and feelings of superiority compared with their friends, to a growing capacity in adolescence for collaboration. Collaboration involves adjusting ones' behaviours to respond to the question "What should I do to contribute to the happiness or to support the prestige and feelings of worthwhileness of my chum" (Sullivan, 1953, p. 245). Friends who are antidotes to loneliness as companions in shared activities in childhood become antidotes to existential anxiety in early adolescence. Self-disclosure increases and friends share personal concerns, desires, and beliefs and can affirm each other's self-worth (Buhrmeister, 1996; Hartup, 2005). Same-sex friendships are initially the locus of these mutually affirming peer relationships, and young adolescents show an increase in sensitivity to peers' views of themselves. Of course, this sensitivity is not only attuned to the positive affirmations and regard of peers, adolescents also carefully and doggedly track the regard of peers who are not so kind in their feedback, leading to self-questioning and sometimes to negative self-regard, low self-esteem, and even retaliation and aggression.

SOCIAL COGNITIVE CHANGES IN PERSPECTIVE TAKING AND FUTURE ORIENTATION

Young adolescents are also aided in the intimate peer interactions that fuel their identity search by a surge of biological, cognitive, emotional, and social-cognitive advances. In particular, they become more like adults in their social competence, interpersonal intimacy, empathy, perspective taking, and capacity for thinking about future possibilities. Research has shown that social perspective-taking ability shifts between childhood and adolescence from a self-interested or self-serving first-person perspective, to a more reciprocal second-person perspective that can acknowledge the needs and interests of others (Selman, 1980; Selman & Schultz, 1990). The increasing complexity and sophistication of children's interpersonal conflict resolution strategies similarly reflect their increasing competence in such varied skills as: (a) differentiating and coordinating the social perspectives and interests of themselves and others; (b) pursuing long-term prosocial goals that preserve friendship across situational conflicts; (c) accurately encoding and interpreting cues from social situations; (d) generating flexible, alternative strategies or behavioural responses; and (e) anticipating and evaluating potential outcomes, not only in relation to the immediate situation or short term, but also in relation to expected long-term effects or consequences for the self and relationships.

Again these developmental advances are not inevitably positive, or even neutral, in their valence. Young adolescents' peer groups are characterized both by greater equity than is experienced in adult-child relationships and also by more concerns with group homogeneity, personal power, and popularity than are experienced in child–child relationships. Liking and being "liked by" one peer can also highlight being disliked by or different from another. Emerging skills in perspective taking and future-oriented, consequence-based reasoning can also fuel increases in interpersonal sensitivity that lead to such problems as jealousy, peer conflicts, in-group and out-group cliques, and sensitivity to peer rejection and neglect, or power and status imbalances (Bukowski & Sippola, 2001). Similarly, children's growing awareness of multiple perspectives and their increased recognition of their own and others' potentially different emotional responses to the same events can advance interpersonal understanding and empathy, but these skills can also provide the understandings that are needed to manipulate others' emotions. In contrast to research suggesting that aggressive children generally have poor peer relationships and hold negative or distorted cognitions about peers (e.g., Hoglund & Leadbeater, 2007; Lochman & Dodge, 1998), accumulating evidence shows that a subgroup of aggressive children actually have a good understanding of others' internal worlds and emotional states (Björkqvist, Österman, & Kaukiainen, 2000; Dunn, Cutting, & Fisher, 2002; Pepler, Craig, & Roberts, 1998; Pettit, Bakshi, Dodge, & Coie, 1990; Sutton, Smith, & Swettenham, 1999). Research also demonstrates that social aggression is positively associated with social intelligence (Björkqvist et al., 2000; Kaukiainen et al. 1999). For instance, research from Sutton et al. (1999) with seven- to ten-year-old children found that physically aggressive "bullies," assessed from self- and peer-nominations, demonstrated higher levels of understanding of others' mental and emotional states (assessed by theory-of-mind tasks) than either children who supported the bully, defended the victim, or were victims themselves. It has also been shown that socially aggressive preadolescents may overestimate the intentions of their peers to aggress against them (Yeung & Leadbeater, 2007).

Items for assessing social aggression from the widely used Social Experiences Questionnaire (SEQ; Crick & Grotpeter, 1996) illustrate the need for perspective taking and understanding others' unexpressed intentions. For example, one item that asks "How often does a classmate tell lies about you *to make other kids not like you anymore?*" requires a prediction about a known other's intention. Similarly, the request to indicate "How often does a kid who is mad at you try to get back at you by not letting you be in their group anymore?" requires the tricky task of rapidly shifting perspectives by standing in the shoes of the angry kid to understand his or her intention (to get back at you) and then to anticipate the perspective of that kid's entire group that will shun you. Research also indicates that social aggression may have a role in establishing and maintaining popularity with peers.

BUT POPULARITY IS NOT THE SAME AS PEER ACCEPTANCE

In early adolescence, peer groups have a salient role in confirming burgeoning identities and self-esteem and this is done in part by conferring or denying group membership, popularity, and status. Group processes that serve either to establish group identity and homogeneity or to award popularity and status to group members have been associated with the use of aggression. The tensions between individual and group needs are regulated by two mechanisms that are controlled by the group: rewarding individuals who contribute to group maintenance with privileges and power, and punishing individuals who threaten group maintenance with social ostracism or isolation (Bukowski & Sippola, 2001).

Links between physical, social, and instrumental aggression and peer ratings of popularity have been demonstrated widely in both quantitative (Cillessen & Mayeux, 2004; Farmer, Estell, Bishop, O'Neal, & Cairns, 2003; LaFontana & Cillessen, 2002; Parkhurst & Hopmeyer, 1998) and qualitative studies (P.A. Adler & Adler, 1995; P.A. Adler, Kless, & Adler, 1992; Evans & Eder, 1993; Merten, 1997). Researchers note an apparent paradox: aggressive children are more likely to be nominated as "least liked" by peers than non-aggressive children; however, aggressive children are frequently also nominated as "popular" (Cillessen & Mayeux, 2004; Farmer et al., 2003; Pelligrini & Long 2002; Rodkin, Farmer, & Pearl, 2000; Rose, Swenson, & Waller, 2004). For example, Parkhurst and Hopmeyer (1998) found that seventh- and eighth-grade students who were rated as "liked" by their peers were also rated as kind and trustworthy, while students who were identified as popular in the school's social hierarchy, but who were "not liked," were judged more likely to start fights and to be stuck up. Socially prominent adolescent leaders appear to be able to use both prosocial and aggressive strategies instrumentally to maintain their influence and popularity with peers (Farmer et al., 2003; Hawley, 2003; Pelligrini, Bartini, & Brooks, 1999; Repacholi, Slaughter, Pritchard, & Gibbs, 2003; Rodkin et al., 2000). Hawley (2003) reported that although socially prominent adolescents admit to being aggressive and are identified by their peers as among the most aggressive children at school, they possess above-average self-concepts and are relatively popular. These socially central adolescents are well known across the peer network, and they are granted the desirable popular status and are also afforded numerous opportunities to assert socially dominant behaviours without being censored by their less popular peers.

The observed associations between popularity and aggression appear to peak in middle school. LaFontana and Cillessen (2002) examined the correlations of peer ratings of aggression (relational and physical) with peer ratings of popularity and social preference (liking) in fourth- to eighth-grade children in a single public school. Physical aggression was negatively correlated with popularity in younger fourth- and fifth-grade students, but was positively correlated in sixth-, seventh-, and eighth-grade students, with the strongest associations in sixth-grade students ($r = .54$). Physical aggression was negatively correlated with social preference (being liked or accepted) in all grades, with the exception of sixth grade ($r = .03$).

STRUCTURAL CHANGES IN FRIENDSHIP NETWORKS

In the transition from elementary school to middle school, many aspects of children's social contexts are also evolving: new social groups are formed, new social hierarchies are established, and peer relationships are renegotiated. At the same time, fewer adults manage more children and children spend greater amounts of time in unstructured and unsupervised activities. The effects of context differences on children's use of interpersonal aggression has not yet been the focus of much attention (but see Dhami, Hoglund, Leadbeater, & Boone, 2005; Leadbeater et al., 2003). Nevertheless, growing research demonstrates that the use of physical aggression is influenced by differences in classroom, school, family, and neighbourhood characteristics (Aber, Jones, Brown, Chaudry, & Samples, 1998; Hoglund & Leadbeater, 2004; Kellam, Ling, Merisca, Brown, & Ialongo, 1999). For example, aggregated classroom-level behaviours and attitudes affect the emergence and continuation of aggression in childhood and adolescence. In an evaluation of a classroom intervention (the Good Behaviour Game) directed at reducing children's aggressive behaviours, Kellam et al. (1999) found that placement in first-grade classrooms with higher aggregate levels of physically aggressive peers (as rated by teachers) contributed to boys' (but not girls') aggressive behaviours in middle school—independent of family- and school-level poverty. Similarly, Aber et al. (1998) investigated the effects of classroom and neighbourhood contexts on the effectiveness of a violence prevention program (Resolving Conflicts Creatively) for second- to sixth-grade children in New York City. Findings showed that the positive effects of high levels of program lessons taught on limiting children's aggressive cognitions were diminished for children in classrooms in which more children rated the use of aggression as "perfectly OK," as well as for children who lived in poorer, more violent neighbourhoods. Hoglund and Leadbeater (2004) examined the direct and interacting effects of differences in classroom, school, and family contexts on changes in children's behaviour problems (disruptiveness and aggression) across first grade. Increases in behaviour problems were greater for children who had more behaviour problems at the beginning of grade one, but also for children who had experienced multiple family moves or who attended schools with more children on income assistance (controlling for family income). Family moves may disrupt protective friendships, and entering a new school may subject children to the tendency of others to exclude "new" children, both of which further reduce children's exposure to prosocial peers. Differences in services, school climate, and peers' norms and interactions that support aggression in schools serving low-income neighbourhoods warrant further investigation.

Research specific to bullying also demonstrates that bystanders can create a context of tolerance for bullying in school playgrounds either through active support or as silent witnesses. Salmivalli, Lagerspetz, Björkqvist, Osterman, and Kaukiainen (1996) have argued that bullying should be viewed as a peer-group process, and that efforts to intervene should be aimed at reducing peer-group support for bullying by raising group awareness of bystander roles. Children who hold values against bullying may also require opportunities to practise acting against bullying through role-playing and rehearsal of behaviours that discourage bullying (Salmavalli, Kaukiainen, & Voeten, 2005). Family, school, classroom, or neighbourhood contexts that support bullying have been largely overlooked as a target for bullying prevention programs. Efforts to change these contexts may require levels of school-district and community support that are difficult to achieve, but that may be imperative to their success (Leadbeater, Schellenbach, Maton, & Dodgen, 2004).

To summarize: dramatic increases in the capacity for social perspective taking, emotional understanding, interpersonal intimacy, mutual respect, and consequence-based reasoning occur in early adolescence. These changes can fuel compassion and self-regulation and can influence the process of identity development that builds on mutual affirmations of self-worth in peer relationships. The centrality of social feedback from peers in defining budding identities also underlies an enhanced sensitivity to the views of others for middle school students that is perhaps stronger than at any other period of life. At the same time, these young adolescents are frequently required by school transitions to move into new, larger school networks where anxieties about not belonging or about being invisible or anonymous can threaten self-esteem. Aggression appears to work to preserve social dominance, peer regard, and popularity at least in the short term. Beyond individual differences, adult and peer norms in these new social contexts can support the use of aggression to maintain status and popularity. Is there any wonder that bullying has not been easy to stop?

CAN BULLYING PREVENTION PROGRAMS BE SENSITIVE TO MIDDLE SCHOOLS STUDENTS' DEVELOPMENTAL NEEDS?

Given the developmental tasks and sensitivities of middle school students and the contextual changes for middle school students that may even favour bullying, it is not surprising that programs that work only to increase empathy or social competence by enhancing children's social-cognitive skills often show weak or no effects on bullying (Miller, Brehm, &

Whitehouse, 1998; D.J. Smith, Schneider, Smith, & Ananiadou, 2004). Programs that target wider social networks including family, classroom, and bystander contexts of children's and adolescents' lives appear to be more promising in reducing aggression (Dodge, Dishion, & Langford, 2006; Olweus, 1993). The collaboration and co-operation of the nested ecologies that support the reduction of aggression in middle schools may be hard to mobilize, but inadequate levels of participation can undermine the implementation of comprehensive school or community-wide approaches to reducing classroom-levels of victimization (Aber et al., 1998; Leadbeater et al., 2003) and bully-victim-bystander problems (see Vernberg & Gamm, 2003).

Developmentally and contextually sensitive approaches to reducing bullying behaviours in early adolescence are clearly needed. Youth struggling with identity development depend on others' feedback for self-definitions and peer opinions and group membership become highly salient. Middle school adolescents need proactive assistance from adults to manage the challenges of their needs for acceptance in the contexts of the new friendships, expanding social networks, and widening ecologies. Yet, these needs emerge at the very point when adult-to-child ratios in middle schools and parent participation and monitoring at home frequently drop off. We often believe that children learn the interpersonal skills that they need in vivo, as they interact with their peers, school, families, and media. Typically, youth are left to experiment with "what works" to maintain their social status and self-esteem. Research findings suggest that both physical and social interpersonal aggression do work, to a degree, in achieving popularity and social status in desired peer networks—even if this is at the expense of being well-liked (Leadbeater, Boone, Sangster, & Mathieson, 2006; Vaillancourt & Hymel, 2006). However, the costs and harmful consequences of aggression for young people may not be immediately evident to those who are encountering heightening opportunities for equity or dominance in peer relationships often for the first time. Adult guidance in negotiating peer-group process is rarely proactive, and it often does not come about until something goes wrong. While school authorities strive to manage the most negative consequences of interpersonal aggression in middle schools with warnings, suspensions, and police involvement, often they are less certain of how to take steps to restore offenders to the community life of the school (Leadbeater, 2000).

Active steps beyond efforts to enhance social perspective taking, tolerance for differences, and empathy are needed to reduce interpersonal aggression. To date, few bullying prevention programs and interventions for children and adolescents have addressed both social and physical aggression. However, several theory-based programs have begun to identify the necessary ingredients of promising programs (Jaffe, Wolfe, Crooks, Hughes, & Baker, 2004; Leadbeater et al., 2003; Salmivalli et al., 2005).

Based on a theoretically and empirically informed understanding of the developmental tasks and contextual challenges of middle school students, we can begin to explicate several strategies that intervention programs need to consider in order to prevent and reduce experiences of aggression with middle school students. Developmentally sensitive prevention programs for middle school students need to target multiple levels of their ecologies and address not only personal differences in developmental capacities and interpersonal skills but also differences in the peer, family, school, and community contexts in which young people are developing. Hence, I divide developmentally appropriate strategies for reducing peer aggression and victimization into personal, peer, and contextual targets.

Personal targets for the prevention of aggression and victimization need to take account of the sensitivities of young adolescents to the regard of their peers and use the developmental advances in social and cognitive sophistication of mid- to late childhood to help them to understand others' internal worlds and the personal and interpersonal consequences of bullying. Information about bullying needs to focus on the prevention of social aggression and cyber-bullying in addition to physical aggression and increase children's abilities to identify the social and personal costs of all types of interpersonal aggression for their relationships. In other words, the first step, perhaps paradoxically, is to raise young people's awareness of the nature of instrumental and social aggression and the emotional and interpersonal harms done by these forms of interpersonal aggression.

Peer targets include the need to identify and influence peer values specifically about all types of interpersonal aggression in the contexts in which children interact; to foster bystander roles that reduce rather than support aggression (see Salmivalli et al., 2005); and to bring socially competent and less competent children together in co-operative, meaningful, and overt social actions. Multiple opportunities are needed for ongoing, cross-clique, adult-guided, and supervised experiences that engage youth in healthy relationships with different groups of peers (e.g., through direct participation with a variety of different peers engaged in their varied interests in team sports, drama, music, mentoring groups, community service, etc.).

Contextual targets include the need to broaden meaningful opportunities for youth to interact in ongoing, meaningful activities that reach across boundaries created by school-based or classroom cliques and to foster social responsibility and opportunities for prosocial leadership. Adult participation in, and facilitation of, these opportunities may also be central to their success. Parents and non-parent adults need to be involved in positive ways in young people's lives. Joint efforts that involve children, youth, parents, teachers, and other community members as experts are needed to create and support non-violent schools and communities, and to create multi-level contexts that are responsive to children's requests for help (Leadbeater et al., 2003). There is a tendency to think of social aggression, in particular, as outside the purview of adult intervention; however, proactive guidance in late elementary school is needed to help boys and girls to recognize social aggression and to be aware of its temporary benefits for popularity as well as its costs for peer acceptance, reputations, and self-esteem. Opportunities for co-operative engagement and prosocial leadership in differing settings are also needed for youth who are identified as involved in peer aggression. Rather than zero tolerance of aggression, direct adult participation as models of prosocial leadership strategies for peacefully and creatively resolving peer conflicts are needed at this developmental stage. Meaningful, group-based involvement in community service offers opportunities for leadership and follower-ship that recognize students' strengths and abilities to contribute to the well-being of their communities.

More research is needed to assess how community involvement can reduce bullying. Anecdotally, for example, local middle schools girls who were about to be suspended for their involvement in internet bullying, which threatened to foment violence across several middle schools, were assigned a community service task. With adult mentors, they wrote passionately for the school newspaper about their hopes for protecting their friends from the consequences of violence and discussed ways to reduce violence with school personnel and police, but their own aggression continued in their peer groups. Used as an isolated punishment, community service without adult support and follow-up may not be useful in creating the changes in youth and school cultures needed to reduce or prevent bullying.

Coordinated efforts are also needed to enhance socially responsible and interpersonally respectful behaviours across the layered contexts that surround youth. Interventions are needed to assist the important adults in children's and adolescents' social networks (parents, teachers, coaches) to reject aggression as normative in peer relationships (Boone & Leadbeater, 2006). Adults also need help to understand how to respond proactively to aggressive behaviours in early adolescence and how to act on their requests for help. Children who ask for help may fear retaliation from peers or be discouraged by adults for "tattling." However, research shows that even young children rarely ask for help to get others into trouble; they are more likely to be seeking adult support or information to deal with a real problem that they do not know how to solve (Leadbeater, Ohan, & Hoglund,

2006). Adults frequently believe that influencing adolescents' peer-group processes are far beyond their reach. Programs are needed that raise adults' awareness of the characteristics and function of the identity and social goals that are related to peer-group processes and interpersonal aggression in this age group. Adults also need to learn about and be engaged in alternative activities that provide opportunities and group-based experiences for adolescents that can serve their developmental needs for mutual recognition.

Furthermore, adults need to participate in ensuring that young adolescents are exposed to contexts that demonstrate alternate values to social aggression, violence, and self-aggrandizement. Children are surrounded by cultural and media supports for interpersonal violence. In a recent study by Coyne et al. (2006), children reported witnessing an average of 50.2 acts of social, relational, and indirect aggression each week while the incidence of these acts on television programs that they watched averaged 319.2 per week. In the new wave of "reality TV," America's next top models, rock stars, and business magnates daily demonstrate the use of social aggression in dyadic and group contests where only one winner can emerge. While media literacy programs can be used to raise awareness of harms done by interpersonal aggression, reality TV has instead opened a new world of interpersonal violence in which social aggression, put-downs, and humiliation by adult judges are normative, and these can serve as training grounds for learning how to use it. As passive spectators, adults become bystanders in support of this interpersonal aggression. Adult participation is needed to help adolescents recognize the harm done by these behaviours and forego them both in interpersonal relationships and internet messaging (see Willard, 2007, for a summary of approaches to cyber-bullying).

Efforts to reduce interpersonal aggression clearly need to reflect the salient developmental advances and possibly normative (but undesirable) use of aggression in early adolescence. In the Victoria, BC, area, we have worked to develop a community-based approach to the prevention of victimization: the WITS and WITS-LEADS programs. The WITS program is a kindergarten to third-grade peer-victimization-prevention program created though a community alliance with the University of Victoria, Greater Victoria School District 61, and the Rock Solid Foundation (a community-based police group). Through this collaboration we have developed and evaluated both the WITS and WITS-LEADS programs, which are now used widely in the greater Victoria area. The WITS program aims to create multi-contextual support (school, classroom, community, and family) to help children to Walk away, Ignore, Talk out conflicts, and/or Seek help when bullied by peers (see www.uvic.ca/wits). By taking a community-based approach to the prevention of peer victimization, it engages parents, school personnel, and representatives from the community (e.g., student athletes and emergence service personnel) in creating environments that respond quickly, positively, and effectively to children's reports of peer victimization. Our findings from a three-year longitudinal evaluation of the WITS program showed that peer victimization can be reduced through this universal, multi-setting program. Importantly, greater program-effect sizes were evident in the schools located in higher poverty neighbourhoods, pointing to the efficacy in these schools of consistent, community-level messages to both adults and children about how to cope with peer victimization (Leadbeater et al., 2003; Leadbeater & Hoglund, 2006). We are currently evaluating the extension of the WITS peer-victimization-prevention program that is developmentally appropriate for fourth and fifth grade students. Called the WITS-Leadership Program or "WITS-LEADS," the new initiative takes an innovative approach that specifically targets relational victimization (e.g., gossiping, rumour spreading, social exclusion) and seeks to increase children's understanding of the "internal worlds" of their peers. LEADS stands for Look and Listen, Explore points of view, Act, Did it work? and Seek help.

There is a need for developmentally sensitive, theory-based approaches that acknowledge differences in the meaning and significance of aggression from preschool to late adolescence. Questions remain about within-group differences in aggression among youth that can only be answered by large-scale longitudinal projects. Research, both qualitative and experimental, should also move beyond single assessments to investigations of short- and long-term changes in the use of aggression by groups of friends. Continued evidence of bullying and its negative consequences for children's development underline the urgency of this work.

KEY MESSAGES

1. Key developmental transitions influence middle school students' sensitivities to and use of interpersonal aggression. These changes usher in opportunities for growth, but they also create vulnerability to victimization and occasions for aggression.

2. Changes from elementary school to middle school contexts provide important points for interventions that enhance prosocial leadership and opportunities for youth to work in meaningful ways with adults to reduce bullying and enhance healthy relationships.

3. Developmentally sensitive prevention programs for middle school students need to target multiple levels of their ecologies and address not

only individual differences in developmental capacities and interpersonal skills but also differences in the peer, family, school, and community contexts in which young people are developing.

REFERENCES

Aber, J.L., Jones, S.M., Brown, J.L, Chaudry, N., & Samples, F. (1998). Resolving conflict creatively: Evaluating the developmental effects of a school-based violence prevention program in neighborhood and classroom context. *Development and Psychopathology*, *10*(2), 187–213.

Adler, P.A., & Adler, P. (1995). Dynamics of inclusion and exclusion in preadolescent cliques. *Social Psychology Quarterly*, *58*, 145–162.

Adler, P.A., Kless, S.J., and Adler, P. (1992). Socialization to gender roles: Popularity among elementary school boys and girls. *Sociology of Education*, *65*, 169–187.

Archer, J. (2004). Sex differences in aggression in real-world settings: A meta-analytic review. *Review of General Psychology*, *8*, 291–322.

Björkqvist, K., Lagerspetz, K., & Kaukiainen, A. (1992). Do girls manipulate and boys fight? Developmental trends in regard to direct and indirect aggression. *Aggressive Behaviour*, *18*, 117–127.

Björkqvist, K., Österman, K., & Kaukiainen, A. (2000). Social intelligence— empathy = aggression? *Aggression and Violent Behavior*, *5*(2), 191–200.

Boone, E., & Leadbeater, B. (2006). Game on: Diminishing risks for depressive symptoms in early adolescence through positive involvement in team sports. *Journal of Research on Adolescence*, *16*(1), 79–90.

Bukowski, W.M., & Sippola, L.K. (2001). Groups, individuals, and victimization: A view of the peer system. In J. Juvonen & S. Graham (Eds.), *Peer harassment in school: The plight of the vulnerable and victimized* (pp. 355–377). New York: Guilford Press.

Buhrmeister, D. (1996). Need fulfillment, interpersonal competence, and the developmental contexts of early adolescent friendship. In W.M. Bukowski, A.F. Newcomb, & W.W. Hartup (Eds.), *The company they keep: Friendship in childhood and adolescence* (pp. 158–186). Cambridge: Cambridge University Press.

Cillessen, A.H., & Mayeux, L. (2004). From censure to reinforcement: Developmental changes in the association between aggression and social status. *Child Development*, *75*, 147–163.

Coyne, S.M., Archer J., & Eslea, M. (2006). "We're not friends anymore! Unless...": The frequency and harmfulness of indirect, relational and social aggression. *Aggressive Behavior*, *32*, 294–307.

Crick, N.R., & Grotpeter, J.K. (1996). Relational aggression, overt aggression and friendship. *Child Development*, *67*, 2328–2338.

Dhami, M.K., Hoglund, W.L., Leadbeater, B.J., & Boone, E.M. (2005). Gender-linked risks for peer physical and relational victimization in the context of school-level poverty in first grade. *Social Development*, *14*, 532–549.

Dodge, K.A., Dishion, T.J., & Langsford, J.E. (2006). Deviant peer influences in intervention and public policy for youth. *Social Policy Report, 20*(1), 3–19.

Dunn, J., Cutting, A.L., & Fisher, N. (2002). Old friends, new friends: Predictors of children's perspective on their friends at school. *Child Development, 73,* 621–635.

Erikson, E.H. (1975). *Life history and the historical moment.* New York: Norton.

Evans, C., & Eder, D. (1993). "No exit": Processes of social isolation in middle school. *Journal of Contemporary Ethnography, 22*(2), 139–170.

Farmer, T.W., Estell, D.B., Bishop, J.L., O'Neal, K.K., & Cairns, B.D. (2003). Rejected bullies or popular leaders? The social relations of aggressive subtypes of rural African American early adolescents. *Developmental Psychology, 39*(6), 992–1004.

Harachi, T.W., Fleming, C.B., White, H.R., Ensminger, M.E., Abbott, R.D., Catalano, R.F., & Haggerty, K.P. (2006). Aggressive behavior among girls and boys during middle childhood: Predictors and sequelae of trajectory group membership. *Aggressive Behavior, 32,* 270–293.

Hartup, W.W. (2005). The development of aggression: Where do we stand? In R.E. Tremblay, W.W. Hartup, & J. Archer (Eds.), *Developmental origins of aggression* (pp. 3–22). New York: Guilford Press.

Hawley, P.H. (2003). Prosocial and coercive configurations of resource control in early adolescence: A case of the well-adapted Machiavellian. *Merrill-Palmer Quarterly, 49*(3), 279–309.

Hoglund, W.L., & Leadbeater, B.J. (2004). The effects of family, school, and classroom ecologies on changes in children's social competence and emotional and behavioral problems in first grade. *Developmental Psychology, 40,* 533–544.

Hoglund, W.L., & Leadbeater, B.J. (2007). Managing threat: Do social-cognitive processes mediate the link between peer victimization and adjustment problems in early adolescence? *Journal of Research on Adolescence, 17,* 525–540.

Haynie, D., Nansel, T., Eitel, P., Crump, A., Saylor, K., Yu, K., & Simons-Morton, B. (2001). Bullies, victims, and bully/victims: Distinct groups of at-risk youth. *Journal of Early Adolescence, 21*(1), 29–49.

Jaffe, P., Wolfe, D., Crooks, C., Hughes, R., & Baker, L. (2004). The fourth R: Developing healthy relationships through school-based interventions. In P. Jaffe, L. Baker, & A. Cunningham (Eds.), *Protecting children from domestic violence: Strategies for community intervention* (pp. 200–218). New York: Guilford Press.

Kaukiainen, A., Björkqvist, K., Lagerspetz, K., Osterman, K., Salmivalli, C., Rothberg, S., & Ahlbom, A. (1999). The relationships between social intelligence, empathy, and three types of aggression. *Aggressive Behaviors, 25,* 81–89.

Kellam, S.G., Ling, X., Merisca, R., Brown, C.H., & Ialongo, N. (1999). The effect of the level of aggression in the first grade classroom on the course and malleability of aggressive behavior into middle school: Erratum. *Development and Psychopathology, 11*(1), 193.

LaFontana, K.M., & Cillessen, A.H. (2002). Children's perceptions of popular and unpopular peers: A multimethod assessment. *Developmental Psychology, 38*, 635–647.

Leadbeater, B.J., (2000). Can restorative justice approaches be used as alternatives to elementary school suspensions? *Advocate, 23*, 6–8.

Leadbeater, B.J., Boone, E.M., Sangster, N.A., & Mathieson, L.C. (2006). Sex differences in the costs and benefits of relational and physical aggression in high school. *Aggressive Behaviors, 32*, 409–419.

Leadbeater, B., & Hoglund, W. (2006). Changing the social contexts of peer victimization. *Journal of the Canadian Academy of Child and Adolescent Psychiatry / Journal de l'Académie canadienne de psychiatrie de l'enfant et de l'adolescent, 15*(1), 21–26.

Leadbeater, B.J., Hoglund, W.L., & Woods, T. (2003). Changing contexts? The effects of a primary prevention program on classroom levels of peer relational and physical victimization. *Journal of Community Psychology, 31*, 397–418.

Leadbeater, B.J., Ohan, J., & Hoglund, W. (2006). How children's justifications of the "best thing to do" in peer conflicts relate to their emotional and behavioral problems in early elementary school. *Merrill Palmer Quarterly, 52*(4), 721–754.

Leadbeater, B., Schellenbach, C., Maton, K., & Dodgen, D. (2004). Research and policy for building strengths: Processes and contexts of individual, family, and community development. In K. Maton, C. Shellenbach, B. Leadbeater, & A. Solzar (Eds.) *Investing in children, youth, families and communities: Strengths-based research and policy* (pp. 13–30). Washington: American Psychological Foundation.

Lochman, J.E., & Dodge, K.A. (1998). Distorted perceptions in dyadic interactions of aggressive and nonaggressive boys: Effects of prior expectations, context, and boys' age. *Development and Psychopathology, 10*, 495–512.

Merten, D.E. (1997). The meaning of meanness: Popularity, competition, and conflict among junior high school girls. *Sociology of Education, 70*, 175–191.

Miller, G.E., Brehm, K., & Whitehouse, S. (1998). Reconceptualizing school-based prevention for antisocial behavior within a resilience framework. *School Psychology Review, 27*(3), 364–379.

Nagin, D., & Tremblay, R.E. (1999). Trajectories of boys' physical aggression, opposition, and hyperactivity on the path to physically violent and nonviolent juvenile delinquency. *Child Development, 70*(5), 1181–1196.

Nansel, T., Haynie, D., & Simons-Morton, B. (2003). The association of bullying and victimization with middle school adjustment. *Journal of Applied School Psychology, 19*(2), 45–61.

Nansel, T., Overpeck, M., Pilla, R., Ruan, W., Simons-Morton, B., & Scheidt, P. (2001). Bullying behaviors among US youth: Prevalence and association with psychosocial adjustment. *Journal of the American Medical Association, 285*(16), 2094–2100.

NICHD Early Child Care Research Network. (2004). Trajectories of physical aggression from toddlerhood to middle childhood: Predictors, correlates, and outcomes. *Monographs of the Society for Research in Child Development, 69* (Whole No. 4, Serial No. 278), 1–129.

Olweus, D. (1993). *Bullying at school: What we know and what we can do.* Cambridge, MA: Wiley-Blackwell.

Oyserman, D. (2007). Social identity and self-regulation. In A.W. Kruglanski & E. Higgins (Eds.), *Social psychology: Handbook of basic principles* (pp. 432–453). New York: Guilford Press.

Oyserman, D., Bybee, D., & Terry, K. (2006). Possible selves and academic outcomes: How and when possible selves impel action. *Journal of Personality and Social Psychology, 91*(1), 188–204.

Parkhurst, J.T., & Hopmeyer, A. (1998). Sociometric popularity and peer-perceived popularity: Two distinct dimensions of peer status. *Journal of Early Adolescence, 18*(2), 125–144.

Pellegrini, A.D., Bartini, M., & Brooks, F. (1999). School bullies, victims, and aggressive victims: Factors relating to group affiliation and victimization in early adolescence. *Journal of Educational Psychology, 91*, 216–224.

Pellegrini, A.D., & Long, J.D. (2002). A longitudinal study of bullying, dominance, and victimization through secondary school. *British Journal of Developmental Psychology, 20*, 259–280.

Pepler, D.J., Craig, W.M., & Roberts, W.L. (1998). Observations of aggressive and nonaggressive children on the school playground. *Merrill-Palmer Quarterly, 44*(1), 55–76.

Pettit, G.S., Bakshi, A., Dodge, K.A., & Coie, J.D. (1990). The emergence of dominance in young boys' play groups: Developmental differences and behavioral correlates. *Developmental Psychology, 26*, 1017–1025.

Repacholi, B., Slaughter, V., Pritchard, M., & Gibbs, V. (2003). Theory of mind, Machiavellianism, and social functioning in childhood. In B. Repacholi and V. Slaughter (Eds.), *Individual differences in theory of mind: Implications for typical and atypical development* (pp. 67–97). New York: Psychology Press.

Rodkin, P.C., Farmer, T.W., & Pearl, R. (2000). Heterogeneity of popular boys: Antisocial and prosocial configurations. *Developmental Psychology, 36*(1), 12–24.

Rose, A.J., Swenson, L.P., & Waller, E.M. (2004). Overt and relational aggression and perceived popularity: Developmental differences in concurrent and prospective relations. *Developmental Psychology, 40*, 378–387.

Salmivalli, C., & Kaukainen, A. (2004). Female aggression revisited: Variable- and person-centered approaches to studying gender difference in different types of aggression. *Aggressive Behavior, 30*(2), 158–163.

Salmivalli, C., Kaukiainen, A., & Voeten, M. (2005). Anti-bullying intervention: Implementation and outcome. *British Journal of Educational Psychology, 75*(3), 465–487.

Salmivalli, C., Lagerspetz, K., Björkqvist, K., Osterman, K., & Kaukiainen, A. (1996). Bullying as a group process: Participant roles and their relations to social status within the group. *Aggressive Behavior, 22*, 1–15.

Selman, R.L. (1980). *The growth of interpersonal understanding*. New York: Academic Press.

Selman, R.L., & Schultz, L.H. (1990). *Making a friend in youth: Developmental theory and pair therapy*. Chicago: University of Chicago Press.

Smith, D.J., Schneider, B.H., Smith, P.K., & Ananiadou, K. (2004). The effectiveness of whole-school antibullying programs: A synthesis of evaluation research. *School Psychology Review, 33*, 548–561.

Sullivan, H.S. (1953). *The interpersonal theory of psychiatry*. New York: Norton.

Sutton, J., Smith, P.K., & Swettenham, J. (1999). Social cognition and bullying: Social inadequacy or skilled manipulation? *British Journal of Developmental Psychology, 17*, 435–450.

Underwood, M.K. (2003). *Social aggression among girls*. New York: Guilford Press.

Underwood, M.K., Galen, B.R., & Paquette, J.A. (2001). Top ten challenges for understanding gender and aggression in children: Why can't we all just get along? *Social Development, 10*(2), 248–266.

Unnever, J., & Cornell, D. (2004). Middle school victims of bullying: Who reports being bullied? *Aggressive Behaviour, 30*(5), 373–388.

Vaillancourt, T., Brendgen, M., Boivin, M., & Tremblay, R.E. (2003). A longitudinal confirmatory factor analysis of indirect and physical aggression: Evidence of two factors over time? *Child Development, 14*(6), 1628–1638.

Vaillancourt, T., & Hymel, S. (2004). The social context of children's aggression. In M.M. Moretti, C.L. Odgers, & M.A. Jackson (Eds.), *Girls and aggression: Contributing factors and intervention principles* (pp. 57–73). New York: Kluwer Academic/Plenum.

Vaillancourt, T., & Hymel, S. (2006). Aggression and social status: The moderating role of sex and peer valued characteristics. *Aggressive Behaviour, 32*, 396–408.

Vernberg, E.M., & Gamm, B. (2003). Resistance to violence prevention interventions in schools: Barriers and solutions. *Journal of Applied Psychoanalytic Studies, 5*, 125–138.

Willard, N. (2007). *Cyberbullying and cyberthreats: Responding to the challenge of online social aggression, threats, and distress*. Champaign, IL: Research Press.

Xie, H., Cairns, R.B., & Cairns, B.D. (2005). The development of aggressive behaviours among girls: Measurement issues, social functions, and differential trajectories. In D.J. Pepler, K.C. Madsen, C. Webster, & K.S. Levene (Eds.), *The development and treatment of girlhood aggression* (pp. 105–136). Mahwah, NJ: Lawrence Erlbaum Associates.

Yeung, R.S., & Leadbeater, B.J. (2007). Does hostile attributional bias for relational provocations mediate the short-term association between relational victimization and aggression in preadolescence? *Journal of Youth and Adolescence, 36*(8), 973–983.

CHAPTER NINE

SCHOOL-BASED INTERVENTIONS

COMMENTARY BY
LEENA AUGIMERI AND MARGARET WALSH

ON
USING EVIDENCE TO REDUCE THE BULLYING BEHAVIOUR EXPERIENCED BY GIRLS
D. CROSS, T. SHAW, H. MONKS, S. WATERS, AND L. LESTER

AND
MATCHING THE PREVENTION OF INTERPERSONAL AGGRESSION TO CRITICAL DEVELOPMENTAL AND CONTEXTUAL TRANSITIONS IN MIDDLE SCHOOL
B. LEADBEATER

It is evident that the development and implementation of anti-aggression and anti-bullying school based interventions represents a complex undertaking that requires commitment, dedication, and knowledge of what works and what doesn't. In their chapters, Bonnie Leadbeater and Donna Cross and colleagues emphasize the need to promote prosocial leadership and social responsibility as they relate to school-based anti-bullying programs. At the same time, they encourage us to take into account an ecological framework that looks at factors such as the individual traits of the child, family interactions, and school climate (including teacher and peer interactions), as well as how these factors are influenced by the greater environment and community (e.g., media, culture, economics, society, and political system)—all in an effort to better understand how to target personal, peer, and contextual factors within and across gender in order to affect positive outcomes. These researchers bring to light the complexity of effectively addressing bullying and aggression within schools and ask the straightforward question: "Is there any wonder that bullying has not been easy to stop?" (see Chapter 8, p. 123).

Over the past 25 years, the Centre for Children Committing Offences (CCCO) at the Child Development Institute (CDI) in Toronto has focused its research, clinical practice, and community mobilization efforts on elementary school-age children with disruptive behaviour problems (e.g., conduct, oppositional, and aggressive) (Augimeri, Walsh, & Slater, 2011). We have learned that what is required to successfully develop, implement, and sustain evidence-based programming (e.g., gender sensitive SNAP® models; see www.stopnowandplan.com) and crime prevention strategies is a collaborative, comprehensive community of practice approach. This approach should take into account the early identification of risks, targeted gender sensitive treatment interventions, and community partnerships (Augimeri, Walsh, Liddon, & Dassinger, 2011; Koegl, Augimeri, Ferrante, Walsh, & Slater, 2008). Such approaches are fundamental for the healthy development of vulnerable young children, their families, and their supporting communities and service providers that bear responsibility for the healthy development of these children.

The implications to society of not taking action on issues pertaining to aggressive children and youth can be enormous (Loeber, Slot, van der Laan, & Hoeve, 2008). For example, Dodge (2008) found that it cost society approximately two million dollars in services for each chronically violent individual over the course of his or her lifetime, and Welsh et al. (2008) report that early-onset offenders can cause significantly higher average victim costs than other offenders. Most research on bullying and aggressive behaviour focuses on the adolescent years when these behaviours are prominent and well established (Farrington, 2008). In a recent analysis, a strong linkage was discovered between bullying behaviour during childhood years and subsequent criminal offences after the age of 12 (Jiang, Walsh, & Augimeri, 2011). Criminal convictions were found to be twice as high for those who were identified by a parent as often engaging in bullying behaviours, as compared to those identified as non-bullies. Longitudinal research has also shown that minor problems starting by the age of 7 can lead to moderate behaviour problems by age 9, which can then evolve into serious delinquency and aggression issues by age 14 (Loeber, Farrington, & Petechuk, 2003).

From ages 7 to 14 years, children spend the majority of their time in school where they are monitored by trained educators qualified to educate and support them. Today, educators are also required to be both knowledgeable and skilled in identifying and managing child aggression and bullying, especially when related to such complex issues as sexism, racism, faithism, heterosexism, classism, ableism, and ageism. It is not that bullying behaviours are new to the school culture—rather, it is the intensity, severity, and variety of methods used (e.g., cyber-bullying and persistent social aggression) that are of major concern. We are increasingly being faced with media accounts of children engaging in dangerous, aggressive, bullying, and violent behaviours at home, at school, and in the community. These behaviours, of course, do not suddenly appear. So, why are we not applying early prevention principles/approaches? Could it be that we are not recognizing, acknowledging, and/or acting on the early warning signs? Or is it that schools may not be equipped with the right tools and programs to deal effectively with mental health issues? Or could it be that there is not a sufficient number of active community partners in place to support our community schools (e.g., local mental health centres)?

In 2009, an article by Rosie DiManno in the *Toronto Star* entitled "Creba murderer's life in detail" not only highlighted the early warning signs for at-risk children who engage in bullying, aggressive, and anti-social behaviour, but also emphasized the number of adults and professionals these children are exposed to during the course of their school career. For example, in this article, the media report stated that the troubled young man awaiting sentencing for murder had undergone many behavioural assessments at school to evaluate his anti-social and violent tendencies. By age 9, there were "30 multiple school suspensions" for rudeness, defiance, verbal and physical aggression towards other students counted on the young man's transcript (pp. GT1–2). Also highlighted was his history of estranged and often chaotic relationships. Our own research and clinical experience (Augimeri, Jiang, Koegl, & Carey, 2006) has demonstrated the importance of building strong and healthy relationships and support systems for all children, especially those classified as being high risk. With our knowledge of the many risks that make children vulnerable, it behooves us to act in a way that ensures high-risk children are provided with positive mentors and are connected to effective interventions to meet their level of risk and need.

For many children, the school system may be the only place and means to access services (Hoagwood, Burns, Kiser, Ringeisen, & Schoenwald, 2001). Building strong relationships and making schools the "hub" of the community versus their status as simply academic facilities may be a way to ensure that at-risk children will receive the necessary attention and services. Another way to think of this is through the scientist-practitioner framework, where schools become the "heart and mind" of the community. For this to work, we would need to saturate schools with resources, supports, specialized programs, and professionals trained to deal with the variety of complex issues plaguing our children, families, and schools. Investing in school-based sustainable and promising programs (e.g., Roots of Empathy, PATHS, SNAP®) that build on each other's strategies to complement and support the learnings' scaffolding (e.g., empathy, problem-solving, and self-control skills) and community partnerships (e.g., mental health centres, child welfare, policing, recreation) will help to create a healthy and caring school culture that could then also impact home and community.

For example, based on the positive outcomes of our SNAP® gender-sensitive treatment models (e.g., Augimeri, Farrington, Koegl, & Day, 2007; Pepler et al., 2010), interest has grown regarding adapting SNAP® for school-based settings. This adaptation of the SNAP® program is a demonstration of a "partners for success" model between various school boards and children's mental health centres (e.g., SNAP® Niagara Collaborative–John Howard Society of Niagara, Pathstone Mental Health and Niagara School Boards, Canadian Safe Schools Network). In these partnership programs, the lead organizations are sent to specific schools identified by the school board, and they work alongside teachers in designated classrooms with high-risk children to deliver the SNAP® program. This combined prevention and intervention program allows SNAP® facilitators to work in the designated classrooms to enhance the environment both as a whole, by teaching all children SNAP® strategies, and individually, by mentoring those identified students whose need is the greatest. The school also participates in SNAP® activities such as assemblies and theme events. The SNAP® for Schools (SNAP®-S) collaborative approach of working with school personnel to create a SNAP® culture is based on two decades of learning (Pepler, King, & Byrd, 1991) and is the beginning of a community of practice model. This model currently in development is generating promising results. For example, preliminary findings indicate that children participating in the SNAP®-S program have significantly fewer behavioural and discipline problems, including a decrease in suspension rates, and show overall improvement in behaviour in and outside the classroom and playground (Child Development Institute, 2012). The majority of children indicated that what they liked best about what they learned was "to stop bullying." Children also reported that, after being taught methods of SNAP®, they have better relationships with their teachers and peers, deal more effectively with conflict and controlling their anger, and are better able to calm down. Teachers reported that some of the most helpful topics of the program were "dealing with anger" and "dealing with bullying." Moreover, teachers found the SNAP®-S program to be a positive tool for change across the following domains: getting along better with teachers, getting along better with peers, calming down when feeling angry, having more control over feelings of anger, and students being able to deal with conflict more positively. The SNAP®-S program continues to evolve, supporting the changing needs of our schools and communities through teaching emotional regulation and self-control skills that promote healthy and positive choices.

No matter how promising a program may be, its success is limited if sustainable infrastructures within the school system are not taken into account: (a) building a community of practice around the school, including collaborative community partnerships with specialized services for children and families (e.g., children's mental health, recreation, child welfare, and policing); (b) providing specialized training and support for school personnel in how to assess and respond effectively to aggressive behaviours in elementary school-age children (see Bardick & Bernes, 2008) utilizing concern or risk assessment tools to help identify children at great risk for anti-social behaviour such as the Early Assessment Risk Lists: EARL-Pre-Checklist (policing and education), EARL-20B for boys and EARL-21G for girls (Augimeri, Walsh, Koegl, & Logue, 2011; Augimeri, Webster, Koegl, & Levene, 2001; Levene et al., 2001); (c) implementing evidence-based gender and culturally sensitive programs that target all aggressive children versus a "flavour of the month" mentality; (d) ensuring that the intervention's philosophy and strategies become part of the school culture as it relates to the *Universal Design* in education and *Differentiated Instruction* (Ontario Ministry of Education, 2005); (e) ensuring that the intervention's skills are incorporated into the school curriculum including *Individual Education Plans (IEP)* and alternative programming; (f) documenting and assessing skills within standardized academic report cards; (g) implementing universal anti-bullying programming and awareness campaigns for the whole school and community that target the various forms of bullying (e.g. cyber-bullying, face-to-face); and (h) securing parent involvement in activities such as parent education, support groups, parent associations, and advisory groups.

Lastly, we need to consider the many complex and diverse needs of schools and recognize that there is no one program that can meet "one size fits all" criteria. Schools need to carefully consider where funding gets allocated (e.g., high concentration on academics versus specialized school programs), as it is the anti-social, emotional, and behavioural children that are the most vulnerable to failure. Evaluation and research is critical to ensuring that schools have the most up-to-date knowledge on effective programs to ensure success for all their students. We need to continue building on the pioneering, innovative research championed by lead investigators such as

Craig and Pepler (1996) as well as other researchers (e.g., Leadbeater, Cross and colleagues) in developing school-based experimental studies that involve students, teachers, administrators, and parents to help us understand what works, what doesn't, and for whom, with regard to aggression, bullying, and victimization. Developing a scientist-practitioner framework within schools whereby research informs practice and vice versa is warranted. This will put us in a better position to understand the issues and solutions pertaining to school-based aggression, violence, and bullying. Attempting to do research within a school setting by outside partners can be extremely challenging, even in the most controlled research settings. To be successful, it requires the full support of school boards, government bodies, and school officials.

Leadbeater's and Cross and colleagues' chapters help to shape our thinking on the issues related to bullying and effective interventions to deal with aggression and bullying in schools. In this discussant, we highlight the need to be cautious around the selection of programs, how they are sustained, and how we (e.g., researchers, educators, government, recreation leaders, mental health professionals, police, child welfare workers, communities) must work together to create a culture whereby schools become the "heart and mind" of a community. We offer a number of suggested strategies that can be implemented within schools to deal with bullying and to develop a positive school culture. We recognize that some of what we propose is already being done, while other aspects require much consideration (e.g., adding intervention programming to the school curriculum, building a community of practice around schools). Investing in sustainable programs that have proven to be effective and that focus on the determinants of mental health and learning, thus creating a caring school culture, will be a means of eradicating aggression and violence and, most importantly, keeping our children safe, in school, and out of trouble.

REFERENCES

Augimeri, L.K., Farrington, D.P., Koegl, C.J., & Day, D.M. (2007). The Under 12 Outreach Project: Effects of a community based program for children with conduct problems. *Journal of Child and Family Studies, 16,* 799–807.

Augimeri, L.K., Jiang, D., Koegl, C.J., & Carey, J. (2006). *Differential effects of the Under 12 Outreach Project (ORP) associated with client risk and treatment intensity* (Report submitted to the Provincial Centre of Excellence for Child and Youth Mental Health). Toronto: Child Development Institute.

Augimeri, L.K., Walsh, M., Koegl, C., & Logue, L. (2011). Early assessment risk list—Pre checklist (EARL-PC). Toronto, ON: Child Development Institute.

Augimeri, L.K., Walsh, M.M, Liddon, A.D., & Dassinger, C.R. (2011). From risk identification to risk management: A comprehensive strategy for young children engaged in antisocial behavior. In A. Roberts & D. Springer, (Eds.), *Juvenile delinquency and juvenile justice: Policies, programs, and intervention strategies* (pp. 117–140). Sudbury, MA: Jones and Bartlett.

Augimeri, L.K., Walsh, M., & Slater, N. (2011). Rolling out SNAP® an evidence-based intervention: A summary of implementation, evaluation and research. *International Journal of Child, Youth and Family Studies, 2*(2.1), 162–184.

Augimeri, L.K., Webster, C.D., Koegl, C.J., & Levene, K. (2001). *Early assessment risk list for boys: EARL-20B* (Version 2). Toronto: Earlscourt Child and Family Centre (now called Child Development Institute).

Bardick, A.D., & Bernes, K.B. (2008). A framework for assessing violent behaviors in elementary school-age children. *Children and Schools, 30*(2), 83–91.

Child Development Institute. (2012, June). *Responding to children with externalizing behaviours within the classroom from research to practice: SNAP® for Schools (SNAP®-S).* Poster session presented at the Third National Symposium on Child and Youth Mental Health, Child Welfare League of Canada, Calgary, AB.

Craig, W.M., & Pepler, D.J. (1996). Understanding bullying at school: What can we do about it? In S. Miller (Ed.), *Safe by design: Building interpersonal skills* (pp. 205–230). Seattle, WA: Committee for Children.

DiManno, R. (2009, April 7). Creba murderer's life in detail. *Toronto Star,* pp. GT1–2.

Dodge, K.A. (2008). Framing public policy and prevention of chronic violence in American youth. *American Psychologist, 63*(7), 573–590.

Farrington, D.P. (2008). Foreword. In R. Loeber, N.W. Slot, P. van der Laan, & M. Hoeve (Eds.), *Tomorrow's criminals: The development of child delinquency and optimal interventions* (pp. xvii–xviii). Aldershot: Ashgate.

Hoagwood, K., Burns, B.J., Kiser, L., Ringeisen, H., & Schoenwald, S.K. (2001). Evidence-based practice in child and adolescent mental health services. *Psychiatric Services, 52*(9), 1179–1189.

Jiang, D., Walsh, M., & Augimeri, L.K. (2011). The linkage between bullying behaviour and future offending. *Criminal Behaviour and Mental Health, 21,* 128–135. doi: 10.1002/cbm.803

Koegl, C.J., Augimeri, L.K., Ferrante, P., Walsh, M., & Slater, N. (2008). A comprehensive strategy for children under 12 in conflict with the law: Referral protocols, gender-specific risk assessment and gender specific clinical interventions. In R. Loeber, N.W. Slot, P. van der Laan, and M. Hoeve (Eds.), *Tomorrow's criminals: The development of child delinquency and optimal interventions* (pp. 285–300). Aldershot: Ashgate.

Levene, K.S., Augimeri, L.K., Pepler, D.J., Walsh, M.M., Koegl, C.J., & Webster C.D. (2001). *Early assessment risk list for girls: EARL-21G* (Version 1, Consultation Edition). Toronto: Earlscourt Child and Family Centre.

Loeber, R., Farrington, D.P., & Petechuk, D. (2003, May). *Child delinquency: Early intervention and prevention* (Child Delinquency Bulletin Series No. 186162). Washington, DC: Office of Juvenile Justice and Delinquency Prevention, US Department of Justice.

Loeber, R., Slot, N.W., van der Laan, P.H., & Hoeve, M. (2008). Child delinquents and tomorrow's serious delinquents: Key questions addressed in this volume. In R. Loeber, N.W. Slot, P.H. van der Laan, & M. Hoeve (Eds.), *Tomorrow's criminals: The development of child delinquency and effective interventions* (pp. 3–17). Hampshire: Ashgate.

Ontario Ministry of Education (2005). *Education for all: The report of the expert panel on literacy and numeracy instruction for students with special education needs, kindergarten to Grade 6* (Reference No. 05-19). Retrieved from http://www.edu.gov.on.ca/eng/document/reports/speced/panel/index.html

Pepler, D.J., King, G., & Byrd, W. (1991). A social-cognitively based social skills training program for aggressive children. In D. Pepler & K. Rubin (Eds.), *The development and treatment of childhood aggression* (pp. 411–448). Hillsdale, NJ: Erlbaum.

Pepler, D., Walsh, M., Yuile, A., Levene, K., Vaughan, A., & Webber, J. (2010). Bridging the gender Gap: Interventions with aggressive girls and their parents. *Prevention Science, 11*, 229–238.

Welsh, B.C., Loeber, R., Stevens, B., Stouthamer-Loeber, M., Cohen, M.A., & Farrington, D.P. (2008). Costs of Juvenile Crime in Urban Areas: A Longitudinal Perspective. *Youth Violence and Juvenile Justice, 6*(1), 3–27.

CHAPTER TEN

UNDERSTANDING SOCIAL AGGRESSION IN ELEMENTARY SCHOOL GIRLS: IMPLICATIONS FOR INTERVENTION

TINA DANIELS AND DANIELLE QUIGLEY

Prior to 1990 only a handful of researchers considered the possibility that girls might be aggressive (R.B. Cairns & Cairns, 1984; Lagerspetz, Björkqvist, & Peltonen, 1988). This changed in the early 1990s when researchers began to talk and write about female aggression (Björkqvist & Niemela, 1992; Lagerspetz & Björkqvist, 1994). Researchers started to consider the possibility that girls could in fact be aggressive but that their aggression took a form aimed at hurting others' social relationships. The terms "indirect" (Lagerspetz & Björkqvist, 1994), "relational" (Crick & Grotpeter, 1995) and "social" (R.B. Cairns, Cairns, Neckerman, Ferguson, & Gariépy, 1989; Galen & Underwood, 1997) were used to describe different aspects of this type of covert, non-physical, relationship-based aggressive behaviour. Since then common beliefs and perceptions about female aggression have come under question as we have struggled to acknowledge and find ways to understand how girls use social aggression, what it means for them (Hadley, 2003), and how to effectively address it.

Since research into social and relational aggression began, there has been considerable confusion in the use of these two overlapping terms and they are frequently used interchangeably in the literature. Crick and her colleagues (Crick, 1997; Crick & Grotpeter, 1995) have identified relational aggression as behaviours that are intended to cause harm through manipulation or damage to another's social relationships or feelings of inclusion and acceptance. This includes angrily retaliating against a peer by excluding someone from the peer group, threatening to not be a person's friend anymore, or spreading hurtful rumours designed to alienate someone from the friendship group. Crick has identified the hurt in this form of aggression as damage to the relationship. In contrast, Underwood and colleagues (Galen & Underwood, 1997; Underwood, 2003) have used the term social aggression to refer to behaviours directed toward damaging another's self-esteem, social status, or both. She believes this type of aggression can be either direct or indirect. Direct forms include acts such as verbal rejection, facial expressions of distain, and body movements intended to be hurtful such as the cold shoulder, hair flip, or evil eye; and indirect forms include such things as cruel gossip, manipulation of friendship patterns, or social exclusion.

In general, social aggression, as Underwood (2003) defines it, represents a broader construct than relational aggression as defined by Crick (1997). Both terms, however, refer to hurtful acts that are perpetrated with the intent to cause harm that is social in nature whether it is damage to one's social relationships with others, damage to one's social position, and/or damage to one's self-esteem. Throughout this paper we will use the term social aggression (originally proposed by Cairns, Cairns, Neckerman, Ferguson, & Gariépy, 1989) to represent all non-physical socially-based forms of aggression.

UNDERSTANDING SOCIAL AGGRESSION

Often referred to as "girls' aggression" by the popular press, social aggression has often been portrayed as being only the foray of girls (Hadley, 2003). Recently however, two meta-analyses have been conducted to examine gender differences in this form of behaviour (referred to by these authors as indirect aggression: Archer, 2004; Card, Stucky, Sawalani, & Little, 2008). Both of these studies have demonstrated that the gender differences are not as large or as consistent as one might expect. It appears that within school-based samples the mean levels of social aggression may or may not differ between boys and girls depending on age, methodology, and setting (Archer, 2004) and that the differences are generally small.

Further examination of this issue suggests that when we move beyond comparing means across normative samples to examining children who are highly aggressive (more than one standard deviation above the mean) gender differences are evident. Spence (2002) found that the number of grades 4, 5, and 6 boys and girls identified by teacher ratings as extremely aggressive differed as a function of the form of aggression rated. Of all children identified as highly socially aggressive, 87% were girls whereas 94% of the highly physically aggressive children identified were boys. Of those who were identified as both extremely physically and socially aggressive 82% were boys and 18% were girls. These numbers suggest that for highly aggressive elementary school girls the aggression of choice is most frequently social aggression, although there is also a small group of girls who are both socially and physically aggressive. While in this study the largest majority of socially aggressive girls were not physically aggressive, other researchers have reported that when girls are highly physically aggressive they are very likely to be highly socially aggressive as well (Pepler, Jiang, Craig, & Connolly, 2009). This research suggests that if we are interested in understanding aggression in girls, in working with girls who are at risk, and in preventing high levels of aggression in girls, we need to better understand social aggression and its use by girls either as a sole aggression strategy or when combined with physical aggression.

Until now most treatment programs for aggressive girls have focused on those who are highly physically aggressive and on reducing the incidence of physically aggressive behaviour. In the past, physically aggressive girls were thought to be more severely disturbed than equally physically aggressive boys and were more likely to incur negative social sanctions and negative sentiments from peers and adults (Crick, 1997; Crick & Dodge, 1994). Now, however, it seems pertinent to consider the use of social aggression as a risk factor for girls and to develop prevention and intervention programs for girls who are at risk for this form of aggression. Although there is a need to know more about social aggression in boys, the goal of this chapter is to profile what we know about social aggression as it relates to girls in order to inform best practices for those who work with girls engaged in high levels of this behaviour.

Many adults believe that social aggression is not an important concern for girls' development, but there is now evidence that social aggression can have serious repercussions for perpetrators and recipients, as well as for those who are drawn into the conflict. For girls who are the focus of socially aggressive behaviours, a host of adjustment problems have been reported including: peer rejection, peer relationship problems, and low peer acceptance (Crick, Casas, & Ku, 1999); social anxiety (Craig, 1998); depression symptoms and low self-esteem (Prinstein, Boergers, & Vernberg, 2001); social avoidance, loneliness, psychological distress, self-restraint issues, and internalizing and externalizing difficulties (Crick & Nelson, 2002).

For children who perpetrate socially aggressive behaviours, a host of adjustment problems have also been identified including social anxiety

(Craig, 1998), peer rejection and loneliness (Crick & Bigbee, 1998; Crick & Grotpeter, 1995), depression (Crick & Grotpeter, 1995; van der Wal, de Wit, & Hirasing, 2003), isolation (Crick & Grotpeter, 1995), teacher-perceived maladjustment (Crick, 1997; Murray-Close, Ostrov, & Crick, 2007), delinquency (Crick, 1997), anti-social behaviour (Werner & Crick, 1999), and symptoms of oppositional defiant disorder and conduct disorder (Prinstein et al., 2001). Comorbid problems can be particularly serious, including self-harm and eating disordered behaviour (Sourander et al., 2006; Werner & Crick, 1999), as well as personality disorders and symptoms of borderline personality disorder (Crick, Murray-Close, & Woods, 2005; Werner & Crick, 1999).

Affiliating with a socially aggressive peer can also cause problems for youth. For example, girls in middle childhood who befriended socially aggressive peers were found to engage in higher levels of social aggression a year later compared to those who did not have this experience (Werner & Crick, 2004). In addition, the friendships of highly socially aggressive girls are characterized by negative behaviours such as high levels of exclusivity, jealousy, and social victimization (Grotpeter & Crick, 1996; Daniels, Quigley, Menard, & Spence, 2010).

These problems of both an internalizing and externalizing nature have been identified most commonly in early and middle childhood (Geiger, Zimmer-Gembeck, & Crick, 2003) and have been found to continue well into adulthood (Anderson, 2005; Werner & Crick, 1999). Such long-term negative effects for the perpetrators of social aggression, as well as those who are targeted and their friends, support an argument for the development and implementation of research-informed interventions for elementary school girls.

The developmental trajectories of social aggression are only just starting to be explored and our understanding is not as well developed as that of physical aggression. There is, however, clear evidence that girls come to view social aggression as a more normative form of angry behaviour as they move through middle elementary school (Crick, Bigbee, & Howes, 1996). The incidence of social aggression has been found to increase through the fourth and fifth grades for girls (Murray-Close et al., 2007). Increases in intimate exchange between friends were found to be associated with these increases in social aggression over this time period. These findings support the idea that the social context of girls during this developmental period may facilitate the use of socially aggressive strategies. As cognitive capacity, verbal skills, and perspective taking increase, girls are better able to recall specific information and to retaliate in response to past events and perceived slights. In addition, increasing knowledge of others' intimate information may provide an opportunity for the use of socially aggressive behaviours. Thus middle elementary school years, especially grades 4 and 5, may provide a critical and opportune age for the initiation of socially aggressive acts and thus an ideal time for prevention and intervention efforts.

At present most of what we know about the inner workings of social aggression within girls' groups is based on the qualitative work of Owens and his colleagues (Owens, Shute, & Slee, 2000; Owens, Slee, & Shute, 2000). They have found that girls report using socially aggressive behaviours to alleviate boredom and create excitement, to seek attention from their peers, to be included in the group, to belong to the right group, to respond to jealousy they experience over friendships or romantic relationships, to secure self-protection, and to seek revenge for a perceived slight. The use of socially aggressive strategies as a function of these motivations leads to highly desirable ends for many girls including popularity, status, power, and control (Vaillancourt, Hymel, & McDougall, 2003). Thus, addressing these needs is a great but critical challenge for any intervention. If interventions are going to be effective, they must focus on replacing this source of power and control with a more socially desirable alternative. Also, to promote girls' use of more prosocial behavioural strategies, there must be an alternative way for girls to meet these overriding needs.

The motivations and goals for the use of social aggression differ from those held for physical aggression. Delveaux and Daniels (2000) found that children's key motivations in using socially aggressive strategies to resolve conflict were to avoid getting in trouble with adults, while at the same time maintaining their relationship with the rest of the peer group. Our most recent research in the prediction of social aggression (Quigley, 2008) indicates that the underlying motivations for the use of social aggression also differ as a function of context. Children reported that they would be motivated to use socially aggressive strategies in response to the threat of an interloper in their best friendship as a function of jealousy (this was especially true for girls) and anger. In contrast, in the larger peer group, children's desire for power over others predicted their use of socially aggressive strategies. Clearly, jealousy, anger, and the desire for power over others are important areas of focus for prevention and intervention programs and the context within which these behaviours take place is an important consideration as well.

In summary, children identify social aggression as a distinct form of aggression, the intent of which is to cause harm by damaging someone's social relationships or self-esteem. Highly aggressive middle-school girls tend to use social aggression rather than physical aggression. The use of this social form of aggression increases with age and is particularly evident in grades 4 and 5. The ramifications of being the perpetrator or recipient of social aggression, or a friend of a socially aggressive girl, all predict to both short- and long-term poor prognoses. Furthermore, the use of social aggression is related to avoiding being detected by teachers or peers while at the same time achieving self-interest, control, and revenge goals. The peer group is important to those who perpetrate socially aggressive behaviours and to the individuals' ability use socially aggressive strategies. This form of aggression is often used to control the dynamic of the peer group, and aggressors are only able to be aggressive with the cooperation of the group. Xie (1998) notes that although most physical aggression takes place within the dyad, the majority of conflicts involving social aggression have a triangular or even more complicated social structure. Thus, understanding the relationship aspect of social aggression may be critical to enabling us to develop effective, successful intervention programs for those who perpetrate or experience acts of social aggression. Taken together, what does all this mean in terms of our intervention efforts?

INTERVENING

Intervention approaches to social aggression are currently just starting to be developed. Ten years ago, Geiger et al. (2003) suggested that we were at a point where researchers could begin to direct the design, implementation, and evaluation of small-scale intensive interventions as well as larger information campaigns. At the same time, they noted that we should move forward cautiously as our knowledge of the antecedents of social aggression was limited.

To date there have been five published prevention/intervention programs that have been developed to address social aggression in middle-elementary school girls and they are at various stages of implementation and evaluation. These programs include the Social Aggression Prevention Program (SAPP; Cappella & Weinstein, 2006), Club Ophelia (Dellasega & Adamshick, 2005), the Friend-to-Friend (F2F) program (Leff et al., 2007), the Psychoeducational group for aggressive adolescent girls (Cummings, Hoffman, & Leschied, 2004), and the Girls United program (Girl Guides of Canada; Daniels & Quigley, 2009). What can we learn from these first intervention attempts designed to address social aggression in girls' groups that can help to inform future endeavours? We review these programs in an effort to develop a set of best practices for addressing social aggression among girls.

Table 10.1 summarizes the various aspects and components of each of these programs and enables comparisons across the five programs.

TABLE 10.1   SUMMARY OF SOCIAL AGGRESSION PROGRAM SPECIFICS

	Focus	Target	Grade	Age	Gender	Total Sessions	Mins/session	Sessions/wk	Location	Qualif. of facilitators	# Facilitators	Structure	Activities	Goals	Peer Mentors
SAPP	P	All girls	4, 5, 6	10.5	G	10	40	1	S	C	1	SG 4–7	C/D/G/M/RP	1/2/3/4/5	N
Club Ophelia	P	Referred SAG or self-selected	Middle school	13.2	G	12	40	1	S	C/T	2	SG 5–8	A/AB/D/G/RP	1/2/3/4/6/12/13	Y
Friend-to-Friend	I	SAG + pos. role models	3, 4, 5		G	20 + 8	30	2	S	R/T	2	CB and SG 8–10	A/CA/F/M/V	1/5/6/13/14	Y
Psycho-educational	I	SAG in residential care	Middle school	14.7	G	8	60	2	R	C	2	SG 8	AB/D/G/RP	1/5/7/8/9/10/11	N
Girls United	P	All girls	1–8	5–16	G	2–3	60	1	C	T	2	SG 8–12	A/C/D/G/RP/V	1/2/3/4/5/6/7/9/10/11/12/13/14	Y

Legend:

SAPP = Social Aggression Prevention Program (Cappella & Weinstein, 2006)
Club = Club Ophelia (Dellasega & Adamshick, 2005; Nixon & Werner, 2010)
Ophelia
Friend-to-Friend = Friend-to-Friend (Leff, Angelucci, Goldstein, Cardaciotto, Paskewich, & Grossman, 2007)
Psycho-educational = Psychoeducational Group for Aggressive Adolescent Girls (Cummings, Hoffman, & Leschied, 2004)
Girls United = Girls United Program (Daniels & Quigley, 2009)

Focus = intervention (I) or prevention (P)
Target = highly socially aggressive girls (SAG) or all girls
Grade = grade of students program is designed for
Age = age (mean age of sample evaluated)
Gender = program is designed for girls only (G) or everyone (E)
Total Sessions = number of sessions for total program
Mins/session = minutes per session
Sessions/wk = number of sessions per week
Location = where activities took place (C = community, R = residential centre, S = school)
Qualif. of facilitators = qualifications of the program facilitator (C = counsellor, R = researcher, T = teacher)
# Facilitators = number of facilitators per group
Structure = structure of program administration (CB = classroom-based, SG = small group; numbers represent size of group)
Activities = List of activities used in program (A = assignments, AB = art-based activities, C = collaboration, CA = cartoons, D = discussion, F = participant-led facilitation, G = games, M = modelling, RP = role-playing, V = videos)
Goals = Goals of the program (1 = increase knowledge of social aggression [SA] or recognize different types of aggression, 2 = build emotional understanding of oneself and others, 3 = promote positive communication and behaviour, 4 = provide opportunities to observe, model, and practise social skills, 5 = teach social problem-solving, 6 = find less aggressive solutions to conflict situations, 7 = understand gender role socialization and its effects, 8 = understand impact of violence on their lives, 9 = teach prosocial coping strategies, 10 = promote positive self-image, 11 = promote safe space in which girls can relate and talk about experiences, 12 = promote healthy relationships, 13 = challenge existing normative beliefs related to SA, 14 = reduce level of SA)
Peer Mentors = Peer mentoring used in the program? Yes (Y) or No (N)

Table 10.2 summarizes the results of the evaluations that have been conducted on four of the programs. The Girls United program does not yet have a published evaluation. Each aspect of these five programs was considered and the relationship between program elements and results was examined. Based on the evaluation results and the researchers' observations, a set of best practices was extracted from these studies and these best practices are discussed below.

TABLE 10.2   RESULTS OF EVALUATIONS

	N	Measures	Data	Control	Participants	Outcome
1. SAPP	134	• Peer report social behaviour questionnaire • SPS scale • Self-report thoughts and feelings survey • Teacher ratings of behaviour and achievement	T	Y	V	• Improved SPS for all subjects • More prosocial behaviour and empathy and less SA for high SA subgroup
2. Club Ophelia	42	• Girls Relationship Scale (GRS) • knowledge about relationships • beliefs about self • beliefs about relationships • self-report of SA	S	N	R/V	No significant differences found although outcomes were in the expected direction
3. Friend-to-Friend	32	• Children's Social Behaviour Questionnaire (Crick, 1996) • Hostile Attribution Bias measure (Crick, 1995) • Loneliness Scale (Asher & Wheeler, 1985) • Depression Inventory (Kovacs, 1985)	S/T	Y	R	Decrease in teacher reports of RA, decrease in teacher reports of PA, increase in teacher ratings of likeability, decrease in hostile attributions, decrease in loneliness compared to control group, slight decrease in depression
4. Psycho-educational	8	• Beliefs and Attitude Scale (Butler & Leschied, 1997)	S	N	R	Significantly fewer anti-social beliefs

Legend:

1 = Social Aggression Prevention Program (Cappella & Weinstein, 2006)
2 = Club Ophelia (Dellasega & Adamshick, 2005; Nixon & Werner, 2010)
3 = Friend-to-Friend (Leff, Angelucci, Goldstein, Cardaciotto, Paskewich, & Grossman, 2007; Leff, Gullan, Paskewich, Abdul-Kabir, Jawad, Grossman, Munro, & Power, 2009)
4 = Psychoeducational Group for Aggressive Adolescent Girls (Cummings, Hoffman, & Leschied, 2004)

N = sample size for evaluation
Measures = outcome measures
Data = source of data (S = Self-report, T = Teacher)
Control = control group used for evaluation (Y = Yes, N = No)
Participants = source of subjects (R = Referral, V = Volunteer)

Recommendations for Best Practices

The five programs highlighted in the tables above together provide some preliminary suggestions for best practices for the intervention and prevention of social aggression. We have extracted seven key recommendations from this body of research and propose that a prevention or intervention program will be most effective when these are in place. They include developing programs that: (1) focus only on girls, (2) focus on early intervention, (3) address all girls' needs not just highly socially aggressive girls, (4) involve multiple sessions over a 2–3 month period, (5) use female peer mentors, (6) build an awareness of the problem, and (7) focus on strengthening skills that are that are incompatible with the use of social aggression. Each of these recommendations is discussed below.

1. Programs should include only girls

While it is true that both boys and girls are targets and perpetrators of social aggression, the study of these behaviours and experiences has developed to the point that we now understand that boys and girls may experience these events differently (Crick, Bigbee, & Howes, 1996), and as such it is important that we take a gender-sensitive approach to intervention and prevention techniques. Also it is apparent that in order for girls to feel comfortable in speaking and talking about their experiences they do not want boys present in the group. All the programs reviewed to date were designed specifically for girls. This is not to say that boys would not benefit from similar programs, but that the groups should be run separately.

Walsh, Pepler, and Levene's (2002) research findings support this suggestion. They evaluated an intervention program called Earlscourt Girls Connection, a program for girls with conduct problems run by the Toronto-based Earlscourt Child and Family Centre. Although the Centre initially began their program as a gender-neutral one, it was met with high attrition rates and increased aggression among the girls. These negative outcomes prompted a gender-specific redesign of the program and, when stringently evaluated, the researchers found that girls' externalizing and internalizing behaviours decreased and their prosocial behaviours increased. Girls may feel more relaxed about expressing honest feelings about themselves without boys present in the group. Girl-only groups also allow for the creation of a safe space for girls and provide an opportunity to cater to the needs of girls.

2. Early intervention, ideally in grades 4 and 5, is better than later intervention

Intervention is most successful if it is implemented early in the history of the group and early in the child's life. Of the five intervention programs summarized, all focused on the middle elementary school years. Leff et al. (2007) targeted girls in grades 3 through 5; Dellasega and Adamshick (2005) focused on girls in middle school; and Cappella and Weinstein (2006) recommended intervening when girls were in fifth grade so that they are capable of recognizing social aggression (having had limited experience with it) but do not yet have long-standing histories of receiving and/or perpetrating acts of social aggression. We have found that girls in grades 4 and 5 are particularly receptive to participating in discussions about social aggression and the dynamics of girls' groups, and are willing and able to change their behaviour. By grades 7 and 8 we have found that attitudes are more severely entrenched and change is harder to achieve.

3. Programs should be designed to address all girls rather than targeting only highly socially aggressive girls

Two of the intervention programs summarized chose to target the larger population of girls while three programs targeted only highly socially aggressive girls. One of the three programs that targeted socially aggressive girls (Leff et al., 2007) reported that it was critical that other non-aggressive girls be included in the intervention to provide prosocial models. Cappella and Weinstein (2006) reported that "the universal inclusion of all girls in their programme…may have been critical, allowing teaching and modelling to occur between participants as well as from the group leader" (p. 454).

Social aggression is not a problem with the individual, but rather, it is a problem in the functioning of the dynamic of the group within which the girl is situated. Thus interventions need to focus on all members of the group. If a targeted intervention is preferred or felt necessary we caution against singling out socially aggressive girls, as it is the entire group dynamic that needs to shift. A targeted intervention should include all of the girls within the group that is experiencing conflicts of a socially aggressive nature so that the ecology of the group may evolve into one that fosters healthy, positive relationships. If your program is specifically focused on highly socially aggressive girls, be aware of the need to include prosocial role models. Cappella and Weinstein (2006) highlight that including female classmates in a flexible small group program that focuses on the perspective of multiple peers' experiences within girls conflicts can have a positive impact especially for girls with the most problems.

4. Programs should spread their sessions out over a minimum of 10 weeks

Three of the programs summarized were implemented over a 10- to 12-week period. Cappella and Weinstein (2006) provided 40-minute sessions once a week for 10 weeks; Leff et al. (2007) offered 30- to 35-minute sessions twice a week for 10 weeks; and Dellasega and Adamshick (2005) provided 40-minute weekly sessions for 12 weeks. Thus it appears that effective programs require intensive programming over an extended period of time.

Research also suggests that blitzing the material over a short period of time such as a two-day workshop does not lead to lasting effects. In 2005, the 10-week Club Ophelia program was compared to a program similar in content but completed over two days (Nixon & Werner, 2010). Evaluations showed an initial decrease in social aggression in both groups, but those who participated in the two-day program showed a return to the original level of social aggression at subsequent follow-up. In contrast, a significant long-term (12-week post-test) decrease in these behaviours was found for the 10-week program. Children may need time to digest the material and information provided as well as to observe and reflect on the program before change can be achieved. Thus it is recommended that programs be implemented over a 2–3 month period, meeting at least once a week.

5. Female peer mentors may be more effective than adult instructors

Three of the programs reviewed (SAPP, F2F, and Club Ophelia) utilized peer mentors to model prosocial behaviour and reported it as being critical to the program's success. In addition, Salmivalli (2001) has reported that female mentors were effective in achieving positive change for grade 7 girls when implementing an anti-bullying program that focused on verbal and social bullying as well as physical bullying.

6. Focus on awareness of the problem as a first step

There is good evidence to suggest that promoting awareness may be an important first step in addressing issues of social aggression (Geiger et al., 2003). Promoting awareness of the problem among parents and teachers is critical, as adult attitudes will shape child behaviour. Promoting awareness among the peer group in order to mobilize the bystanders may also be effective as has been shown with anti-bullying programs (Salmivalli & Voeten, 2004). Whether specific programs are needed that focus only on social aggression or whether including a focus on social aggression in already existing anti-bullying programs can be equally as effective remains to be seen.

7. Build skills that are incompatible with the use of social aggression

Program content should include questioning beliefs about the normative role that social aggression can play in some girls' lives (Daniels & Quigley, 2009; Dellasega & Adamshick, 2005; Leff, Angelucci, Goldstein, Cardaciotto, Paskewich, & Grossman, 2007; Leff et al., 2009; Nixon & Werner, 2010). Unrealistic expectations for friendships and socio-cultural pressures that may drive aggression underground should be explored, as well as focusing on developing skills incompatible with social aggression such as empathy, acceptance of diversity, and inclusion. Emphasis can be placed on finding other activities and interests to keep girls actively involved, as boredom and excitement are reported by girls as some of the reason why they use these behaviours (Owens, Shute, & Slee, 2000). Finally, efforts must be made to meet the needs of intimacy, group belonging, and group cohesion, as well as the power and status that can be achieved by the use of social aggression. Unless these needs can be met in other ways, social aggression will continue to be used within the group.

CONCLUSION

Adults often find it difficult to believe that girls who are otherwise popular and nice can be mean to a friend. Some think that children need to learn to handle these things themselves while others believe that girls' conflicts are "normal" and they minimize the seriousness of such behaviour. At this point in time, however, there is adequate research to demonstrate that social aggression interferes with success at essential developmental tasks of middle childhood: for both those who receive and perpetrate social aggression, it adversely affects the forming and maintaining of intimate, close relationships, and it facilitates the development of internalizing and externalizing difficulties including psychiatric symptoms in young adulthood (Geiger et al., 2003). It is critical that adults recognize this behaviour as aggressive in intent and focus on helping girls to deal with it in effective ways. It is still early in the study of social aggression and some may feel it is too soon to be developing intervention programs, but the need is there. Care and caution is advised in this endeavour (Geiger et al., 2003). We believe that we are ready to move forward, but intervention programs must be carefully developed using strategies that have been informed by research and evaluated systematically. To date, interventions have been modestly successful. As we think about moving forward, this paper is a call for more research-based interventions to address social aggression in girls' friendships that include comprehensive evaluations.

We dedicate this chapter to our friend and mentor Dr. Nicki Crick, whose pioneering work greatly influenced our thinking in this field.

NOTE

Correspondence concerning this chapter should be directed to Tina Daniels, Department of Psychology, Carleton University, Ottawa. Email: tina_daniels@carleton.ca.

REFERENCES

Anderson, M.N. (2005). *Long-term effects on the psychosocial adjustment of women who have experienced social victimization as young girls: A qualitative research study* (Unpublished doctoral dissertation). Argosy University, Seattle.

Archer, J. (2004). Sex differences in aggression in real-world settings: A meta-analytic review. *Review of General Psychology, 8*(4), 291–322.

Asher, S.R., & Wheeler, V.A. (1985). Children's loneliness: A comparison of rejected and neglected peer status. *Journal of Consulting and Clinical Psychology, 53*, 500–505.

Björkqvist, K., & Niemela, P. (Eds.). (1992). *Of mice and women: Aspects of female aggression*. San Diego, CA: Academic Press.

Butler, S., & Leschied, A.W. (1997). The Beliefs and Attitudes Scale. Unpublished manuscript, Clarke Institute, Toronto, ON.

Cairns, R.B., & Cairns, B.D. (1984). Predicting aggressive patterns in girls and boys: A developmental study. *Aggressive Behaviour, 10,* 227–242.

Cairns, R.B., Cairns, B.D., Neckerman, H., Ferguson, L., & Gariépy, J. (1989). Growth and aggression: 1. Childhood to early adolescence. *Developmental Psychology, 25,* 320–330.

Cappella, E., & Weinstein, R. (2006). The prevention of social aggression among girls. *Social Development, 15*(3), 434–462.

Card, N.A., Stucky, B.D., Sawalani, G.M., & Little, T.D. (2008). Direct and indirect aggression during childhood and adolescence: A meta-analytic review of gender differences, intercorrelations, and relations to maladjustment. *Child Development, 79*(5), 1185–1229.

Craig, W.M. (1998). The relationship among bullying, victimization, depression, anxiety, and aggression in elementary school children. *Personality and Individual Differences, 24,* 123–130.

Crick, N.R. (1995). Relational aggression: The role of intent attributions, feelings of distress, and provocation type. *Development and Psychopathology, 7,* 313–322.

Crick, N.R. (1997). Engagement in gender normative versus gender non-normative forms of aggression: Links to social-psychological adjustment. *Developmental Psychology, 33,* 610–617.

Crick, N.R., & Bigbee, M.A. (1998). Relational and overt forms of peer victimization: A multi-informant approach. *Journal of Consulting and Clinical Psychology, 66*(2), 337–347.

Crick, N.R., Bigbee, M.A., & Howes, C. (1996). Children's normative beliefs about aggression: How do I hurt thee? Let me count the ways. *Child Development, 67,* 1003–1014.

Crick, N.R., Casas, J.F., & Ku, H.C. (1999). Relational and physical forms of peer victimization in preschool. *Developmental Psychology, 35*(2), 376–385.

Crick, N.R., & Dodge, K. (1994). A review and reformulation of social-information processing mechanisms in children's social adjustment. *Psychological Bulletin, 115,* 74–101.

Crick, N.R., & Grotpeter, J. (1995). Relational aggression, gender, and social-psychological adjustment. *Child Development, 66,* 710–722.

Crick, N.R., Murray-Close, D., & Woods, K. (2005). Borderline personality features in childhood: A short-term longitudinal study. *Development and Psychopathology, 17,* 1051–1070.

Crick, N.R., & Nelson, D.A. (2002). Relational and physical victimization within friendships: Nobody told me there'd be friends like these. *Journal of Abnormal Child Psychology, 30*(6), 599–607.

Cummings, A., Hoffman, S., & Leschied, A. (2004). A psychoeducational group for aggressive adolescent girls. *Journal for Specialists in Group Work, 29*(3), 285–299.

Daniels, T., & Quigley, D. (2009). Girls United: Creating a nation-wide intervention program to address the use of social aggression within girls' groups. In W. Craig, D. Pepler, & J. Cummings (Eds.), *Rise up for respectful relationships: Prevent bullying* (pp. 145–167). Ottawa: National Printers.

Daniels, T., Quigley, D., Menard, L., & Spence, L. (2010). "My best friend always did and still does betray me constantly": Examining relational and physical victimization within a dyadic friendship context. *Canadian Journal of School Psychology, 25*(1), 70–83.

Dellasega, C., & Adamshick, P. (2005). Evaluation of a program designed to reduce relational aggression in middle-school girls. *Journal of School Violence, 4*(3), 63–76.

Delveaux, K.D., & Daniels, T. (2000). Children's social cognitions: Physically and relationally aggressive strategies and children's goals in peer conflict situations. *Merrill-Palmer Quarterly, 46*(4), 672–692.

Galen, B.R., & Underwood, M. (1997). A developmental investigation of social aggression among children. *Developmental Psychology, 33*(4), 589–600.

Geiger, T., Zimmer-Gembeck, M., & Crick, N. (2003). The science of relational aggression: Can we guide intervention? In M. Moretti, C. Odgers, & M. Jackson (Eds.), *Girls and aggression: Contributing factors and intervention principals* (pp. 27–40). New York: Kluwer Academic/Plenum.

Grotpeter, J.K., & Crick, N.R. (1996). Relational aggression, overt aggression, and friendship. *Child Development, 67*, 2328–2338.

Hadley, M. (2003). Relational, indirect, adaptive or just mean: Recent work on aggression in adolescent girls—Part I. *Studies in Gender and Sexuality, 4*(4), 367–394.

Kovacs, M. (1985). The Children's Depression Inventory. *Psychopharmacology Bulletin, 21*, 995–998.

Lagerspetz, K.M., & Björkqvist, K. (1994). Indirect aggression in boys and girls. In L.R. Huesmann (Ed.), *Aggressive behaviour: Current perspectives* (pp. 131–150). New York: Plenum Press.

Lagerspetz, K.M., Björkqvist, K., & Peltonen, T. (1988). Is indirect aggression typical of females? Gender differences in aggressiveness in 11- to 12-year-old children. *Aggressive Behaviour, 14*, 403–414.

Leff, S., Angelucci, J., Goldstein, A.B., Cardaciotto, L., Paskewich, B., & Grossman, M.B. (2007). Using a participatory action research model to create a school-based intervention program for relationally aggressive girls—The Friend to Friend Program. In J.E. Zins, M.J. Elias, & C.A. Maher (Eds.), *Bullying, victimization, and peer harassment: A handbook of prevention and intervention* (pp. 199–218). New York: Haworth Press.

Leff, S.S., Gullan, R.L., Paskewich, B.S., Abdul-Kabir, S., Jawad, A.F., Grossman, M., . . . Power, T.J. (2009). An initial evaluation of a culturally adaptive social problem solving and relational aggression prevention program for urban African American relationally aggressive girls. *Journal of Prevention and Intervention in the Community, 37*(4), 260–274.

Murray-Close, D., Ostrov, J.M., & Crick, N.R. (2007). A short-term longitudinal study of growth of relational aggression during middle childhood: Associations with gender, friendship intimacy and internalizing problems. *Development and Psychopathology, 19*, 187–203.

Nixon, C.L., & Werner, N.E. (2010). Reducing adolescents' involvement with relational aggression: Evaluating the effectiveness of the Creating a Safe School (CASS) intervention. *Psychology in the Schools, 47*(6), 606–620.

Owens, L., Shute, P., & Slee, R. (2000). "Guess what I just heard!": Indirect aggression among teenage girls. *Aggressive Behavior, 26*, 67–83.

Owens, L., Shute, R., & Slee, P. (2000). "I'm in and you're out ..." Explanations for teenage girls' indirect aggression. *Psychology, Evolution & Gender, 2*, 19–46.

Pepler, D., Jiang, D., Craig, W., & Connolly, J. (2009, April). Developmental trajectories of physical and relational aggression: Gender differences and associated factors. In E. Menesini & C. Spiel (Chairs), Patterns of aggressive behaviour in adolescence: Contextual and longitudinal correlates. Symposium conducted at the Society for Research in Child Development 2009 Biennial Meeting, Denver, CO.

Prinstein, M.J., Boergers, J., & Vernberg, E.M. (2001). Overt and relational aggression in adolescents: Social-psychological adjustment of aggressors and victims. *Journal of Clinical Child Psychology, 30*(4), 479–491.

Quigley, D. (2008). Behind the hurt: Children's underlying emotions and desires and their reported use of relationally as compared to physically aggressive strategies. (Unpublished master's thesis). Carleton University, Ottawa.

Salmivalli, C. (2001). Peer-led intervention campaign against school bullying: Who considered it useful, who benefited? *Educational Research, 43*(3), 263–278.

Salmivalli, C., & Voeten, M. (2004). Connections between attitudes, group norms, and behavior in bullying situations. *International Journal of Behavioral Development, 28*(3), 246–258.

Sourander, A., Aromaa, M., Pihlakoski, A., Haavisto, A., Rantava, P., Helenius, H., & Sillanpaa, M. (2006). Early predictors of deliberate self-harm among adolescents: A prospective follow-up study from age 3 to age 15. *Journal of Affective Disorder, 93*(1–3), 87–96.

Spence, L. (2002). The dynamics of relationally aggressive girls' friendships and social networks. (Unpublished doctoral dissertation). Carleton University, Ottawa.

Underwood, M. (2003). Social aggression among girls. New York: Guilford Press.

Vaillancourt, T., Hymel, S., & McDougall, P. (2003). Bullying is power: Implications for school-based intervention strategies. *Journal of Applied School Psychology, 19*(2), 157–176.

van der Wal, M.F., de Wit, C.A., & Hirasing, R.A. (2003). Psychosocial health among young victims and offenders of direct and indirect bullying. *Pediatrics, 111*, 1312–1317.

Walsh, M.M., Pepler, D.J., & Levene, K.S. (2002). A model intervention for girls with disruptive behaviour problems: The Earlscourt Girls Connection. *Canadian Journal of Counselling, 36*(4), 297–311.

Werner, N.E., & Crick, N.R. (1999). Relational aggression and social psychological adjustment in a college sample. *Journal of Abnormal Psychology, 108*(4), 615–623.

Werner, N.E., & Crick, N.R. (2004). Maladaptive peer relationships and the development of relational and physical aggression during middle school. *Social Development, 13*(4), 495–512.

Xie, H. (1998). The development and functions of social aggression: A narrative analysis of social exchange in interpersonal conflicts. (Unpublished doctoral dissertation). University of North Carolina, Chapel Hill, NC.

Xie, H., Cairns, B., & Cairns, R. (2005). The development of aggressive behaviours among girls: Measurement issues, social functions, and differential trajectories. In D. Pepler, K. Madsen, C. Webster, & K. Leven (Eds.), *Development and treatment of girlhood aggression* (pp. 105–136). Mahwah, NJ: Lawrence Erlbaum Associates.

Xie, H., Cairns, R.B. & Cairns, B.D. (2002). The development of social aggression and physical aggression: A narrative analysis of interpersonal conflicts. *Aggressive Behavior, 28*(5), 341–355.

CHAPTER ELEVEN

REDUCING RISK OF ADOLESCENT AGGRESSION AND VIOLENCE: A BRIEF ATTACHMENT-FOCUSED TREATMENT PROGRAM FOR PARENTS AND CAREGIVERS

MARLENE M. MORETTI

CIHR SENIOR RESEARCH CHAIR, DEPARTMENT OF PSYCHOLOGY,
SIMON FRASER UNIVERSITY

AND

INGRID OBSUTH

DEPARTMENT OF PSYCHIATRY, HARVARD MEDICAL SCHOOL,
AND DEPARTMENT OF PSYCHOLOGY,
SIMON FRASER UNIVERSITY

Rates of aggression and violence in children, teens, and young adults remain a pressing concern in the vast majority of developed countries. Canada is no exception. From 1997 to 2006, violent crime rates among youth in Canada increased by 12%, setting them 30% higher than those recorded in 1991 (Milligan, 2008). Youth charges for assault accounted for the bulk of this increase, representing 80% of apprehensions for violent crime in 2006. Among assault charges, a 21% increase occurred for aggravated assault and a 40% increase for assault with a weapon. Homicides also increased by 41%; however, they accounted for less than 1% of violent youth crime with fewer than 100 youth charged per year.

Rates of bullying and victimization in school contexts also remain at high levels. In a 2006 survey of Canadian youth in grades 6 to 9 conducted as part of the International Youth Health Survey, students responded to questions about bullying at school, assaults requiring medical assistance, threats of extortion, and being the victim of theft (Savoie, 2007). Over 40% reported victimization in the 12 months preceding the survey, with two thirds of these students reporting repeated victimization. Perpetration of violent behaviours was also high with 13% of students admitting to carrying a weapon. Students reported that they typically began engaging in these behaviours at age 12 or 13. These results are generally consistent with the 2007 Ontario Student Drug Use and Health Survey (Adlaf, Paglia-Boak, Beitchman, & Wolfe, 2007) of students in grades 7 to 12, in which 9% of students reported carrying a weapon in the past 12 months; 11% reported perpetrating an assault; and 5% reported engaging in gang-related violence. Canada is certainly not alone with respect to the problem of youth violence and bullying. In a 2005 report by the United States Center for Disease Control (CDC, 2006), 35.9% of youth in grades 9 to 12 reported being in a physical fight in the preceding 12 months and 18.5% reported carrying a weapon (gun, knife, or club) within the preceding 30 days.

Although many assume that aggression and violence is a problem restricted primarily to boys, the past two decades of research have shown otherwise. Rates of violent offending continue to remain substantially higher for boys, but trends show that female violent offending is increasing disproportionately in Canada, the US, and elsewhere (Adlaf et al., 2007; Snyder & Sickmund, 2006). The shrinking gap between boys and girls in rates of violence is concerning, particularly in conjunction with recent studies of young women's aggressive behaviour in romantic relationships. For example, Straus and Ramirez (2007) found that severe physical attacks toward romantic partners among young adults were comparable for males (11.0%) and females (11.6%). In cases where only one partner reported engaging in severe aggressive acts, it was substantially more likely to be the female (29.8%) rather than male partner (13.7%). These findings concur with Archer's (2000) conclusion based on his meta-analytic review of 82 studies examining sex differences in perpetration of intimate partner violence: women were slightly more likely than men to perpetrate violence toward their partners, but also slightly more likely to be injured in violent partner altercations. In sum, youth violence continues to present a significant challenge nationally and internationally.

The economic costs of youth violence, including social and criminal justice services, are substantial and rising. These costs extend into the future because of long-term social, economic, and health related problems that emerge as high-risk violent youth mature into adulthood (e.g., Trulson, Marquart, Mullings, & Caeti, 2005), and are particularly concerning when one considers associated costs of increased risk for partner and child abuse (e.g., Gebo, 2007; Thornberry, 2005). Prevention is clearly a priority, but risk reduction programs are also important. It is imperative that these programs draw from the most compelling research evidence and target factors with clear concurrent and prospective relations to risk onset and/ or exacerbation. Furthermore, given the rising rates of female aggression and violence, intervention programs need to target risk factors that are relevant to both girls and boys. Gender-tailored programs may be necessary in some domains; however, we also emphasize that there are many risk and protective factors in common across girls and boys and these should not be disregarded.

Some factors that increase risk for aggression and violence in children and teens are immutable, such as difficult temperament (van Zeijl et al., 2007), but exposure to socially determined risk factors can be altered. Family influences, including adverse parenting behaviour and exposure to family violence, have garnered much attention in research on the roots of aggression and violence. In this chapter, we discuss the facets of parenting and parent–child relationships that may pose risk for aggression and violence in teens. Our discussion focuses on how parenting behaviours shape children's attachment representations, which in turn regulate children's cognitive, affective, and behavioural functioning, particularly in interpersonal contexts. We move from research to intervention, provide a rationale for a brief manualized program that supports parents and caregivers of high-risk teens, and present evidence of its effectiveness across communities in Canada.

PARENTING AND CHILD AND ADOLESCENT AGGRESSION

Research on parenting styles has consistently revealed key features that either place children at risk or buffer them from adversity with respect to social-psychological health in general, and aggression and violence in particular. Parenting characterized by high warmth, behavioural control, and autonomy promotion—that is, "authoritative parenting"—predicts a range of positive child outcomes (e.g., Dornbusch, Ritter, Leiderman, Roberts, & Fraleigh, 1987; Maccoby & Martin, 1983). In contrast, parenting that is low in warmth, high in behavioural control, and low in autonomy promotion—that is, "authoritarian parenting"—places children at risk for many negative outcomes, including aggression (Barber, 2002; Grolnick, 2003). Similarly, children suffer when parenting is neglectful or disengaged, low in warmth, and low in behavioural control and autonomy promotion (Baumrind, 1972; Brown & Whiteside, 2008; Gray & Steinberg, 1999; Steinberg, Lamborn, Darling, Mounts, & Dornbush, 1994).

Looking more specifically at the components of general parenting styles, distinct parenting behaviours have been shown to predict child outcomes (Steinberg, Elmen, & Mounts, 1989). The most robust finding in this regard is the central importance of parental warmth as a protective factor across childhood age, sex, and culture (Khaleque & Rohner, 2002; Scaramella, Conger, & Simons, 1999; Stattin & Kerr, 2000). Parental warmth protects youth from developing aggressive behaviours during adolescence and prospectively buffers them from responding to conflict with aggression (Scaramella et al., 1999).

A number of other aspects of parent–child relationships and family functioning have deep and lasting effects on child and adolescent aggression and violence. Most important among these is exposure to family violence. Meta-analytic reviews clearly show that exposure to family violence is concurrently and prospectively related to increased risk for aggression and violence in childhood and adolescence (Kitzmann, Gaylord, Holt, & Kenny, 2003). Of note is the fact that exposure to parental partner violence produces negative effects on par with those found for direct maltreatment, including physical and sexual abuse (e.g., Carroll, 1994; Kitzmann et al., 2003). For example, Maxwell and Maxwell (2003) compared the effects of child physical abuse with observing family violence and found that the latter was the most significant predictor of adolescent aggression. Not only do such studies underscore the profound effects of exposure to family violence on child and youth aggressive behaviour, but they have also led some researchers to argue that exposure to family violence is potentially even more damaging than either direct abuse or neglect alone (Somer & Braunstein, 1999). The strong effects of observing family violence may be due to implicit lessons learned within these emotionally provocative and personally salient contexts, lessons that guide the future use and meaning of aggression within close relationships (Moretti & Obsuth, 2011; Moretti, Penney, Obsuth, & Odgers, 2006). As we discuss later, such experiences can have deep effects on the adolescents' emerging belief systems and interpersonal response patterns.

THE MEDIATING ROLE OF ATTACHMENT REPRESENTATIONS

As research has progressed, interest had moved beyond the mere identification of which specific parenting behaviours increase versus buffer risk, to a search for the *mechanisms* that mediate the impact of parenting behaviours on child adjustment. A number of theoretical models propose that internalized beliefs and expectations exert lasting and substantial influences on adjustment and behaviour over the course of development, and thus are likely at play in mediation processes. Attachment theory focuses on the intrapersonal and interpersonal beliefs and expectations that emerge from parent–child interactions. Over time, beliefs—sometimes referred to as "if-then" interpersonal contingency beliefs (Baldwin & Sinclair, 1996)—consolidate into "internal working models" that embody rich and multi-faceted relational information (Bowlby, 1973). These representational structures guide attention, encoding, and interpretation of relational events; they also give rise to affective experiences of emotional arousal and provoke behavioural sequences of approach or avoidance. Although the foundations of internal working models are based on experiences within early caregiving relationships and set the course for navigating subsequent close relationships (Hamilton, 2000; Waters, Merrick, Treboux, Crowell, & Albersheim, 2000), later experiences such as interpersonal loss, adversity, and experiences in intimate relationships also influence attachment representations and interpersonal behaviour (Waters et al., 2000; Weinfield, Sroufe, & Egeland, 2000).

Many of the parenting behaviours associated with aggressive and violent behaviour are similarly associated with insecure attachment in young children and adolescents (Benson, Buehler, & Gerard, 2008; Doyle & Markiewicz, 2005; Karavasilis, Doyle, & Markiewicz, 2003). Exposure to family violence and maltreatment also has deleterious effects on child attachment (e.g., Cicchetti, Toth, & Lynch, 1995; Lyons-Ruth & Jacobvitz, 1999). Research has shown that parenting and attachment style each uniquely predict child adjustment, including aggressive behaviour (Muris, Meesters, Morren, & Moorman, 2004; Muris, Meesters, & van den Berg, 2003; Roelofs, Meesters, ter Huurne, Bamelis, & Muris, 2006), suggesting that once established, attachment representations carry forward—or mediate—the impact of parenting on adjustment.

Given the common pathway between parenting and aggression on the one hand, and parenting and attachment on the other, it is not surprising that studies reveal significant relationships between various types of insecure attachment and aggressive and delinquent behaviour (e.g., Greenberg,

Speltz, DeKlyen, & Endriga, 1991; Greenberg, 1999). For example, Allen et al. (2002) found that anxious-preoccupied attachment at age 16 predicted increasing delinquent behaviour between the ages of 16 to 18 years. Others have shown that avoidant patterns of attachment relate to aggressive and delinquent behaviour as well. For example, early studies revealed that anxious-avoidant attachment was related to non-compliant behaviour in very young children both concurrently and prospectively from infancy to grades 1 to 3 (Greenberg, Speltz, DeKlyen, & Jones, 2001; Renken, Egeland, Marvinney, Mangelsdorf, & Sroufe, 1989; Speltz, DeKlyen, & Greenberg, 1999). Further, Rosenstein and Horowitz (1996) found that avoidant-dismissing attachment was characteristic of male adolescents diagnosed with conduct disorder, substance abuse, and anti-social and narcissistic personality disorders.

Several processes may be related to the mediating role of attachment in the relation between parenting and risk for aggression and violence. First, these effects may be mediated at the cognitive level. As previously noted, beliefs formed on the basis of repeated experiences within the caregiver-child relationship form a working model (i.e., a set of expectations and behaviours to draw upon) for interpersonal relationships within and outside of the family. For example, some children may have learned that their caregivers only respond to their needs when their pleas for attention are amplified through increasingly aggressive and demanding behaviours, as in anxious-preoccupied attachment. Hence, they come to believe that others only respond to dire and demanding expressions of need; for these children aggression and intimacy become interwoven over time. These children learn that aggressive and potentially destructive behaviour has a functional role in attachment relationships and use it to demand and sustain the engagement of others with them. Other children who experience their caregivers as rejecting withdraw from them, as in anxious-avoidant attachment, and come to anticipate similar behaviours from others. They are thus unlikely to seek others for comfort (i.e., high avoidance) and may interpret ambiguous social cues as motivated by hostile and controlling intentions. Aggressive behaviour becomes a way to stave off potential rejection or attack and close relationships offer little in the way of trusted comfort.

Second, attachment may mediate or moderate the relation between parenting and risk through its effects on emotion regulation. A number of researchers have argued that attachment representations are regulatory mechanisms that modulate emotional arousal (e.g., Bowlby, 1973; Cassidy, 1994; Grossman & Grossman, 1993; Zimmermann, 1999). Early in development, these regulatory functions are largely performed by parents, but over time they become consolidated and internalized as a component of the attachment representation, providing a degree of autonomy in self-regulation (Spangler & Zimmerman, 1999). Parenting that optimizes attachment security also optimizes healthy emotion regulation (e.g., Allen, Hauser, Eickholt, Bell, & O'Connor, 1994; Calkins & Bell, 1999; Morris, Silk, Steinberg, Myers, & Robinson, 2007); conversely, parenting that is inconsistent and parenting that is rejecting and controlling is linked to insecure attachment and provides little scaffolding in the development of adaptive emotion regulation. As insecurely attached children move into adolescence and adulthood they are poorly equipped to manage emotionally provocative events often present in increasingly complex social interactions. As a result, they are vulnerable to respond with aggression to challenging situations.

Finally, attachment may mediate the relation between parenting and aggressive behaviour through its relation to children's moral development and development of prosocial values and attitudes (Laible & Thompson, 2000). Parenting that is sensitive and mindful of the psychological world and autonomy of the child provides an ideal context for moral development, empathy, and care and respect for others (e.g., Fonagy, 2000). On the other hand, parenting that disregards the internal psychological world of the child and instead focuses on managing or controlling their behaviour, will miss important opportunities to engage the child in moral reasoning and will limit the internalization of morality and prosocial reasoning. Fonagy (2000) argued that the caregivers' capacity for reflective awareness of their own and their child's internal world increases the likelihood of the child's secure attachment and facilitates the development of mentalization, or reflective function, in the child. Thus, insecure attachment places children at risk for aggression and violence by limiting their exposure to healthy relational experiences that promote a sense of social responsibility, social connection, and empathy.

An important advantage of attachment theory is that it provides an integrated model for understanding the cognitive, emotional, and social effects of parenting on child development over time. It also emphasizes the fact that child development—and most notably, a particular child's relative level of risk and resilience—is dynamically embedded in relational contexts. As a result, an attachment perspective demands a developmental and systemic appreciation of risky behaviour which can be readily applied to the development of treatment programs. Next we briefly note the application of attachment theory to intervention for children and youth, and describe a program specifically developed to reduce teen risk for aggression and violence.

ATTACHMENT-FOCUSED TREATMENT PROGRAMS
FOR CHILDREN AND YOUTH

Over the past two decades, a number of attachment focused treatment programs have been developed primarily for mothers of infants or young children. A meta-analytic review of 70 studies of attachment-based interventions revealed a medium effect size for enhancing parental sensitivity and a small effect size for increasing attachment security (Bakermans-Kranenburg, van IJzendoorn, & Juffer, 2003). Other programs, with similar results, have been developed and evaluated since this review. For example, van Zeijl et al. (2006) used Video-Feedback Intervention to Promote Positive Parenting and Sensitive Discipline (VIPP-SD) with mothers from highly distressed families and found that it enhanced maternal sensitivity and reduced infant overactive behaviours (e.g., cannot sit still, quickly shifts activity), particularly for infants with a reactive temperament. Comparable findings emerged using VIPP-SD with mothers of seven- to ten-month olds: compared to control mothers, mothers who completed VIPP-SD became more sensitive, particularly if their infants were reactive in temperament (Klein Velderman, Bakermans-Kranenburg, Juffer, & van IJzendoorn, 2006).

The Circle of Security program (COS; Marvin, Cooper, Hoffman, & Powell, 2002) adopts a more tailored approach based on the attachment pattern of each child with his or her mother, the mother's working model of the parent-child relationship, and maternal attachment behaviours toward the child. Parents are encouraged to reflect on their child's needs for attachment and autonomy and to pay attention to the role of anxiety in provoking behaviour. Videotaped feedback is used to help parents identify and reflect on sequences of caregiver-child interaction surrounding problem behaviour and develop alternate parenting strategies. Toddler and preschool children whose parents completed the COS program showed significant increases in attachment organization and security (Hoffman, Marvin, Cooper, & Powell, 2006).

Few programs have been developed for adolescents. Apart from the program we describe later in this chapter, only two attachment-based programs for adolescents and their families are evident in the literature to date. Attachment-Based Family Therapy (ABFT; Diamond, Reiss, Diamond, Siqueland, & Isaacs, 2002), originally modelled on Multidimensional Family Therapy (MDFT; Liddle, 2002), helps parents "reframe" problem behaviour in terms of relational issues, strengthen the working alliance between parent and teen, revisit and repair ruptures in the attachment relationship, and help parents provide a secure base for autonomy development in their children. Results have been promising showing decreases in depression, family conflict and other problem behaviors following their family's completion of ABFT (Diamond, Wintersteen, Brown, Diamond, Gallop, Shelef, & Levy, 2010; Diamond, Diamond, Levy, Closs, Ladipo, & Siqueland, 2012).

The Multiple-Family Group Intervention (MFGI; Keiley, 2007) is also a brief manualized program, specifically designed for caregivers of incarcerated adolescents and delivered prior to the teens' release. Keiley (2002) argues that enhancing parent–teen bonds and reducing coercive interaction patterns may promote greater attachment security and in turn reduce risk for anti-social and delinquent behaviour. Through role plays and behavioural coaching during problematic scenarios, caregivers and teens develop skills necessary to avoid the escalation of negative affect and acting-out behaviour. Promising findings emerged from a recent pre- and post-treatment evaluation of MFGI (Keiley, 2007) in a sample of 67 caregivers of 73 incarcerated teens. Six months post-treatment, recidivism was only 44% for the treatment group compared to the national norm of 65% to 85%. Results also showed significant declines in the teens' externalizing behaviour and enhancement of teen–mother attachment.

As promising as these programs appear, further development of attachment-based approaches for adolescents and their families is well overdue. Below we describe a manualized short-term intervention for parents and other caregivers of teens at high risk for aggressive and violent behaviour.

CONNECT©: SUPPORTING PARENTS AND CAREGIVERS OF YOUTH AT RISK FOR AGGRESSION

Connect (Moretti, Braber, & Obsuth, 2009) is a 10-week manualized attachment-focused program for caregivers of teens engaged in aggressive, violent, and anti-social behaviours. It was developed based on evidence of the importance of parent–adolescent attachment in supporting healthy development, specifically in relation to engagement in aggressive and anti-social behaviour, and builds on the success of attachment-focused treatments for younger children. Connect focuses on the enhancement of the core components of secure attachment: parental sensitivity, parental reflective function and mindfulness, and dyadic affect regulation. Rather than simply teach parents a set of parenting techniques, it provides guidance in considering the parent–teen relationship and the growing autonomy of their child, so basic parenting strategies can be tailored and used constructively to support the relationship and provide structure and safety.

Each session begins with the introduction of an attachment principle geared to capture key aspects of the parent–teen relationship and common parenting challenges. The program coaches parents to attend to attachment issues related to their adolescent's behaviour; to reflect on these issues as they relate to their child's state of mind and life experiences; to be mindful of their own emotional and cognitive reactions to their child's behaviour; and to respond, rather than react, with empathy and clear limit-setting. Experiential activities, including role plays and reflection exercises are utilized to illustrate each principle. For example, one session focuses on conflict in relationships. In this session, parents are encouraged to reframe conflict as a natural part of all relationships that is particularly acute during periods of transition, such as adolescence. The message is clearly not to accept any degree of conflict or aggressive behaviour by their teen; however, parents are asked to: (a) "step back" in emotionally charged situations; (b) consider their teen's behaviour in relation to his or her psychological world and attachment needs; (c) reflect on their own psychological experience and emotional response; (d) weigh different response options in terms of their impact on their current and future relationship with their teen, their teen's receptivity to feedback, and maximizing the development of healthy autonomy for their teen; and (e) think about how they can set appropriate limits with empathy and support. By anticipating domains of conflict and proactively navigating these hot spots in a shared partnership with their teen, parents are better equipped to sidestep coercive interaction patterns that spin out of control. Being mindful of their own emotional response to their youth's problem behaviour and the need to balance their own needs with those of their teen helps parents to move from a stance of anger, frustration, and blame to one of greater self- and mutual understanding and proactive choice in parenting.

Our first evaluation of the effectiveness of Connect was based on a wait-list control study with 20 caregivers (17 females and 3 males) and their teens (7 females and 13 males, mean ages 15 and 14 years old, respectively) with follow-up at one year post-treatment (Moretti & Obsuth, 2009). Caregivers completed measures of parenting and youth externalizing and internalizing problems at four time-points: at the beginning of their wait-list placement (approximately 4–6 months prior to treatment), at the beginning of treatment, at the end of treatment, and at one year following treatment.

Analyses revealed a small but insignificant decline in parent reports of teen problem behaviour during the wait-list period. In contrast, parent ratings of youth behaviour problems pre- and post-treatment on the *Child Behaviour Checklist (CBCL*; Achenbach & Edelbrock, 1981) revealed significant declines in youths' externalizing and internalizing problems. Specifically, caregivers reported significant reductions in youths' anxiety/ depression, social problems, rule-breaking behaviour, aggressive behaviour, oppositional defiant problems, and conduct problems. Further, caregivers reported significant increases in their sense of parenting satisfaction and efficacy as measured by the *Parenting Sense of Competence Scale* (PSOC; Johnston & Mash, 1989). Not only were all post-treatment gains maintained one year later at follow-up, but caregivers also reported additional decreases in youths' total problems, including anxiety and depression, social problems, rule-breaking behaviours, and conduct problems. Results confirmed that the program was equally effective with youth who scored above the 70th percentile on the CBCL as rated by their caregivers prior to treatment, thus ruling out the concern that the program was only effective for those with less severe aggressive, violent, and anti-social behaviour and not for youth in the clinical range on these indicators.

In response to the increasing demand for evidence-based, cost-effective, and accessible programs for caregivers and parents of at-risk youth, a standardized training program was developed to train mental health professionals to lead Connect groups across the province of British Columbia (for more information about Connect© research, training, and implementation see: http://adolescenthealth.ca/connect). Mandatory program evaluation, with standardized measures included in the treatment manual, was integrated into program delivery. Over the course of a two-year trial, 50 leaders in 17 communities were trained to deliver Connect. Results based on pre-post-treatment reports from 309 parents and caregivers (279 females and 30 males) of 309 adolescents (135 females and 174 males, mean ages 13.73 and 15.53 years old, respectively) replicated our initial findings confirming treatment effectiveness (Moretti & Obsuth, 2009). Based on the *Brief Child and Family Phone Interview* (BCFPI; Cunningham, Pettingill, & Boyle, 2000), significant pre-post-treatment reductions were found in youths' externalizing and internalizing problems. In addition, significant increases were reported in youths' social participation, quality of relationships, school participation, and global functioning. Following treatment, parents also reported significant decreases in youths' suppression of affect as well as significant increases in youths' ability to regulate their affect and reflect on their emotional experiences as measured by the *Affect Regulation Checklist* (ARC; Moretti, 2003). Further, based on an adapted version of the *Conflict Tactics Scale* (Straus, 1979) parents reported that after treatment their teens were significantly less verbally and physically aggressive toward them and they were significantly less verbally and physically aggressive toward their teens.

Results also revealed changes in parenting experiences: parents reported significantly greater satisfaction and competence in parenting their teens as measured by the PSOC (Johnston & Mash, 1989) and significantly less objective and subjective strain (e.g., anger, resentment, embarrassment, missing work or neglecting other duties, interruption of personal time, feelings of sadness, guilt, and fatigue) as measured by the *Caregiver Strain Questionnaire* (CGSQ; Brannan, Heflinger, & Bickman, 1997).

Regular attendance and satisfaction with programs is essential to their success. Attendance in both trials was excellent, with low dropout rates of 14% and with 84% of participants (excluding those who dropped out) attending at least 70% of Connect sessions. Our community sample of 309 caregivers uniformly reported high levels of satisfaction with the program. All participants reported that the program was helpful or very helpful, 97% felt that Connect helped them to understand their child a great deal better, and 86% noted a positive change in their relationship with their child as a result of applying what they learned in the program. Similar findings were reported in the wait-list control study.

It is not yet clear what processes promote change in attachment. Investigating these questions offers an unparalleled opportunity to learn more about the basic process of attachment. Thus, intervention trials are valuable beyond demonstrating treatment effectiveness—they offer unique opportunities to manipulate conditions and processes that we believe are critical to secure attachment. Research on intervention and attachment change thus far has suggested that caregiver sensitivity, or the ability of caregivers to cognitively represent the relation of their child's behaviour to attachment needs and to respond appropriately, is central to moving children toward attachment security. However, other studies suggest that there may be more at play than just caregiver sensitivity (e.g., van IJzendoorn, 1995).

Fonagy and others (Fonagy, Gergely, Jurist, & Target, 2002; Slade, Grienenberger, Bernbach, Levy, & Locker, 2005) believe that the capacity of the caregiver to mentalize and reflect on the child's emotional state, that is the capacity for "reflective function," is crucial to attachment security. When caregivers can understand their child's behaviour in relation to their child's feelings and needs, this gives meaning to the child's affective experience and provides opportunities for the caregiver to modulate these states with the child, thereby providing optimal conditions for the development of attachment security and emergent autonomy. However, in order for this process to unfold successfully, caregivers must themselves be able to access and modulate their own emotional experiences in relation to their own attachment experiences and feelings. This perspective suggests that the processes underlying change be deeper than simply changing caregiver behaviour. Changes in caregiver "state of mind" may also be critical to treatment success. Our current research looks precisely at these issues with the hope that we might soon be able to understand why some caregivers, but not others, benefit from treatment.

In two recent studies (Moretti & Obsuth, under review; Moretti, Obsuth, Mayseless, & Scharf, 2012), we investigated the importance of parenting representations, attachment insecurity (anxiety and avoidance), and affect regulation as key targets of intervention and essential mechanisms in the change process. In the first study (Moretti & Obsuth, under review), we examined change processes in a sample of 784 caregivers who attended the Connect Program and completed pre- and post-treatment question-naires of adolescent parent attachment (*The Comprehensive Adolescent-Parent Attachment Inventory*, CAPAI; Moretti, McKay, & Holland, 2000), youth affect regulation (*Affect Regulation Checklist*, ARC; Moretti, 2003), and youth externalizing and internalizing problems (*The Brief Child and Family Phone Interview*, BCFPI; Cunningham, Pettingill, & Boyle, 2000). Analyses revealed that decreases in attachment avoidance (i.e., fear of inti-macy and discomfort with closeness and/or dependence) were related to decreases in externalizing problems while decreases in attachment anxiety (i.e., dependence and fear of rejection and/or abandonment) were related to decreases in internalizing problems. Furthermore, decreases in youth affect dysregulation were related to decreases in youth externalizing and internalizing problems following treatment.

In the second study (Moretti et al., 2012), 31 caregivers completed the Parenting Representations Interview–Adolescence (PRI-A; Scharf & May-seless, 1997, 2000, cited in Mayseless & Scharf, 2006, 2007) prior to and following their completion of the Connect program. The PRI-A is a semi-structured interview that assesses parental representations of the child, the parent, and the child–parent relationship. Interviews are coded along dimensions related to attachment security and parenting behaviours. Fol-lowing completion of the program, parents viewed their relationships with their adolescents as more secure across a number of dimensions. They reported fewer conflicts and increased levels of mutuality, reciproc-ity, and open communication in their relationships. Interestingly, they reported increased levels of monitoring of their adolescents coupled with increased autonomy-granting and their teens' increased acceptance of parental authority, suggesting that their capacity for a shared partner-ship (between parents and teens) was enhanced through treatment. In the interviews following treatment, parents also conveyed a significantly greater self-understanding, understanding of their child, as well as a more elaborate perception of their child currently and going into the future.

Furthermore, they viewed their relationship with their child more posi-tively, with less idealization and role-reversal. Overall, parents' narratives following treatment were more secure and less anxious-preoccupied or dismissing. Importantly, changes in parental representations were related to changes in youth behaviour following treatment. Specifically, decreases in youth externalizing problems were related to increases in partnership and mutuality between parents and adolescents and increases in parents' positive feelings about their relationship. Decreases in youth externalizing problems were also related to increases in youths' acceptance of parental authority, and decreases in conflicts and power struggles in the parent-teen relationship. Similarly, decreases in youth internalizing problems were related to: increases in positive feelings and youths' acceptance of parental authority; decreases in conflicts and power struggles in the parent–teen relationship; decreases in parent-reported experiences of pain and dif-ficulties in their relationship with their teen; and decreases in parental self-sacrifice.

SUMMARY AND FUTURE DIRECTIONS

Attachment theory offers a perspective that helps us to understand the development and function of aggression and violence. It is inherently a developmental perspective and therefore provides an understanding of how behaviour patterns unfold over time and in relation to a wide range of cognitive, social, and emotional risk and protective factors embedded in relational contexts. Furthermore, because it does not preclude other levels of analysis, it provides a framework for integrating seemingly diverse mod-els. For example, an attachment perspective is not necessarily in opposition with coercion theory, which argues that aggressive behaviour is shaped by parental responses to child behaviour and the relational consequences of such action (van Zeijl et al., 2006).

The findings reported in this chapter are promising, particularly given the serious and long-standing nature of aggressive and violent behaviour in these teens and the stress and difficulties experienced by their care-givers. Aggression and violence of this nature and magnitude often pro-vokes strong reactions in caregivers and clinicians to contain, control, and eradicate such behaviour. Yet such efforts often escalate the very problems they seek to diminish. Paradoxically, an attachment-focused approach that guides parents away from increasing control and toward connection with their teens reduces aggression in teens and their caregivers.

The evaluation of behavioural and other outcomes associated with treatment is important, but in-depth and careful evaluation of the underlying processes is equally important. Building on solid theoretical roots, attachment-based interventions not only offer an effective evidence-based treatment but also allow for the examination of theoretically predicted change processes. Understanding these processes will help to refine basic theory and to hone our intervention strategies to better prevent and reduce the burden of suffering in children and families.

KEY MESSAGES:

1. Parenting behaviours shape children's attachment representations, which in turn regulate children's cognitive, affective, and behavioural functioning.
2. Secure parent–child relationships play a key role in child and adolescent development—they serve as major protective factors and can buffer teens from newly emerging or continued engagement in risky behaviours.
3. Effective treatment programs focusing on parent-teen relationships are key to maintaining and enhancing healthy adolescent development and supporting youth through the transition to young adulthood.
4. Over the past two decades, evidence has grown for the effectiveness of attachment-based programs in reducing the severity of emotional and behavioural problems in young children. Brief, manualized treatment programs that target parent–teen attachment, such as the Connect program, also offer promise in reducing youth problem behaviours and enhancing caregivers' experiences of parenting.
5. More research is required to understand which treatment components and underlying change processes are most significant in accounting for and maintaining treatment effects.

ACKNOWLEDGEMENTS
Support for this chapter was provided by the Canadian Institutes of Health Research (CIHR), Institute of Gender and Health (IGH), New Emerging Team grant (#54020), and CIHR Operating Grant (#84567).

NOTE
For further information, contact Dr. Moretti at moretti@sfu.ca or at Department of Psychology, Simon Fraser University, 8888 University Drive, Burnaby, BC, Canada V5A 1S6 (Phone: 778-782-3604).

REFERENCES

Achenbach, T.M., & Edelbrock, C.S. (1981). Behavioral problems and competencies reported by parents of normal and disturbed children aged four through sixteen. *Monographs of the Society for Research in Child Development, 46*, 1–78.

Adlaf, E.M., Paglia-Boak, A., Beitchman, J.H., & Wolfe, D. (2007). *OSDUH Highlights: The mental health and well-being of Ontario students 1991–2007* (Centre for Addiction and Mental Health [CAMH] Research Document Series No. 23). Toronto: CAMH.

Allen, J.P., Hauser, S.T., Eickholt, C., Bell, K.L., & O'Connor, T.G. (1994). Autonomy and relatedness in family interactions as predictors of expressions of negative adolescent affect. *Journal of Research on Adolescence, 4*, 535–552.

Allen, J.P., Marsh, P., McFarland, C., McElhaney, K., Land, D.J., Jodl, K.M., & Peck, S. (2002). Attachment and autonomy as predictors of the development of social skills and delinquency during midadolescence. *Journal of Consulting and Clinical Psychology, 70*(1), 56–66.

Archer, J. (2000). Sex differences in aggression between heterosexual partners: A meta-analytic review. *Psychological Bulletin, 126*(5), 651–680.

Bakermans-Kranenburg, M.J., van IJzendoorn, M.H., & Juffer, F. (2003). Less is more: Meta-analysis of sensitivity and attachment interventions in early childhood. *Psychological Bulletin, 129*(2), 195–215.

Baldwin, M.W., & Sinclair, L. (1996). Self-esteem and "if ... then" contingencies of interpersonal acceptance. *Journal of Personality and Social Psychology, 71*(6), 1130–1141.

Barber, B.K. (2002). Reintroducing parental psychological control. In B.K. Barber (Ed.), *Intrusive parenting: How psychological control affects children and adolescents* (pp. 3–14). Washington, DC: American Psychological Association.

Baumrind, D. (1972). An exploratory study of socialization effects on Black children: Some Black-White comparisons. *Child Development, 43*, 261–267.

Bowlby, J. (1973). *Attachment and loss: Vol. 2. Separation, anxiety, and anger.* New York: Basic Books.

Boyle, M.H., Cunningham, C.E., Georgiades, K., Cullen, J., Racine, Y., & Pettingill, P. (2009). The Brief Child and Family Phone Interview (BCFPI): 2. Usefulness in screening for child and adolescent psychopathology. *Journal of Child Psychology and Psychiatry, 50*(4), 424–431.

Brannan, A.M., Heflinger, C.A., & Bickman, L. (1997). The caregiver strain questionnaire: Measuring the impact on the family of living with a child with serious emotional disturbance. *Journal of Emotional and Behaviour Disorders, 4*, 212–222.

Brown, A.M., & Whiteside, S.P. (2008). Relations among perceived parental rearing behaviors, attachment style, and worry in anxious children. *Anxiety Disorders, 22*, 263–272.

Calkins, S.D., & Bell, K.L. (1999). Developmental transitions as windows to parental socialization of emotion. *Psychological Inquiry, 10*, 368–372.

Carroll, J. (1994). The protection of children exposed to marital violence. *Child Abuse Review, 3*(1), 6–14.

Cassidy, J. (1994). Emotion regulation: Influences of attachment relationships. *Monographs of the Society for Research in Child Development, 59*(2–3), 228–249.

Centers for Disease Control and Prevention. (2006). Youth risk behavioral surveillance—United States, 2005. *Morbidity and Mortality Weekly Report (MMWR), Surveillance Summaries, 55*(no. SS-5).

Cicchetti, D., Toth, S.L., & Lynch, M. (1995). Bowlby's dream comes full circle: The application of attachment theory to risk and psychopathology. *Advances in Clinical Child Psychology, 17,* 1–75.

Cunningham, C.E., Pettingill, P., & Boyle, M. (2000). *The Brief Child and Family Phone Interview.* Hamilton, ON: Canadian Centre for the Study of Children at Risk, Hamilton Health Sciences Corporation, McMaster University.

Diamond, G.M., Diamond, G.S., Levy, S., Closs, C., Lapido, T., & Siqueland, L. (2012). Attachment-based family therapy for suicidal lesbian, gay, and bisexual adolescents: A treatment development study and open trial with preliminary findings. *Psychotherapy, 49*(1), 62–71.

Diamond, G.S., Reiss, B., Diamond, G.M., Siqueland, L., & Isaacs, L. (2002). Attachment-based family therapy for depressed adolescents: A treatment development study. *Journal of the American Academy of Child and Adolescent Psychiatry, 41,* 1190–1196.

Diamond, G.S., Wintersteen, M.B., Brown, G.K., Diamond, G.M., Gallop, R., Shelef, K., & Levy, S. (2010). Attachment-based family therapy for adolescents with suicidal ideation: A randomized controlled trial. *Journal of the American Academy of Child and Adolescent Psychiatry, 49,* 122–131.

Dornbusch, S.M., Ritter, P.L., Leiderman, P.H., Roberts, D.F., & Fraleigh, M.L. (1987). The relation of parenting style to adolescent school performance [Special issue: Schools and development]. *Child Development, 58*(5), 1244–1257.

Doyle, A.B., & Markiewicz, D. (2005). Parenting, marital conflict and adjustment from early- to mid-adolescence: Mediated by adolescent attachment style? *Journal of Youth and Adolescence, 34*(2), 97–110.

Fonagy, P. (2000). Attachment and borderline personality disorder. *Journal of the American Psychoanalytic Association, 48,* 1129–1146.

Fonagy, P., Gergely, G., Jurist, E., & Target, M. (2002). *Affect regulation, mentalization, and the development of the self.* New York: Other Books.

Gebo, E. (2007). A family affair: The juvenile court and family violence cases. *Journal of Family Violence, 22*(7), 501–509.

Gray, M.R., & Steinberg, L. (1999). Unpacking authoritative parenting: Reassessing a multidimensional construct. *Journal of Marriage and the Family, 61*(3), 574–587.

Greenberg, M.T. (1999). Attachment and psychopathology in childhood. In J. Cassidy & P.R. Shaver (Eds.), *Handbook of attachment: Theory, research, and clinical applications* (pp. 469–496). New York: Guilford Press.

Greenberg, M.T., Speltz, M.L., DeKlyen, M., & Endriga, M.C. (1991). Attachment security in preschoolers with and without externalizing problems: A replication. *Development and Psychopathology, 3,* 413–430.

Greenberg, M.T., Speltz, M.L., DeKlyen, M., & Jones, K. (2001). Correlates of clinic referral for early conduct problems: Variable- and person-oriented approaches. *Development and Psychopathology, 13(2),* 255–276.

Grolnick, W.S. (2003). *The psychology of parental control: How well-meant parenting backfires.* Mahwah, NJ: Lawrence Erlbaum Associates.

Grossmann, K.E., & Grossmann, K. (1993). Emotional organization and concentration on reality from an attachment theory perspective. *International Journal of Educational Research, 19,* 541–554.

Hamilton, C.E. (2000). Continuity and discontinuity of attachment from infancy through adolescence. *Child Development, 71(3),* 690–694.

Hoffman, K.T., Marvin, R.S., Cooper, G., & Powell, B. (2006). Changing toddlers' and preschoolers' attachment classifications: The Circle of Security intervention. *Journal of Consulting and Clinical Psychology, 74(6),* 1017–1026.

Johnston, C., & Mash, E.J. (1989). A measure of parenting satisfaction and efficacy. *Journal of Clinical Child Psychology, 18,* 167–175.

Karavasilis, L., Doyle, A.B., & Markiewicz, D. (2003). Associations between parenting style and attachment to mother in middle childhood and adolescence. *International Journal of Behavioral Development, 27(2),* 153–164.

Keiley, M.K. (2002). The development and implementation of an affect regulation and attachment intervention for incarcerated adolescents and their parents. *The Family Journal: Counseling and Therapy for Couples and Families, 10(2),* 177–189.

Keiley, M.K. (2007). Multiple-family group intervention for incarcerated adolescents and their families: A pilot project. *Journal of Marital and Family Therapy, 33(1),* 106–124.

Khaleque, A., & Rohner, R.P. (2002). Perceived parental acceptance-rejection and psychological adjustment: A meta-analysis of cross-cultural and intra-cultural studies. *Journal of Marriage and Family, 64(1),* 54–64.

Kitzmann, K.M., Gaylord, N.K., Holt, A.R., & Kenny, E.D. (2003). Child witnesses to domestic violence: A meta-analytic review. *Journal of Consulting and Clinical Psychology, 71,* 339–352.

Klein Velderman, M., Bakermans-Kranenburg, M.J., Juffer, F., & van IJzendoorn, M.H. (2006). Effects of attachment-based interventions on maternal sensitivity and infant attachment: Differential susceptibility of highly reactive infants. *Journal of Family Psychology, 20(2),* 266–274.

Laible, D.J., & Thompson, R.A. (2000). Mother–child discourse, attachment security, shared positive affect and early conscience development. *Child Development, 71,* 1424–1440.

Liddle, H.A. (2002). *Multidimensional family therapy for adolescent cannabis users: Cannabis youth treatment series (Vol. 5)* (Publications No. [SMA] 02-3660). Rockville, MD: United States Department of Health and Human

Services, Substance Abuse and Mental Health Services Administration, Center for Substance Abuse Treatment.

Lyons-Ruth, K., & Jacobvitz, D. (1999). Attachment disorganization: Unresolved loss, relational violence, and lapses in behavioral and attentional strategies. In J. Cassidy & P.R. Shaver (Eds.), *Handbook of attachment: Theory, research, and clinical applications* (pp. 520–554). New York: Guilford Press.

Maccoby, E.E., & Martin, J. (1983). Socialization in the context of the family: Parent-child interactions. In E.M. Hetherington & P.H. Mussen (Series Eds.), *Handbook of child psychology: Vol. 4. Socialization, personality, and social development* (pp. 1–101). New York: Wiley.

Marvin, R., Cooper, G., Hoffman, K., Powell, B. (2002). The Circle of Security project: Attachment-based intervention with caregiver–preschool child dyads. *Attachment and Human Development, 4*(1), 107–124.

Maxwell, C.D., & Maxwell, S.R. (2003). Experiencing and witnessing familial aggression and their relationship to physically aggressive behaviors among Filipino adolescents. *Journal of Interpersonal Violence, 18,* 1432–1451.

Mayseless, O., & Scharf, M. (2006). Maternal representations of parenting in adolescence and psychosocial functioning of mothers and adolescents. In O. Mayseless (Ed.), *Parenting representations: Theory, research, and clinical implications* (pp. 208–238). New York: Cambridge University Press.

Mayseless, O., & Scharf, M. (2007). Adolescents' attachment representations and their capacity for intimacy in close relationships. *Journal of Research on Adolescence, 17*(1), 23–50.

Milligan, S. (2008). Youth custody and community services in Canada, 2005/2006. *Juristat, 28*(8). (Cat. No. 85-002-X). Ottawa, ON: Statistics Canada. Retrieved from the Statistics Canada website: http://www.statcan.gc.ca/pub/85-002-x/85-002-x2008008-eng.pdf

Moretti, M.M. (2003). Affect regulation checklist. Unpublished research measure, Simon Fraser University, Burnaby, BC, Canada.

Moretti, M.M., Braber, K., & Obsuth, I. (2009). *Connect: An attachment focused treatment group for parents and caregivers—A principle based manual.* British Columbia: Simon Fraser University.

Moretti, M.M., McKay, S., & Holland, R. (2000). The Comprehensive Adolescent-Parent Attachment Inventory (CAPAI). Unpublished measure and data, Simon Fraser University, Burnaby, BC.

Moretti, M.M., & Obsuth, I. (2009). Effectiveness of an attachment-focused manualized intervention for parents of teens at risk for aggressive behaviour: The Connect program. *Journal of Adolescence, 32,* 1347–1357.

Moretti, M.M., & Obsuth, I. (2011). Attachment and aggression: From paradox to principles of intervention to reduce risk of violence in teens. In M. Kerr, H. Stattin, R.C.M.E. Engels, G. Overbeek, & A.K. Andershed (Eds.), *Understanding girls' problem behaviour: How girls' delinquency develops in the context of maturity and health, co-occuring problems and relationships* (pp. 185–205). UK: John Wiley & Sons.

Moretti, M.M., & Obsuth, I. An attachment-based intervention for parents of adolescents at risk: Exploring mechanisms of change. Manuscript under review.

Moretti, M.M., Obsuth, I., Mayseless, O., & Scharf, M. (in press). Shifting internal parent–child representations among caregivers of teens with serious behaviour problems: An attachment based approach. *Journal of Child and Adolescent Trauma*.

Moretti, M.M., Penney, S., Obsuth, I., & Odgers, C. (2006). Family lessons in attachment and aggression: The impact of interparental violence on adolescent adjustment. In J. Hamel & T. Nicholls (Eds.), *Family therapy for domestic violence: A practitioner's guide to gender-inclusive research and treatment* (pp. 191–214). New York: Springer.

Morris, A.S., Silk, J., Steinberg, L., Myers, S., & Robinson, L.R. (2007). The role of the family context in the development of emotion regulation. *Social Development, 16*(2), 361–388.

Muris, P., Meesters, C., Morren, M., & Moorman, L. (2004). Anger and hostility in adolescents: Relationships with self-reported attachment styles and perceived parenting rearing styles. *Journal of Psychosomatic Research, 57*, 257–264.

Muris, P., Meesters, C., & van den Berg, S. (2003). Internalizing and externalizing problems as correlates of self-reported attachment style and perceived parental rearing in normal adolescents. *Journal of Child and Family Studies, 12*(2), 171–183.

Renken, B., Egeland, B., Marvinney, D., Mangelsdorf, S., & Sroufe, L.A. (1989). Early childhood antecedents of aggression and passive-withdrawal in early elementary school [Special issue]. *Journal of Personality, 57*(2), 257–281.

Roelofs, J., Meesters, C., ter Huurne, M., Bamelis, L., & Muris, P. (2006). On the links between attachment style, parental rearing behaviors, and internalizing and externalizing problems in non-clinical children. *Journal of Child and Family Studies, 15*(3), 331–344.

Rosenstein, D.S., & Horowitz, H.A. (1996). Adolescent attachment and psychopathology. *Journal of Consulting and Clinical Psychology, 64*(2), 244–253.

Savoie, J. (2007). *Youth self-reported delinquency, Toronto, 2006.* (Statistics Canada Catalogue No. 85-002-XPE, Vol. 27, no. 6). Ottawa: Statistics Canada, Canadian Centre for Justice Statistics.

Scaramella, L.V., Conger, R.D., & Simons, R.L. (1999). Parental protective influences and gender-specific increases in adolescent internalizing and externalizing problems. *Journal of Research on Adolescence, 9*(2), 111–141.

Slade, A., Grienenberger, J., Bernbach, E., Levy, D., & Locker, A. (2005). Maternal reflective functioning, attachment, and the transmission gap: A preliminary study. *Attachment and Human Development, 7*(3), 283–298.

Snyder, H., & Sickmund, M. (2006). *Juvenile offenders and victims: 2006 National Report.* Washington, DC: US Department of Justice, Office of Justice Programs, Office of Juvenile Justice and Delinquency Prevention.

Somer, E., & Braunstein, A. (1999). Are children exposed to interparental violence being psychologically maltreated? *Aggression and Violent Behavior, 4*(4), 449–456.

Spangler, G., & Zimmermann, P. (1999). Attachment representation and emotion regulation in adolescence: A psycho-biological perspective on internal working models. *Attachment and Human Development, 1,* 32–46.

Speltz, M.L., DeKlyen, M., & Greenberg, M.T. (1999). Attachment in boys with early onset conduct problems. *Development and Psychopathology, 11*(2), 269–285.

Stattin, H., & Kerr, M. (2000). Parental monitoring: A reinterpretation. *Child Development, 71*(4), 1072–1085.

Steinberg, L., Elmen, J.D., & Mounts, N.S. (1989). Authoritative parenting, psychosocial maturity, and academic success among adolescents. *Child Development, 60*(6), 1424–1436.

Steinberg, L., Lamborn, S.D., Darling, N., Mounts, N.S., & Dornbush, S.M. (1994). Over-time changes in adjustment and competence among adolescents from authoritative, authoritarian, indulgent, and neglectful families. *Child Development, 65,* 754–770.

Straus, M.A. (1979). Measuring intrafamily conflict and violence: The conflict tactics scales. *Journal of Marriage and the Family, 41,* 75–81.

Straus, M.A., & Ramirez, I.L. (2007). Gender symmetry in prevalence, severity, and chronicity of physical aggression against dating partners by university students in Mexico and USA. *Aggressive Behaviour, 33*(4), 281–290.

Thornberry, T.P. (2005). Explaining multiple patterns of offending across the life course and across generations. *Annals of the American Academy of Political and Social Science, 602,* 156–195.

Trulson, C.R., Marquart, J.W., Mullings, J.L., & Caeti, T.J. (2005). In between adolescence and adulthood: Recidivism outcomes of a cohort of state delinquents. *Youth Violence and Juvenile Justice, 3*(4), 355–387.

van IJzendoorn, M.H. (1995). Of the way we were: On temperament, attachment, and the transmission gap: A rejoinder to Fox. *Psychological Bulletin, 117*(3), 411–415.

van Zeijl, J., Mesman, J., Stolk, M.N., Alink, L.R.A., van IJzendoorn, M.H., Bakermans-Kranenburg, M.J., . . . Koot, H.M. (2007). Differential susceptibility to discipline: The moderating effect of child temperament on the association between maternal discipline and early childhood externalizing problems. *Journal of Family Psychology, 21*(4), 626–636.

van Zeijl, J., Mesman, J., van IJzendoorn, M.H., Bakermans-Kranenburg, M.J., Juffer, F., Stolk, M. N., . . . Alink, L. R. A. (2006). Attachment-based intervention for enhancing sensitive discipline in mothers of 1- to 3-year-old children at risk for externalizing behaviour problems: A randomized controlled trial. *Journal of Consulting and Clinical Psychology, 74*(6), 994–1005.

Waters, E., Merrick, S., Treboux, D., Crowell, J., & Albersheim, L. (2000). Attachment security in infancy and early adulthood: A twenty-year longitudinal study. *Child Development, 71*(3), 684–689.

Weinfield, N.S., Sroufe, L.A., & Egeland, B. (2000). Attachment from infancy to early adulthood in a high-risk sample: Continuity, discontinuity, and their correlates. *Child Development, 71*(3), 695–702.

Zimmermann, P. (1999). Structure and functioning of internal working models of attachment and their role for emotion regulation. *Attachment and Human Development, 1*, 55–71.

CHAPTER TWELVE

COMMON AND UNIQUE INTERVENTION TARGETS FOR GIRLS' AGGRESSION

COMMENTARY BY
ISABELA GRANIC

ON
UNDERSTANDING RELATIONAL AGGRESSION IN ELEMENTARY SCHOOL GIRLS: IMPLICATIONS FOR INTERVENTION

T. DANIELS AND D. QUIGLEY

AND
REDUCING RISK OF ADOLESCENT AGGRESSION AND VIOLENCE: A BRIEF ATTACHMENT-FOCUSED TREATMENT PROGRAM FOR PARENTS AND CAREGIVERS

M.M. MORETTI AND I. OBSUTH

Over the last decade, major strides have been made in identifying the risk factors associated with girls' aggression. As the contributors to this volume have documented, a great deal has also been learned about the processes and mechanisms that underlie the development of aggression in girls. The essential next step is to apply our developmental findings to the task of tailoring and implementing prevention and intervention strategies that will effectively target troubled girls' problem behaviours. The authors of the previous two chapters have taken up this challenge and pushed us to consider the real-world applicability of our developmental research. Each of these chapters asks: How can we improve young children's lives and the lives they touch by reducing their angry and aggressive behaviour? The two sets of authors answer this basic question from different angles, each providing a unique perspective, while also converging on several key themes that require further consideration.

First, both chapters make a very clear argument for thinking about the development and treatment of aggressive behaviour as a "relationship" problem. Moretti and Obsuth emphasize the importance of focusing on the parent–adolescent relationship, whereas Daniels and Quigley focus on girls' peer relations. Given the mounting empirical evidence reviewed earlier in this volume about the most important factors that promote, maintain, and amplify aggression in girls, clearly both sets of relationships are essential to consider when designing and implementing treatments.

A second theme that emerges in both chapters is the importance of understanding the developmental context within which girls' aggression is embedded. The risks, long-term outcomes, and treatment implications differ substantially for elementary-aged girls who are physically aggressive, middle-school children who are developing the cognitive capacities to socially manipulate in increasingly hurtful ways, and adolescent girls who engage in fierce forms of social aggression.

A third theme emphasized in both chapters is the importance of targeting interventions and preventions at key developmental transition periods during which many of the most serious developmental problems for youths start to emerge and become further exacerbated. Daniels and Quigley make a strong argument for implementing early prevention programs, before middle school, ideally in grades 4 and 5, when girls are beginning to recognize social aggression around them, but are not yet entrenched in the social dynamics that exacerbate these problems. In contrast, Moretti and Obsuth argue that the adolescent transition period is a critical one during which both increased vulnerabilities and, by extension, increased opportunities arise to intervene with troubled girls' distressed parent–adolescent relationships. A number of scholars have suggested that family relationships during early adolescence go through a period of reorganization during which roles and responsibilities are renegotiated and relationships become realigned to represent a more equal balance of power (Hartup, 1989; Steinberg, 1990; Youniss & Smollar, 1985). This sensitive developmental window may be one of the last opportunities to strengthen adolescents' ties to their parents and buffer them from adjustment problems in the future. The final theme highlighted by the authors is the urgent need for further development and research on evidence-based prevention and intervention programs that work for aggressive children in general, and girls in particular. In the last decade, a great deal of headway has been made by scholars who have insisted on the need for interventions that focus not only the commonalities, but also the unique aspects, of girls' aggression. The two chapters make important contributions to furthering this goal.

Despite the overlapping themes, the previous two chapters also diverge in at least one important way. In particular, one set of authors advocates treatment models that target risk factors and causal mechanisms that are common to both boys and girls while the other set of authors supports gender-specific treatment models. Moretti and Obsuth make a strong case for focusing on risk factors that are relevant to both boys and girls. Although they recognize the potential benefits of gender-tailored programs, they argue that family influences—in particular, harsh, critical parenting and exposure to family violence—are serious risk factors that contribute to the development of violence and aggression in both genders. The authors review a large body of evidence that converges to suggest that parental warmth protects children from negative behavioural outcomes and, conversely, poor parenting practices and harsh discipline put children at risk. They also emphasize the serious long-term consequences for children who are exposed to family violence and note that these negative outcomes relate as much, or more, to exposure to parental partner violence as direct maltreatment. For these authors, these findings point to the importance of the attachment relationship. Specifically, they develop a model that proposes that attachment representations (i.e., the beliefs and expectations a child constructs from experiences with the caregiver) mediate the impact of parenting behaviours on child adjustment. The development of healthy attachment representations is seen as equally important for boys' and girls' developmental outcomes. With this common mechanism in mind, the authors review the promising results from the few attachment-based interventions that have been developed for troubled youths and present their own attachment-oriented program—called Connect—developed to target aggressive adolescents' relationships with their parents.

Moretti and Obsuth present some impressive results from their first evaluation of the effectiveness of Connect. Parents consistently reported improvements in their adolescents' internalizing and externalizing problems, as well as improvements in their own sense of parenting efficacy and satisfaction. This study was then extended to include programs across the province of British Columbia and preliminary findings are likewise promising. The authors did not mention any gender analyses that were conducted; however, it seems reasonable to assume that if no differences were reported, there were probably none found. The lack of gender-specific results would support the authors' contentions that, indeed, attachment processes are common causal mechanisms that can be targeted in treatments for both boys and girls equally.

On the other hand, Daniels and Quigley make a convincing case for the importance of tailoring interventions specifically for girls and their unique needs and developmental challenges (see also Levene, Madsen, & Pepler, 2005). Although girls may share several of the same risk factors and outcomes with aggressive boys, they also may present with unique problem behaviours and thus may require unique targets of treatment. In particular, Daniels and Quigley focus on the prevalence and serious associated outcomes of social aggression, a form of non-physical, indirect aggression that is less common in boys than girls. Their chapter takes us through the growing body of research that has documented the serious adjustment problems associated with girls who engage in, and/or are victims of, high levels of social aggression. Not surprisingly, the authors conclude by emphasizing how important it is to view social aggression as a breakdown in relationships among peers (oftentimes exacerbated by problems with relationships with adults as well). Their review of the literature leads the authors to discuss the small number of programs aimed at preventing social aggression in girls. From this discussion, the chapter concludes with seven thoughtful recommendations for best practices for intervention and prevention programs, the first of which clearly suggests that "programs should include only girls."

These two chapters provide exemplary models of the innovative thinking that is emerging from scholars interested in girls' aggression. Moreover, there are several implications from these discussions that may require further consideration. First, it is important to note that in addition to the arguments made by Daniels and Quigley, there may be other reasons for tailoring prevention and interventions to address aggressive girls' needs. Social aggression is not the only factor that distinguishes girls and boys in their aggressive tendencies. Specifically, aggressive girls' experiences with sexual objectification, sexual abuse, and their view of relationships as constituting alliances of power lead to very different targets of treatment than those for boys (Artz, 2005; Pepler et al., 2010). Moreover, given that girls often find themselves vulnerable in dating relationships, prevention and intervention programs for them may need to specifically focus on the prevention of STDs, HIV, and unplanned pregnancies, issues less relevant for aggressive boys (see, e.g., Artz, 2005; Pepler et al., 2010).

Second, and related to the first point, it may be important to consider the relevant outcomes of treatment and prevention for girls and whether these differ in some important ways from boys. If there are etiological differences between aggressive girls and boys, there may also be unique outcomes to measure when we assess treatment effectiveness for girls. For example, it may be important not only to measure internalizing and externalizing symptoms, but also early pregnancy, risky sexual behaviour, and the choices they make about dating partners.

Third, it seems that when we speak of "aggressive girls," we are not addressing one specific type of girl, with one developmental profile that leads to adjustment problems. The heterogeneity of aggressive girls is highlighted in both chapters. The authors all pointed out the multi-dimensional relationship factors that contribute to girls' aggressive behaviour and the variability of problem behaviours that girls present with when they enter treatment (e.g., concurrent depression and anxiety, social aggression with or without physical aggression). Given this heterogeneity, then, it seems important to begin thinking about tailoring treatments not only based on gender but also based on specific subtypes of girls, with specific constellations of presenting problems and etiologies. Moreover, the authors did an excellent job of arguing for very different targets of intervention (e.g., attachment dynamics versus social aggression), different types of relationships (parents versus peers), and different developmental stages at which to aim our treatment efforts (late childhood versus adolescence). Taking the insights of these two chapters together, it seems essential to develop more comprehensive interventions that take into account all the relationships that are central to girls' lives, as well as the multi-faceted risk profiles with which they present.

Finally, both chapters highlighted the promise of very different treatment and prevention approaches. To continue to move forward in the directions the authors have highlighted, randomized controlled trials seem essential. Such trials have the potential not only to help us pinpoint the extent to which any one intervention is more effective compared to alternative approaches but, if designed correctly, can also help elucidate the mechanisms of change responsible for treatment success. Then, armed with a better understanding of these change mechanisms, we will be able to refine our developmental models of girls' aggression and further strengthen the impact of treatment implementation in real-world contexts.

REFERENCES

Artz, S. (2005). To die for: Violent adolescent girls' search for male attention. In D.J. Pepler, K.C. Madsen, C. Webster, & K.S. Levene (Eds.), *The development and treatment of girlhood aggression* (pp. 135–160). Mahwah, NJ: Erlbaum.

Hartup, W.W. (1989). Social relationships and their developmental significance. *American Psychologist, 44*(2), 120–126.

Levene, K., Madsen, K., & Pepler, D. (2005). Girls growing up angry: A qualitative study. In D.J. Pepler, K.C. Madsen, C. Webster, & K.S. Levene (Eds.), *The development and treatment of girlhood aggression* (pp. 167–188). Mahwah, NJ: Erlbaum.

Pepler D., Walsh M., Yuile A., Levene K., Jiang D., Vaughan A., & Webber J. (2010). Bridging the gender gap: Interventions with aggressive girls and their parents. *Prevention Science, 11*(3), 229–238.

Steinberg, L. (1990). Autonomy, conflict, and harmony in the family relationship. In S. Feldman & G. Elliot (Eds.), *At the threshold: The developing adolescent* (pp. 255–276). Cambridge, MA: Harvard University Press.

Youniss, J., & Smollar, J. (1985). *Adolescent relations with mothers, fathers, and friends*. Chicago: University of Chicago Press.

THE CAPACITY OF RELATIONSHIPS AND CAPACITY FOR RELATIONSHIPS

DEBRA PEPLER AND BRUCE FERGUSON

This collection of chapters has much to teach us about the development of girls' (and boys') aggression and about strategies to support children's and youths' healthy development. For this volume and for the conference that generated it, researchers were challenged to consider the development and treatment of girls' aggression with a focus on relationships. Why a focus on relationships? According to the National Scientific Council on the Developing Child (2004), "relationships are the 'active ingredients' of the environment's influence on healthy human development" (p. 1). In other words, healthy development depends on healthy relationships. We might assume, therefore, that children who have developed unhealthy relationship patterns have experienced unhealthy relationships. Their relationships at home, school, and/or in the community may have failed to support them in developing the skills, understanding, and behaviours that are essential to engage in and sustain positive relationships. In an attempt to integrate the important knowledge from the diverse chapters, we reflect on what the authors have told us about the development of girls' (and boys') aggression based on: the capacity (or lack thereof) of girls' relationships to support their development; girls' capacity (or lack thereof) for healthy relationships; and how through interventions that focus on relationships, we can provide relationship solutions to girls' relationship problems.

THE CAPACITY OF RELATIONSHIPS

If relationships are the "active ingredients" of the environment's influence on children and youths' healthy human development, it is important to consider how relationships function to influence development. Children's relationship experiences begin within their families, but quickly expand to include school (with both teachers and peers) and the broader social contexts of communities, media, and culture. From a developmental perspective, it is important to consider whether the critical relationships in children's lives have the capacity to promote their healthy development. The authors contributing to this volume provide many insights into how girls who develop aggressive behaviour problems might have lacked relationships that would have had the capacity to support these girls' healthy development.

Family

As Odgers (this volume) highlights, girls who have developed aggressive behaviour problems often live in families that are themselves at risk for problems. Aggression tends to be a concerning feature of these families' interactions and girls in these families have an increased likelihood of being victimized. Odgers helps us understand how family adversity, exposure to hostile conflict, and experiences of maltreatment can lead to elevated stress responses in children. The combination of stressful family environments and a lack of appropriate and supportive role models contribute to aggressive girls' risk of developing both mental and physical health problems through adolescence and into adulthood.

The family context plays significantly in Dion's (this volume) exploration of the lives of First Nations girls, who have often learned to use aggression to survive in their challenging worlds. Dion helps us understand how relationships in First Nations communities have been destroyed by the colonization experience. The First Nations girls' voices provide stark insights into the multiple challenges that they and their families face. It is clear that First Nations families have not been supported to heal from oppression and continue to suffer from loss, poverty, and disrupted relationships. Given the lack of opportunities to re-create healthy relationships within families and communities, the cycle of violence is often played out in family interactions between spouses, between parents and children, among siblings, and among peers. Children growing up in these violent environments are likely to suffer from the elevated stress responses described by Odgers and the mental and physical health problems that ensue.

For generations, First Nations children who have grown up in troubled relationships have not been adequately prepared to be parents with the capacity to provide their own children with healthy family relationship contexts. The intergenerational transmission of the cycle of violence is a tragic legacy of colonization and of the practices that removed children from their supportive and caring family contexts. There is much to be done to support First Nations families in re-creating their traditional values which cherished children. These traditional values are based on strong relationship principles of being inclusive, cooperative, collective, egalitarian, harmonious, spirit-centred, interconnected, and interrelated (Dumont, 2005). The First Nations girls in Dion's research reached out to their mothers, grandmothers, sisters, and cousins for guidance, suggesting that the hope for children and youth growing up in these compromised family relationships is to strengthen the capacity of these important family members so they can promote the healthy development of all First Nations children.

Peers

As children move beyond the family in the early years of life, peer relationships become increasingly important, not only for the connections and friendship that they offer, but also for their capacity to shape each other's development. In considering the role of peer relationships in development, Adams, Bukowski, and Bagwell (2005) note that peers offer support and intimacy, as well as stability through childhood and adolescence. There is substantial research showing that peer relationships can promote healthy development or, conversely, lead and maintain children and youth on troubled pathways (Adams et al., 2005; Dodge, Dishion, & Lansford, 2006).

In her chapter on the different paths to aggression for girls and boys, Hay explains how peer rejection may be especially relevant for girls' development of aggressive behaviour problems. She notes that girls generally learn to regulate their emotions and behaviours at an earlier age than boys. Consequently, in the preschool years, girls are more able than boys to persist at tasks, regulate their activity level, and maintain emotional balance. A small proportion of girls, however, does not follow the typical pathway for their gender and continues to use physical aggression with peers. Hay argues that these girls are at risk for being rejected by other girls and that consequently they migrate to the margins of girls' social groupings. At the margins, they have few opportunities to interact with prosocial peers and to access the support and intimacy that positive peer relationships provide. Not only does the experience of rejection place these girls at risk for future aggression, but rejection by girls may also lead them to associate with boys' groups. This in turn increases the likelihood of these girls' aggressive behaviour (Caspi, Lynam, Moffit, & Silva, 1993) and may engage them on a pathway of early sexual behaviour. A similar theme of troubles arising from associating with boys, and particularly aggressive boys, emerged in Dion's interviews with First Nations girls. The girls noted that boys at school often bothered them, which had the effect of increasing their aggression. The challenge for girls with tendencies to be aggressive appears to be that they are pushed away from peers who might have the capacity to promote and reward prosocial behaviours and are drawn instead toward peers who may reinforce and encourage aggressive and other anti-social behaviours. Prevention and intervention efforts are required to shift this balance so that girls can be embedded in relationships both within the family and in broader social contexts that have the capacity to promote healthy development.

THE CAPACITY FOR RELATIONSHIPS

The relationship contexts for girls with aggressive behaviour problems appear to lack the capacity to promote their healthy development. Both within the family and the peer group, there are frequent opportunities to observe and garner reinforcement for being aggressive and relatively few opportunities to observe and be reinforced for prosocial behaviour. We now turn to consider what girls who are aggressive have not been supported to develop in these troubled relationship contexts and alternatively what they may have developed that inhibits their capacity for healthy relationships.

What Have Aggressive Girls Not Developed?

From the early years of life, Hay contends that girls with aggressive behaviour problems have failed to develop typical self-regulation, attentional, verbal, and problem-solving skills. These are the essential social-emotional and executive functioning skills that enable most girls to move away from using aggression at earlier ages than boys. Girls who lag in developing these critical skills are not capable of engaging in developmentally appropriate and positive relationships with peers.

With a focus on the family, Moretti and Obsuth note that, without sensitive parenting and a secure attachment, children fail to develop moral understanding, empathy, respect for others, and prosocial reasoning. They note that troubled families are also unable to provide the supports for children to develop the skills required to avoid interactions in which they escalate negative emotions and act out with troublesome behaviours. Consistent with this, Loeber and colleagues note that girls with disruptive problems have not developed the ability to regulate their emotions—a critical skill for successful social interactions, as well as for mental health and academic success.

Leadbeater also points to the lack of social-emotional development by noting that children who use interpersonal aggression tend to lag behind their peers in the development of perspective-taking abilities and consequence-based reasoning (predicting what will happen in the future). These children may have experienced the insecure attachments highlighted by Moretti and Obsuth. In considering salient developmental issues during the transition to adolescence, Leadbeater notes that developmental changes during this stage provide opportunities for growth for those who are gaining the capacity for more sophisticated relationships. In contrast, they create vulnerability to victimization and occasions for aggression for those who have not been able to keep pace with their peers in social-emotional development. Daniels and Quigley elaborate on this developmental lag by noting that aggressive girls have not learned the skills that are incompatible with aggression, such as empathy, acceptance of diversity, and inclusion. Cross and colleagues indicate that girls involved in bullying, and especially those involved in social bullying, may not have appropriated social norms against bullying or developed assertiveness, conflict resolution skills, and skills to take action instead of remaining bystanders.

Taken together, these chapters provide clarity for our attempts to understand what relationship-capacity skills aggressive girls have failed to develop that may underlie their difficulties in engaging in and sustaining healthy relationships. First, it seems that many girls with aggressive behaviour problems have failed to exhibit the most critical developmental skill: the ability to regulate emotions and behaviours. Girls' lack of self-regulation may in turn underlie the range of social skills in which they experience delays relative to their peers, including the development of attentional, verbal, and assertiveness skills. Consistent with the lag in social skills, these girls also appear to lag in the development of social cognitions and social understanding, with a failure to develop moral understanding, perspective taking, empathy, prosocial and consequence-based reasoning, as well as norms of inclusion and respect that are inconsistent with hurting others through bullying and aggression. These gaps in relationship capacity provide direction for the diverse range of supports required to enable aggressive girls to catch up with their peers, experience positive relationships, and move away from pathways leading to social-emotional problems that further undermine their abilities to find supportive relationships that are so critical for their healthy development.

What Have Aggressive Girls Developed?

An understanding of the development of aggressive behaviour problems requires a consideration of why children develop aggressive strategies in their efforts to thrive in their worlds. As many researchers have pointed out, aggression is adaptive for some children in some ways. It can be an effective means of solving a problem and acquiring resources and social dominance. Patterson (1982) raised a concern for the adaptive nature of aggression in his description of coercive processes between parents and aggressive children. He noted that if children persist with aggressive strategies in response to parents' requests, parents often give up, inadvertently reinforcing the children for their aggression. Peers also provide reinforcement for aggression: some aggressive children acquire social status and support from their peers, and particularly from peers who are similarly aggressive (Rodkin, Farmer, Pearl & Van Acker, 2006). Little, Brauner, Jones, Nock, and Hawley (2003) found that children who used instrumental aggression only and those who were only moderate in their use of aggression were generally well adjusted. Conversely those who were highly reactive in their use of aggression and those who were consistently high on aggression experienced maladjustment across many domains (Little et al., 2003). The latter description characterizes the girls with whom the contributing authors have conducted much of their research. In a review of papers on the adaptive nature of aggression, Bukowski (2003) concluded that children who have developed aggressive behaviour patterns are not well served. Those children who are highly aggressive are not liked by peers and have few positive peer relationships. Although the children who are instrumentally aggressive have some power and status in the peer group, they may not be liked and thus may also not receive the benefits of support and intimacy from their peers. It is important, therefore, to reflect on what is developing for aggressive children and to consider the nature of children's aggression, the contexts in which it unfolds, and how it may be adaptive in the moment but maladaptive in the long run if it does not provide a foundation for healthy relationships.

In her chapter on First Nations girls, Dion provides insight into the adaptive nature of aggression and positive aspects of girls' development. She notes that the First Nations girls who were interviewed had developed aggressive behaviour that was adaptive in the relationship contexts within their homes and communities. These girls had learned that by using aggression, they were able to protect themselves and exert "control" over their lives. Another perspective on what aggressive girls might learn is provided by Moretti and Obsuth. They note that some children with insecure attachments develop internal working models of relationships that reflect an anxious and preoccupied attachment. These children learn that aggressive and destructive behaviours are adaptive and they learn to use aggressive behaviours to demand and sustain others' attention and engagement. Leadbeater's chapter reflects a similar understanding of how children might learn that aggression is adaptive. She highlights that when early adolescents have identity related concerns, some resort to aggression to gain social status, popularity, and access to popular peer groups. Status, access to peer groups, and friendships are also identified by Daniels and Quigley who note that girls learn to use social aggression as a strategy to get attention and be included. They also learn to use social aggression to sustain relationships—girls learn that aggression is an effective response when someone is threatening their close relationships. There are, however, significant costs to the individual and to her relationships in persisting with an aggressive approach within important relationships.

Starting from a consideration of the lack of behavioural and emotional regulation, Loeber and colleagues work us through careful analyses to illustrate how girls who are dysregulated become irritable, which then leads them to become angry and oppositional in their interactions. The oppositional behaviour, in turn, leads them to develop conduct disorder, which keeps them out of step and in conflict with those around them. Conduct problems lead girls to become depressed, magnifying their risks for individual and relationship problems. Odgers provides data to support the development of depressive and other internalizing problems, which she contends emerge as a response to stress within the family and beyond. In addition to mental health problems, Odgers provides evidence that aggressive girls have a range of physical health problems that may be associated with their responses to stress and their lack of self-regulation, as discussed above. In adulthood, women with a history of anti-social behaviour problems are more likely to have poor diets, unprotected sex, and be addicted to alcohol and drugs. In our research on aggressive girls, we found a similar risk for a range of health problems, which was partially explained by the quality of the girls' relationships with their mothers (Pepler, Craig, Jiang, & Connolly, 2011). Consistent with Odger's and Dion's research, our data suggest that girls' mental and physical health problems may be rooted in challenging family dynamics.

The First Nations girls who spoke out in Dion's study provide insights into the processes within the family and other close relationships that may underlie the development of mental and physical health problems. Dion notes that, over the years, these girls had developed fear, vigilance, and anger because of their experiences in relationships. During a sensitive period when these girls grappled with the developmental task of identity formation, they experienced persistent threats to their sense of self through negative comments, false accusations, abuse, and racism. Rather than developing a consolidated sense of self, Dion notes that the First Nations girls developed contradictory emotions, such as shame/pride, denial/affir-mation, fear/comfort, and loss/love. Moretti and Obsuth point to similar conflicting perspectives for youth who have an anxious-avoidant attach-ment. Through years of dysfunctional family interactions, these youths learn not to seek out others for comfort and they develop a social cogni-tive style of interpreting ambiguous behaviours as hostile and as attempts to control them. As Cross and colleagues note, relationship perspectives developed in the family extend to the peer group. They explain that when close peer relationships are troubled and strained, girls become anxious and concerned about losing friendships that are highly valued.

The girls of interest in the present volume are girls who have developed strong patterns of aggression and who have failed to develop critical skills to engage in and sustain healthy relationships. Although aggression can be adaptive for these girls to protect themselves, assert control, and try to achieve social status in the short term, there are many costs associated with their aggressive approach to relationships. Given the individual mental and physical health costs, as well as the relationship costs associated with girls' aggression, we need to identify the prevention and intervention sup-ports we can put in place to enhance the capacity of relationships within the family, peer group, school, and community to promote the healthy development of girls at risk. We also need to consider prevention and inter-vention supports to fill the gaps and shift the maladjusted patterns for those girls who have not had the opportunities to develop the skills and understanding that are critical to their capacity for healthy relationships.

RELATIONSHIP SOLUTIONS FOR RELATIONSHIP PROBLEMS

Enhancing the Capacity of Relationships

A review of the gaps in the capacity of relationships identified in the con-tributions to this volume indicates that numerous aspects of family and peer relationships need strengthening to ensure that they are healthy and are equipped to promote healthy development. Within the family, interac-tions are often caught within a cycle of violence between spouses—which children witness—as well as toward and between children, placing chil-dren at risk for being victimized. These violent interactions provide a weak sense of security, many models of aggression as a problem solving strat-egy, and few experiences to promote relationship capacity. Families often experience many other forms of adversity, placing all family members at risk for stress and health problems. Within the peer group, we need to be concerned about rejection and marginalization of aggressive children, which tips the balance away from experiences in positive relationships and toward experiences in aggressive and unhealthy relationships. The short-comings and struggles in family and peer relationship contexts highlight the need for interventions that reach well beyond the children with aggressive behaviour problems. What can we do to prevent or intervene to stop these negative interactions within the family and peer group? What can we do to promote the capacity of these relationships to support children and youth to feel that they belong, have an active and engaged place in the world, and have a hopeful future.

There are opportunities to support families that are struggling on many fronts to provide the relationship "ingredients" for their children's healthy development. Many of the contributors to this volume have developed prevention and intervention programs with a focus on supporting parents. Moretti and Obsuth's chapter focuses on interventions with parents to help them change their parenting behaviours, which in turn changes their children's attachment representations and promotes children's regulation of cognitions, emotions, and behaviours, particularly in relationships. They describe their attachment-focused program, *Connect*, which supports parents and other caregivers of teens engaged in aggressive, violent, and anti-social behaviours. The program offers parents an understanding of the parent–teen relationship and of their children's growing need for independence. In this way, parents can learn to tailor their parenting approaches to be constructive, responsive, and reparative, providing safety and support for their children. Evidence of the program's effectiveness is provided and research on this program is ongoing.

Although their programs are primarily school based, Leadbeater and colleagues' WITS program, Augimeri and colleagues' SNAP® program, and Cross and colleagues' Friendly Schools Friendly Families program all have a component to support parents in becoming more effective in creating family contexts that promote children's healthy development. In some cases, as Dion points out for First Nations families, parents face too many challenges embedded in generations of dysfunction and therefore cannot take advantage of prevention and intervention efforts. In the case of the First Nations girls, they found that talking to family members, friends, and other significant adults was helpful in navigating the difficulties they experienced. The scope of support for those involved with troubled youth should expand to other relationships in which youth can find safety to explore their feelings and work through their challenges. The Canadian Red Cross has developed a violence prevention program called *Walking the Prevention Circle* (www.redcross.ca) that focuses on building capacity among leaders in Aboriginal communities so that those leaders can coordinate support for children and youth. By enabling those who can provide support, families, extended families, and communities can provide healthy relationships that may provide alternative sources of supports for children and youths' healthy development.

Several chapters provide guidance for prevention and intervention strategies to promote positive relationship contexts within the peer group. Given the natural tendencies for peers to avoid and reject children who are highly aggressive, Cross and colleagues note that there are opportunities to raise peers' understanding, empathy, and support for those who are experiencing difficulties. Aggressive children are often difficult to be with: they are irritable, angry, and most likely unpredictable, as described by Loeber and colleagues. Consequently, peers many not spontaneously develop or demonstrate the understanding and behaviours that will provide support and inclusion for troubled children. It remains, therefore, the responsibility of adults who are responsible for groups of children, such as teachers and coaches, to promote positive peer relationships and to be vigilant for peer dynamics that reject and marginalize troubled children. We have referred to this role as *social architecture* (Pepler, Cummings, & Craig, 2009). The capacity of peer relationships is a focus for the school-based WITS, Friendly Schools Friendly Families, and SNAP® programs. Peer relationships are critical for children's healthy development during childhood and adolescence. If children are not embedded in healthy relationships, they experience a range of difficulties that exacerbate their existing problems. It is critical to find effective ways to promote positive peer relationships, even for the most troubled children and youth, as this is a critical building block for a sense of self, of safety, and of competence and confidence.

Enhancing the Capacity for Relationships
In her commentary, Granic provides guidance for prevention and intervention strategies designed to enhance children's capacity for relationships. She notes that we need to consider: (a) the contexts in which children are developing, (b) the timing of interventions, and (c) the tailoring of interventions to meet girls' specific needs when required. The tailoring of interventions might take into account girls' developmental progress relative to their peers, girls' views of relationships as critical for their alliances of power, as well as girls' sexual development and how others respond to them sexually (e.g., objectification, abuse). As Cross and colleagues indicate, interventions also need to take into account the nature of girls' aggression, which is often social rather than physical. Because children with social-emotional behaviour problems are most vulnerable to failure, Augimeri

and Walsh argue that it is essential to consider what works, what doesn't, and for whom. In addition, it is important to recognize that girls are vulnerable to being both aggressive and victimized in dating relationships and beyond (Josephson & Pepler, in press). When focusing on girls' development in the context of relationships, we need to understand the critical developmental processes and lags that affect girls' abilities to engage in and sustain healthy relationships. This understanding will provide critical direction for prevention and intervention efforts.

In considering interventions to support First Nations girls, Dion asks a critical question: What do the girls want to accomplish? If we wish for these girls to have the capacity for fulfilling and healthy relationships, Dion argues that we need to find ways to provide them with alternatives to aggression to meet their needs. In other words, we need to provide them with safety in their relationships and with opportunities to feel safe and in control without relying on aggression. For these and other girls, it is important to determine whether or not they have the capacity for relationships. They may be socially skilled but choose to be aggressive to achieve goals of control, safety, or status. Conversely, they may lack essential skills of behavioural and emotional control, attention, and assertion, as well as the essential social cognitions of perspective taking, moral reasoning, empathy, and prosocial problem solving. Prevention and intervention efforts must be tailored to scaffold for the capacities that girls require for healthy relationships and effective academic and lifelong achievement.

Although aggressive children are often seen in a clinical setting with their families as in the SNAP® Girls Connection (Pepler et al., 2010), they will need to have many opportunities to practise the skills they are taught with peers. Opportunities to practise newly acquired skills with supportive adults and peers can ideally be provided through the school-based programs, such as the WITS, Friendly Schools Friendly Families, and SNAP® programs. With positive reinforcement from both adults and peers for their positive behaviours, girls may learn to shift from a negative to a positive style of interacting, so that they can develop prosocial leadership and social responsibility, as Augimeri and Walsh advocate.

CONCLUSIONS

We are indebted to the authors for their thoughtful and cutting-edge contributions both to the conference and to this volume. We have benefited by our focus on troubled girls, who have so often been in the shadows in research on and interventions for aggressive behaviour problems. As Stouthamer-Loeber reminds us, much can be learned by looking at the differences among girls in their developmental profiles and pathways, as well as in their relationship experiences. The Pittsburgh Girls Study which Loeber and Stouthamer-Loeber lead will lay the foundation for a much richer understanding of girls' healthy and unhealthy development across numerous relationships.

Although this collection of chapters has focused primarily on girls' development of aggression, it also has implications for boys' development of aggression and highlights the critical role that relationships play in development. When we consider the mental and physical well-being of aggressive children, it becomes apparent that healthy relationships may be more important to buffer their vulnerability and promote their resilience compared to other children whose relationships have been supportive and whose social skills are well developed.

Given that relationships are critical as "the 'active ingredients' of the environment's influence on healthy human development" (National Scientific Council on the Developing Child, 2004, p. 1), we are left with the task of asking *how* do relationships exert their influence and *what* are the critical developmental capacities for healthy relationships. A review of the chapters in this volume provides insights to begin to answer these two questions.

How Do Relationships Exert Their Influence for Healthy Development?
Safety in relationships is the foundation for children's healthy development. Starting from birth, children thrive when they are provided with safe, consistent, trusting, and predictable relationships. Secure attachment relationships enable children to explore the world and approach other relationships with positive confidence and the ability to return to the security of primary relationships in times of distress, with the confidence that they will be kept safe.

Autonomy develops from the moment a child enters the world through a complex dance with those responsible for caring for the child. To support a child's developing autonomy, parents and other adult caregivers must be child-centred in their thinking about what the child needs support with and what the child is capable of handling independently. A developmentally attuned balance between these two considerations provides children with the safety necessary to develop the understanding and skills to move out into the world confidently and gradually. As they do this, children are able to develop a stronger sense of their identity and place in the world.

Positive role models from adults and other children provide moment-to-moment lessons in the complex task of learning how to get along with others. From a child's perspective, parents, other adults, and peers are always on stage and being observed. By modelling self-regulation, positive regard, respect and trust for others, and effective social problem solving, significant members in children's social worlds can provide strong, effective lessons for adaptive social functioning. In addition, positive role models can reinforce positive behaviours and discourage aggressive behaviours, helping children along their journey to become socially competent.

Belonging and inclusion are critical to survival. As a social species, we yearn for social interaction, recognition, and a place in the contexts in which we live. Children need to feel wanted and valued not only in the family, but also in their peer group, school, and community.

What Are the Critical Developmental Capacities for Healthy Relationships?

Emotional and behavioural regulation is the essential building block for children's abilities to function psychologically, socially, and academically. As they learn to regulate their emotions, children are able to think calmly, logically, and constructively about approaches to both social and academic problems. They become increasingly able to attend to and respond to the demands of their worlds in adaptive ways.

Perspective taking and synchrony are essential for effective social interactions. When children are able to take others' perspectives and attune their behaviours to those of others during social interactions, they are able to sustain interactions and build relationships. When adults support children's development of empathy, they provide guidance for moral development, respect, social understanding, and prosocial reasoning.

A sense of identity in relationships develops as children learn more about themselves from the way that others treat them. With an emerging identity that is positive, strong, and cohesive, children are able to make decisions that align with whom they know themselves to be and whom they know caring adults expect them to be. With increasing confidence about themselves and their place in the world, children are able to understand their own position relative to others in relationships and to ensure that their needs and the needs of others are in balance for sustainable, healthy relationships.

There is much work to be done in order to understand what relationship processes are critical for children's healthy development and why. There is much more work to be done to convince decision makers and governments that learning how to relate positively to others is just as important as learning to read and work with numbers; however, learning to understand and get along with others is highly complex and requires focused support from socializing adults. Our vision is that someday the most vulnerable aggressive children will not be marginalized from the safe and supportive systems at school and in the community, but will be included in healthy relationships and supported to learn the relationship skills that their families have not been able to foster. Only then will these children feel safe and trusting, with a view to engaging positively with, rather than reacting negatively to, those around them.

REFERENCES

Adams, R.E., Bukowski, W.M., & Bagwell, C. (2005). Stability of aggression during early adolescence as moderated by reciprocated friendship status and friend's aggression. *International Journal of Behavioral Development, 29,* 139–145.

Bukowski, W.M. (2003). What does it mean to say that aggressive children are competent or incompetent? *Merrill-Palmer Quarterly, 49,* 390–400.

Caspi A., Lynam D., Moffitt, T.E., & Silva, P.A. (1993). Unraveling girls' delinquency: Biological, dispositional, and contextual contributions to adolescent misbehavior. *Developmental Psychology, 29,* 19–30.

Dodge, K., Dishion, T., & Lansford, J. (2006). Deviant peer influences in intervention and public policy for youth. *SRCD Social Policy Reports, 20,* 3–19.

Dumont, J. (2005). *First Nations Regional Longitudinal Health Survey (RHS) Cultural Framework.* Retrieved from http://rhs-ers.ca/english/pdf/rhs2002 -03reports/developing-a-cultural-framework.pdf

Josephson, W., & Pepler, D. (in press). Bullying: A stepping stone to dating aggression? *International Journal of Adolescent Mental Health.*

Little, T.D., Brauner, J., Jones, S.M., Nock, M.K., & Hawley, P.H. (2003). Rethinking aggression: A typological examination of the functions of aggression. *Merrill-Palmer Quarterly, 49,* 343–369.

National Scientific Council on the Developing Child. (2004). *Young children develop in an environment of relationships* (Working Paper No. 1). Retrieved from http://www.developingchild.net

Patterson, G.R. (1982). *Coercive family process.* Eugene, OR: Castalia.

Pepler, D., Craig, W., Jiang, D., & Connolly, J. (2011). Girls' aggressive behavior problems: A focus on relationships. In M. Kerr, H. Stattin, R. Engels, G. Oyerbeek, & A. Andershed (Eds.) *Understanding girls' problem behavior: How girls' delinquency develops in the context of maturity and health, co-occurring problems, and relationships* (pp. 165–183). London: Wiley-Blackwell.

Pepler, D., Cummings, J., & Craig, W. (2009). Steps to respect for everyone by everyone. In W. Craig, D. Pepler, & J. Cummings (Eds.), *Rise up for respectful relationships: Prevent bullying* (PREVNet Series, Vol. 2, pp. 199–206). Kingston, ON: PREVNet.

Pepler, D., Walsh, M., Yuile, A., Levene, K., Jiang, D., Vaughan, A., & Webber, J. (2010). Bridging the gender gap: Interventions with aggressive girls and their parents. *Prevention Science, 11*(3), 229–238. doi: 10.1007/s11121-009-0167-4

Rodkin, P.C., Farmer, T.W., Pearl, R., & Van Acker, R. (2006). They're cool: Social status and group support for aggressive boys and girls. *Social Development, 15,* 175–204.

INDEX

**Titles in the SickKids Community and Mental Health Series
Published by Wilfrid Laurier University Press**

Hearing Voices: Qualitative Inquiry in Early Psychosis, edited by Katherine M. Boydell and H. Bruce Ferguson / 2012 / 156 pp. / ISBN 978-1-55458-263-1

Preventing Eating-Related and Weight-Related Disorders: Collaborative Research, Advocacy, and Policy Change, edited by Gail L. McVey, Michael P. Levine, Nina Piran, and H. Bruce Ferguson / 2012 / 298 pp. / ISBN 978-1-55458-340-9

Youth, Education, and Marginality: Local and Global Expressions, edited by Kate Tilleczek and H. Bruce Ferguson / 2013 / 264 pp. / ISBN 978-1-55458-634-9

Understanding and Addressing Girls' Aggressive Behaviour Problems: A Focus on Relationships, edited by Debra Pepler and H. Bruce Ferguson / 2013 / 210 pp. / ISBN 978-1-55458-838-1